PRAISE FOR *REGENERATIVE TOURISM AND HOSPITALITY*

A much-needed straight-talking guide to the route and rationale for being a regenerative travel business. When we know being sustainable is not enough, insights on how to be nature- and community-positive—featuring stand-out heroes in this space, such as Fogo Island Inn in Canada and The Datai Langkawi in Malaysia—make this essential reading and reference for academics, operators, and agents alike.
Juliet Kinsman, Sustainability Editor and Founder, BOUTECO

This book articulates regeneration not as an abstract principle but as lived practice rooted in place, community, and voices from across the regenerative travel movement itself. What makes Amanda Ho's work essential is the honesty with which it insists we must first question our understanding of what tourism and hospitality mean, how they operate, what places require, and what fundamental shifts are necessary. Read it for the practical cases, yes, but stay with it for the harder work: this book doesn't pretend the transformation is comfortable, only that it is possible, and vital.
Willy Legrand, IU International University of Applied Sciences

Regenerative Tourism and Hospitality is a landmark contribution for the responsible development of the travel and tourism industry. Drawing on her extensive experience as CEO of RegenerativeTravel.com, Amanda proposes an innovative framework of five interconnected pillars to be used as a practical lens for understanding and implementing regenerative travel. A must-read for innovative travel managers.
Alessandro Inversini, Professor, EHL Hospitality Business School

This is a seminal work on regenerative travel and tourism. Amanda powerfully showcases the pioneering practitioners around the world who are ushering in a new era of travel. Her breadth and depth of knowledge make this a foundational read for anyone committed to seeing travel and tourism become a true force for good.
Sarah Dusek, CEO, Few & Far

Regenerative Tourism and Hospitality

Building a Resilient and Positive Impact-Led Travel Industry

Amanda Ho

Publisher's note

Every possible effort has been made to ensure that the information contained in this book is accurate at the time of going to press, and the publishers and authors cannot accept responsibility for any errors or omissions, however caused. No responsibility for loss or damage occasioned to any person acting, or refraining from action, as a result of the material in this publication can be accepted by the editor, the publisher or the author.

First published in Great Britain and the United States in 2026

All rights reserved. No part of this publication may be reproduced, stored in a retrieval system or transmitted in any form or by any means – including electronic, mechanical, photocopying, recording or by any artificial intelligence (AI) or machine learning system – without the prior written permission of the publisher. Unauthorized use, including the use of text or images to train AI models, is strictly prohibited and may result in legal action.

Kogan Page

Kogan Page Ltd, 2nd Floor, 45 Gee Street, London EC1V 3RS, United Kingdom
Kogan Page Inc, 8 W 38th Street, Suite 902, New York, NY 10018, USA
www.koganpage.com

EU Representative (GPSR)

eucomply OÜ, Pärnu mnt 139b–14 11317, Tallinn, Estonia
www.eucompliancepartner.com

Kogan Page books are printed on paper from sustainable forests.

© Amanda Ho 2026

The moral rights of the author have been asserted in accordance with the Copyright, Designs and Patents Act 1988.

ISBNs

Hardback   978 1 3986 2154 1
Paperback   978 1 3986 2152 7
Ebook   978 1 3986 2153 4

British Library Cataloguing-in-Publication Data
A CIP record for this book is available from the British Library.

Library of Congress Cataloging-in-Publication Data
A CIP record for this book is available from the Library of Congress.

Typeset by Integra Software Services, Pondicherry
Print production managed by Jellyfish
Printed and bound by CPI Group (UK) Ltd, Croydon CR0 4YY

CONTENTS

01 The Future is Regenerative 1
The Crisis and the Call to Action 1
Understanding Sustainability: Its Strengths
    and Shortcomings 2
The Emergence of Regeneration: A New Paradigm 3
My Journey into Regenerative Travel 4
Moving Beyond Sustainability: A New Perspective 8
The Paradigm Shift: Changing the Way We Think 14
The Importance of "History of Place" in Regenerative
    Tourism 15
Embracing the Regenerative Journey 20
The Urgency of Regeneration 20
Notes 21

02 The Interconnected Pillars of Regenerative Tourism 23
Capacity-Building for Cultural Resilience 24
Ecological Restoration 29
Holistic Well-Being in Regenerative Travel 32
Economic Viability 34
Community Empowerment 39
Steps Toward Regenerative Travel 42
Key Takeaways 45
Notes 47

03 Capacity-Building in Tourism 50
Shift Away from Mass Tourism Models 52
Preserve Traditions While Preventing Exploitation 63
Engage with Communities Respectfully and with
    Intention 69
Build Partnerships and Support Systems 73
Key Takeaways 81
Notes 83

04 Ecological Restoration: Conservation and Biodiversity 87
  Rewilding and Restoring Ecosystem Health and Biodiversity 89
  Enhancing Climate Resilience and Carbon Sequestration 91
  Reforestation: Restoring Biodiversity and Water Cycles 99
  Wildlife Reintroduction and Biodiversity Conservation 102
  Revitalizing Essential Ecosystem Services 106
  Supporting Livelihoods and Building Resilient Communities 111
  Key Takeaways 118
  Notes 121

05 Holistic Well-Being: The Heart of Regenerative Tourism 124
  Structure 128
  The Symbiosis Between Communities and Conservation 130
  Empowering Employees as the Core of Regeneration 134
  Aligning with Environmental and Cultural Stewardship 143
  Enhancing Guest Experience Through Meaningful Connections 148
  Key Takeaways 151
  Notes 154

06 Economic Viability 155
  Enhancing Local Economic Resilience Through Sustainable Tourism 155
  Tourism as a Tool for Conservation 160
  Driving Conservation and Economic Resilience 166
  Blended Finance: A New Model for Sustainable Funding 172
  Key Takeaways 179
  Notes 181

07 Community Empowerment 183
  Strategies for Engaging Communities 185
  Engage Local Communities from the Outset 185

Invest in Local Education and Capacity-Building 188
Prioritize Local Sourcing and Economic Integration 191
Foster Long-Term Relationships, Not Transactions 202
Key Takeaways 208
Notes 209

08 The Role of Destination Management Companies in Regenerative Tourism 211

The Future of Regenerative Tourism: A Shift in Industry Mindset 213
Disrupting Traditional Tourism Channels 217
Building a Travel Model That Gives Back 219
Marketing Regenerative Tourism: A Shift in Strategy 224
Key Takeaways 226
Notes 229

09 Shifting From Fragmentation to Collective Action 230

Aligning Industry Players for Systems Change 231
The Next Step for Hospitality Giants 235
UNWTO Integrates Industry into National Climate Plans 244
Key Takeaways 247
Notes 249

10 Regenerative Leadership for the Future 251

Honoring Indigenous Wisdom in Regenerative Travel: Restoring Right Relationship with Place 251
Why Indigenous Knowledge Matters 251
Five Systemic Shifts Toward a Regenerative Future 256
How Tourism Can Inspire Change Through Communication 261
Education and Cultural Change in Travel 263
The Future is Regenerative 265
Key Takeaways 267
Notes 270

Index 273

The Future is Regenerative 01

The Crisis and the Call to Action

The early 21st century has brought us face-to-face with a sobering reality: The world as we know it is on the brink of environmental collapse. The signs are unmistakable—rising global temperatures, the melting of polar ice caps, increasingly frequent and severe natural disasters, and the rapid loss of biodiversity. These are not isolated events; they are interconnected symptoms of a planet in crisis. The human footprint has grown too large, and the systems that support life on Earth are faltering under the weight of our consumption and neglect.

Nowhere is this crisis more evident than in the travel industry. What was once seen as a means of cultural exchange, exploration, and adventure has, in many cases, become a significant contributor to environmental degradation. Tourism accounts for approximately 8 percent of global greenhouse gas emissions, underscoring the unsustainable nature of the industry in its current form. But within this crisis lies a unique opportunity for transformation.[1] As we confront the urgent need to mitigate climate change, protect ecosystems and preserve cultural heritage, we are also presented with the chance to redefine what travel can and should be. The time has come to move beyond the outdated model of sustainability, a model that, while well-intentioned, often falls short of addressing the depth of the challenges we face. Instead, we must embrace a new paradigm: regeneration.

Understanding Sustainability: Its Strengths and Shortcomings

To fully grasp the importance of moving beyond sustainability, it is essential to first understand what sustainability is and why it has been the dominant framework for environmental and social responsibility over the past few decades.

Sustainability, as a concept, emerged in the latter half of the 20th century in response to growing concerns about environmental degradation and resource depletion. The Brundtland Commission's 1987 report introduced a now widely accepted understanding of sustainable development: the need to address present demands in a way that does not endanger the ability of future generations to meet theirs.[2] This definition has since become the cornerstone of sustainability efforts worldwide.

At its core, sustainability is about balance—balancing economic growth with environmental protection, balancing the needs of the present with those of the future, and balancing human activity with the natural world's capacity to support it. The goal of sustainability is to maintain this balance over time, ensuring that we do not deplete resources, pollute the environment, or harm ecosystems beyond their ability to recover.

In the travel industry, sustainability has manifested in various forms, from eco-friendly hotels that minimize water and energy use to carbon offset programs that allow travelers to neutralize the emissions from their flights. Many tourism businesses have adopted green certifications, such as Leadership in Energy and Environmental Design (LEED) for buildings or the Global Sustainable Tourism Council's criteria for destinations. These efforts have undoubtedly had a positive impact, raising awareness about the need for environmental stewardship and encouraging more responsible practices.

However, despite these advances, sustainability has significant limitations. One of the most fundamental issues is that sustainability, by definition, aims to maintain the status quo. It is about doing less harm, not necessarily about doing good. It is about maintaining existing conditions rather than improving them. In a world where ecosystems have already been severely damaged, and where climate change is accelerating at an alarming rate, merely sustaining what remains is not enough. We need to go further—we need to regenerate.

The Emergence of Regeneration: A New Paradigm

Regeneration is a concept that goes beyond sustainability by focusing on renewal, restoration, and improvement. While sustainability seeks to minimize harm and achieve neutrality, regeneration aims to create positive outcomes that enhance the well-being of ecosystems, communities, and cultures.

In essence, regeneration is about making things better, not just preventing them from getting worse. It is about healing the damage that has already been done and creating conditions that allow life to thrive. This approach recognizes that everything is interconnected, the health of the environment is linked to the health of communities, economies, and cultures. Regenerative practices seek to restore and enhance these connections, fostering a holistic and integrated approach to travel and tourism.

The concept of regeneration is rooted in whole systems thinking, which views the world as a complex web of relationships and interactions. Instead of focusing on individual components in isolation, systems thinking emphasizes the importance of understanding how these components work together as part of a larger whole. In the context of travel, this means considering not just the environmental impact of a single hotel or tour but also how that hotel or tour fits into the broader ecosystem, community, and economy of the destination.

Regenerative travel is about reimagining the entire travel experience—from the moment a trip is planned to the moment a traveler returns home. It involves rethinking how we choose destinations, how we travel to them, how we interact with local communities and environments, and how we leave a positive legacy in the places we visit. Regeneration is not just an alternative to sustainability; it is a fundamental shift in the way we think about travel and our relationship with the world.

My Journey into Regenerative Travel

My journey in the tourism industry is deeply rooted in my passion for storytelling and love of travel. Born in New York, I identify as an American, but since my childhood, I can recall restlessly sitting on the floor of Cathay Pacific flights when we made the journey back to Hong Kong to visit my family. As a Chinese-American child growing up in the suburbs of Long Island, I often felt a sense of awe traveling to and from Hong Kong with my parents and then counterculture shock returning to a sheltered life in Huntington. I was fortunate that my parents believed in showing me new cultures early on in life and exposing me to the realities of third-world countries.

I've always had an entrepreneurial spirit, which began during my university studies in journalism and communications at the State University of New York at Geneseo. My career started in 2013 shortly after my graduation in New York City, where I launched a print and digital magazine that began as my passion project, serving as its Founder and Editor in Chief for seven years. During this time, I also cut my teeth as a freelance brand strategist, collaborating with agencies like Starworks and Conway and Partners. These roles allowed me to hone my skills as a storyteller and producer, specializing in luxury hospitality, real estate, and lifestyle brands. It was in these early years that I first explored the world of sustainable travel, initially through my work as an ambitious journalist living in the epicenter of the travel world.

I became focused on only telling stories of sustainable travel companies and amplifying these voices through film, writing, and photography. From documenting the efforts of anti-poaching rangers in Kenya to exploring the impact of tourism in Antarctica, my journey as a storyteller led me to spotlight individuals and organizations that were pioneering climate change solutions through travel. The lifestyle magazine went on to partner with organizations like the Moroccan Tourism Board, G Adventures, and Celebrity Cruises, as we worked to connect them with an affluent millennial audience that embodied the 'global generation' and amplify their message of cultural exploration and responsible travel.

In 2015, I met my now Co-Founder of Regenerative Travel, David Leventhal who was the owner of Playa Viva, a boutique hotel on the west coast of Mexico in Zihuatanejo while bringing a press trip to the property through the magazine. Back in 2005, David and Sandra Kahn initiated the development of Playa Viva, inspired by Bill Reed's regenerative development philosophy presented at the Greenbuild Conference. They embraced a holistic "regenerative" approach, formulating a set of core regenerative principles to guide all decisions, with a focus on preserving and enhancing the natural and cultural heritage of the land which I had experienced first-hand during my visit.

In the years that followed, I found myself drawn to only covering independent, owner-run hotels that were led with purpose, embodying the essence of what I believe is now represented by the term regenerative hospitality. A few years later, David and I reconnected on understanding the increased desire for values-driven experiences and we decided to come together in 2019 to create a brand that represented a collection of hotels around the world that all embodied this spirit of regeneration called Regenerative Travel.

As a company, we have taken the helm in spearheading a global movement towards regenerative tourism through instilling a regenerative mindset within travelers, hotels, and the entire travel industry through education, advocacy, and collaboration. My journey as an entrepreneur and CEO of the company has been a continuous process of trial and error, shaped by the invaluable lessons I've learned from the many people I've met around the world and their incredible stories.

The travel industry is a vast and complex ecosystem that is often only learned by working on it. This book attempts to break down what I've come to understand defines regenerative tourism and how the travel industry has to play a critical role in taking significant action and moving towards regenerative models in order to save our planet.

Regenerative Travel: A Stepping Stone Toward a Larger Vision

The inspiration behind co-founding Regenerative Travel stemmed from a profound belief in the transformative power of storytelling as a catalyst for positive change. I recognized early on that to ignite a paradigm shift towards regeneration, we needed more than just a movement—we needed a brand that could genuinely capture and convey the essence of this vision. My conviction has always been that meaningful change arises most effectively from inspiration, the kind that resonates deeply with people, touching their hearts and minds, rather than from tactics rooted in guilt or shame.

Travel, by its very nature, is a lived experience, one that holds the remarkable ability to shape and transform an individual's worldview. When travelers are exposed to environments that are not only sustainable but regenerative—actively restoring and enhancing ecosystems and communities—their experiences can lead to a profound personal shift. This realization was the driving force behind the creation of Regenerative Travel.

What began as a mission to connect travelers with hotels that had a positive environmental and social impact has evolved into a dynamic association and marketplace. Regenerative Travel now aims to foster collaboration and synergy among all key stakeholders in the travel industry, including hotels, travel agents, destination management companies (DMCs), and tour operators such as AndBeyond, Six Senses, and destination management organizations (DMOs) like Procolombia. Our goal is to unite these diverse players under a shared vision: to shape a regenerative future for travel and to transform the industry towards models that not only sustain but also enhance and restore.

In this context, Regenerative Travel serves as a critical stepping-stone toward realizing a broader vision of sustainability within the travel industry. The world is currently grappling with the urgent issue of climate change, with the travel sector alone contributing approximately 8 percent of global greenhouse gas emissions. This stark reality highlights the necessity of shifting from mere sustainability to regeneration, where travel not only minimizes harm but actively contributes to the healing and flourishing of the planet and its communities.

This shift is not just about mitigating negative impacts but about reimagining and redesigning the entire travel experience—from how we plan our trips to how we interact with the places and people we visit. Through Regenerative Travel, we aim to lead this change, inspiring the industry to embrace a model that supports ecological and social regeneration, ensuring that travel becomes a force for good in the world.

The mission of the regenerative tourism movement lies in its ability to foster not only a more sustainable but also a more holistic and prosperous ecosystem for all stakeholders involved. By creating an environment that encourages engagement, interaction, and deep understanding, we lay the foundation for travelers to truly grasp the true essence of a place. This is the crucial first step toward effecting a paradigm shift toward regenerative travel. It's about not just visiting a destination but actively participating in its flourishing, fostering a profound connection between the traveler and the place.

The Role of Regenerative Tourism in Addressing Global Challenges

Regenerative tourism plays a crucial role in addressing the profound global challenges posed by climate change. The urgency of this role is addressed in the latest reports from the Intergovernmental Panel on Climate Change (IPCC), which highlight the alarming trajectory of global warming. Between 2011 and 2020, global surface temperatures increased by 1.09°C compared to the previous 50 years, with the last five years being the hottest on record since 1850. The IPCC warns that, without immediate and substantial reductions in greenhouse gas emissions, the world is on track to exceed the critical threshold of 1.5°C above pre-industrial levels by as early as 2040.[3]

The implications of this warming are severe, including rising sea levels, more frequent and intense heatwaves, and increased water scarcity, all of which disproportionately affect the most vulnerable populations. These challenges demand innovative and holistic solutions, and regenerative travel emerges as a beacon of hope in this context.

Regenerative tourism extends beyond sustainability by actively restoring and improving ecosystems, communities, and economies. It aligns closely with the principles outlined in Paul Hawken's "Project Drawdown," a seminal work that provides a roadmap for reversing global warming. Project Drawdown identifies over 90 climate solutions that, if implemented globally, could begin to reduce atmospheric carbon concentrations by mid-century. Among these solutions are strategies that the travel and hospitality industry can adopt, such as promoting plant-rich diets, which reduce the demand for land-clearing and lower greenhouse gas emissions from livestock.[4] By encouraging travelers to choose plant-based meals, hotels and restaurants contribute to a broader shift towards sustainable agriculture and reduced environmental impact.

Moreover, regenerative travel promotes the protection and restoration of vital ecosystems, such as forests and coastal areas. Forests act as essential carbon sinks, and their preservation and restoration are crucial for sequestering carbon and preventing further deforestation. Similarly, coastal and ocean ecosystems play a vital role in regulating the planet's climate by absorbing heat and carbon. Travel businesses can support these ecosystems by advocating for marine protected areas and investing in conservation projects that help replenish fish stocks and protect biodiversity.

Another significant aspect of regenerative travel is its potential to advance social equity and gender equality. As highlighted by Project Drawdown, empowering women through education, family planning, and leadership opportunities is one of the most effective ways to address climate change. Regenerative travel initiatives that support female entrepreneurs, train women as guides, and create job opportunities in sustainable tourism can have a transformative impact on communities, helping to lift families out of poverty while promoting environmental stewardship.

Regenerative travel embodies a comprehensive response to the climate crisis by integrating environmental, social, and economic goals. As we face the undeniable realities of climate change, regenerative travel provides a tangible and hopeful pathway towards a more sustainable and harmonious future for all.

Moving Beyond Sustainability: A New Perspective

The shift from sustainability to regeneration requires us to fundamentally rethink our roles, not just as travelers but as stewards—or perhaps more aptly, gardeners—of the environments and communities we engage with. This chapter delves deeper into the transformative potential of regenerative tourism, drawing on the insights and experiences of two of the leading voices in this field: Anna Pollock and Bill Reed.

About the Pioneers of Regenerative Thought

ANNA POLLOCK
A Visionary for Conscious Travel

Anna Pollock, the founder of Conscious. Travel, has been a leading figure in the tourism industry for over 45 years. Her work as an independent consultant, strategist, and international speaker has positioned her as one of the foremost proponents of regenerative tourism. Anna's philosophy centers on the idea that tourism, when approached from a regenerative perspective, can become a powerful force for healing and transformative change. Her collaboration with Visit Flanders exemplifies this shift, as she has helped guide the region away from a growth-centric model toward one focused on destination flourishing.

BILL REED
The Architect of Regenerative Development

Bill Reed is a globally recognized consultant, facilitator, and educator in the fields of sustainability and regeneration. As a principal of the Regenesis Group and The Place Fund, Bill's work is centered on creating integrative, whole-system design processes that foster regenerative development. His approach is deeply rooted in understanding and working within the natural systems of a place, ensuring that development not only sustains but enhances the ecological and social fabric of a community. Bill's experience spans over 200 green design commissions, ranging from buildings to city masterplans, making him a pivotal figure in the evolution of regenerative practices.

The Need for Regeneration: Beyond Sustainability

The question that arises from our exploration of sustainability is: Why do we need to move beyond it? Why is sustainability no longer sufficient?

Bill Reed offers a compelling perspective: "The most important thing in regeneration is regenerating our capability as humans to assume our proper role on the planet." He challenges the traditional notion of humans as "stewards" of the Earth, suggesting instead that we think of ourselves as "gardeners." This metaphor of the gardener is powerful because it implies reciprocity—an ongoing, dynamic relationship where we learn from life as much as we give to it. Regeneration, in this sense, is about rebirth—about rethinking and reclaiming our role on this planet as active participants in the cycles of life.

Anna Pollock echoes this sentiment by pointing out the limitations of sustainability. "Everyone needs hope that there is a way out of the mess that we've created," she says. Sustainability, while a step in the right direction, often feels like a halfway measure, a band-aid on a much deeper wound. Even if we were to cover the planet with LEED Platinum buildings, built to the highest levels of sustainability, this would not ensure humanity's long-term survival. Sustainability, as it is often practiced, still allows for continued resource use at unsustainable levels, particularly in industries like tourism, where growth is often equated with success.

Anna highlights a crucial point: We need to redefine what growth means. Rather than focusing solely on economic growth—often measured by GDP—we should consider other forms of growth such as individual and community health and well-being, knowledge, understanding and caring. This is the essence of regenerative thinking; it is not about following a prescribed set of standardized rules or ticking a checklist of actions, but of developing the capacity to sense and respond to the uniqueness of each place and situation, to think critically, to see connections and act in ways that contribute to the flourishing of life in all its forms. It's about growing in ways that are less consumptive and more enriching, not just for ourselves but for the communities and ecosystems we interact with.

"Be hopeful—because we *can* do this. One of the greatest contributions hospitality and tourism can make is to bring people to places where healing and restoration are actively taking place. Right now, 43 percent of the planet's landmass is degraded due to our actions—but the beauty of regeneration is that nature responds quickly when given the chance. We've seen water return to parched landscapes, communities reunite around ancestral knowledge, and ecosystems begin to flourish again," Anna shares. "These stories are happening all over the world. So fill your cup with them—let them inspire you. Then get involved—not to fix, but to learn. Come with humility, curiosity, and an open heart. Once you commit to this path, you'll be surprised by how many opportunities open up before you."

Rethinking Regenerative Travel: A Framework for Change

Regenerative travel, as Bill Reed explains, is about more than just efficiency. At its most basic level, green design—saving energy, recycling, reducing pollution—focuses on efficiency. But efficiency alone does not equate to sustainability. "Efficiency only means we are doing less bad; we are being more efficiently unsustainable," Bill notes. The challenge with most green and sustainable hospitality projects is that they often stop at efficiency, without addressing the larger life systems at play.

Regeneration, on the other hand, is about engaging with and understanding the broader "life shed" of a place—the complex web of natural, social, and cultural systems that define it. When travelers learn to appreciate these systems, they are more likely to take that perspective home with them, fostering renewed relationships with the places they visit and the people they meet. This approach is not just about conserving resources; it's about transforming our relationships with the world around us.

Anna Pollock adds that the true measure of success in regenerative travel is not the quantity of visitors but the quality of their experience and the net impact on the destination. The goal is not merely to attract more tourists but to enhance the capabilities of everyone involved—individuals, businesses and communities alike. A hotel, for example, will naturally go through stages of growth in terms of income and operations. In its early stages, the focus may be on establishing a market presence and increasing visitor numbers. But at a certain point, the traditional measures of success—revenue, occupancy rates—will only take you so far.

To truly create a positive net impact, businesses must look beyond material growth. They must consider how they can contribute to the personal growth of their employees, ensuring that they are not doing the same job in ten years but have expanded their capabilities. Similarly, businesses should look at the communities in which they operate, finding ways to contribute in non-material ways, such as through education, cultural preservation, or community-building initiatives.

Co-Evolution and Continuous Adaptation: The Heart of Regeneration

Bill Reed emphasizes that regeneration is not a one-time effort; it is a continuous process of evolution and adaptation. At its most basic level, traditional tourism often involves extracting value—visitors fly in, enjoy the amenities, and then leave, taking their memories with them but leaving little behind for the community.

This ongoing exchange creates abundance, not just for the present but for the future. "Regeneration is not episodic," Bill explains. "It's continually evolving, and you have to be conscious of that evolution and adjust to it as you move forward." This continuous adaptation is what makes regeneration so powerful—it's a living process, responsive to change and growth.

This idea of co-evolution extends to how we think about our purpose. Regeneration is not just about solving problems; it's about living into the potential of what a place, a community, or a system can become. There are three levels of work in this framework: self-development, organizational development, and the actualization of what you are in service to—whether that's a community, an ecosystem, or a broader system of life.

From Restoration to Capacity-Building and Resonance

The term "regeneration" has gained increasing traction across the tourism, hospitality, and development sectors. Yet as its popularity grows, so too does the risk of dilution. In a compelling conversation with regenerative practitioner and systems thinker Bill Reed, foundational clarity was brought to bear on the misuse and oversimplification of "regeneration." His call to action: To co-conspire in repositioning regeneration not as a trendy rebranding of sustainability or restoration, but as a fundamentally distinct and deeper worldview—rooted in co-evolution, capacity-building, and resonance.

The most urgent distinction Bill makes is that regeneration is not simply about restoring something to a better or previous state. Restoration, while necessary, implies a return. Regeneration, by contrast, is about building the capacity of people and systems to co-evolve—to continuously adapt, respond, and grow in the face of change. As Bill notes, "Life is a continual process of becoming." Regeneration embraces this dynamic truth.

In practical terms, regenerative tourism asks: How do we support local communities not only in healing from past harms, but in developing the leadership, knowledge, and relational systems to shape their own futures? How do we create platforms, such as hotels or tourism experiences, that build ongoing developmental capacity?

This capacity-building approach resonates with the example Bill offers of his work in Costa Rica, where a developer has flipped the traditional paradigm. Rather than imposing a project on the land, he asks: "What is the place asking for?" The outcome is not a master-planned resort, but an emergent design—one rooted in listening, responsiveness, and the intelligence of life itself.

Using the metaphor of a tuning fork, Bill argues that true regeneration creates a field of care, coherence, and potential—a living system of values and energy that inspires others to participate. This includes the sense of belonging, joy, adaptability, and co-creativity within a community.

Perhaps the most powerful metaphor Bill offers is that of a human relationship. After conflict, a couple cannot simply return to how things were. They must grow into something new together. In this analogy, regeneration is not a return or repair—it is a choice to grow forward, to discover a new way of being that honors what has been while reaching for what might yet become.

This ethos underpins regenerative travel. Travelers and hosts enter into a relationship—one that, at its best, does not extract or exploit, but co-creates new meaning, understanding, and possibility. It is this relational ethic—rooted in reciprocity, humility, and evolution—that defines the heart of regeneration.

Bill's feedback challenges us to elevate our discourse, deepen our frameworks, and protect the soul of regeneration from becoming a hollow slogan. It calls us to become co-conspirators in restoring the true meaning of regeneration: a worldview that prioritizes capacity, community, consciousness, and co-evolution over static restoration.

To move forward, regenerative tourism practitioners must commit not only to better metrics and models—but to cultivating deeper presence, deeper listening, and deeper love. The deliverable, as Bill puts it, is not just outcomes, but fields of resonance that transform places and people from within.

The Paradigm Shift: Changing the Way We Think

Anna Pollock argues that much of this work is about changing our perception—about resetting the filters through which we view the world. When we change the way we think, the entire world around us changes as well. Many people, especially those new to regenerative concepts, look for checklists and clear guidelines on what to do. While examples and best practices are certainly helpful, true regeneration requires a deeper understanding of life's working principles and an awareness of life's interconnections.

This shift in perception is crucial for creativity and innovation. When we understand the systems we are a part of—both natural and social—we can respond more effectively and creatively to the challenges we face. This is the essence of regenerative thinking: It's not about following a prescribed set of rules but about developing the capacity to think critically, to see connections, and to act in ways that contribute to the flourishing of life in all its forms.

The Importance of "History of Place" in Regenerative Tourism

David Leventhal, my Co-Founder at Regenerative Travel and Co-Founder of Playa Viva, an independent boutique hotel in Mexico, introduces the concept of the "history of place" as a critical component of regenerative tourism. This process involves looking at a specific location from a long-term perspective—geological, archeological, and cultural. It includes not just written history but also the stories and aspirations of local communities, as told by elders and other residents. By understanding the deep history of a place, hoteliers and developers can better grasp their role as stewards of its future.

> **DAVID LEVENTHAL**
> A Practitioner of Regenerative Hospitality
>
> David Leventhal's journey into regenerative tourism began with his work in emerging media and technology, eventually leading him to focus on real estate and hospitality. As the owner of Playa Viva and the Founder of Regenerative Travel, David has championed the principles of regenerative tourism since 2006. Playa Viva, a regenerative resort in Mexico, embodies a new type of luxury—one that is deeply connected to cultural authenticity, natural immersion, and impeccable service. David's commitment to creating a sense of place, both geographically and historically, has made Playa Viva a model for what regenerative hospitality can achieve.

For David, this understanding requires patience and humility. When coming into a new place, he advises hoteliers to "sit on the land for a full year to understand the life cycle of that place." This same principle should be applied to the community. It's about co-evolving with the land and the people, recognizing that a hotel is not separate from the community but a part of it, extending well beyond the boundaries of its property line.

This approach is crucial for creating a truly regenerative experience. It ensures that tourism development is not just about extracting value—enjoying the beach, savoring the local cuisine—but about contributing to the long-term flourishing of the place and its people.

In the early 2000s, David Leventhal stood on a stretch of untamed coastline along Mexico's western Pacific shore. The property—200 acres of raw, sun-drenched terrain with a mile of beachfront—offered sweeping views of the ocean and was flanked by rolling hills with subtle north–south contours. To the casual observer, it may have seemed like a perfect setting for a luxury resort. But to David and his wife Sandra Kahn, it was a sacred invitation—a blank canvas awaiting purpose. "So much about Playa Viva is what you don't get in pictures," David would later explain. "It's what you feel in the land. That presence of history, of potential, of calling."

Their initial intent was grounded in conservation and eco-conscious development, shaped by prior work in environmental and social impact. But regeneration? That language hadn't yet entered their vocabulary. The paradigm shift occurred after Sandra attended the Greenbuild Conference and met Bill Reed and the Regenesis Group, a pioneering consultancy in regenerative design. Sandra returned home visibly moved. "You've got to talk to these people," she told David. "They brought land back to life."

David, ever the pragmatist, approached with skepticism. "Aren't you destroying a place in the process of building?" he asked Bill during a call. Bill's response marked a turning point: "If you understand the history of place and how it got to be that way, then you can understand your role in bringing back the abundance that was once there."

This resonated deeply. From there, the couple brought Regenesis on board to lead two intensive design charrettes. These sessions weren't mere architectural consultations—they were immersive, multi-stakeholder forums that brought together anthropologists, archeologists, geologists, hydrologists, biologists, permaculture experts, local elders, youth, artists, and potential guests. They studied soil layers, solar patterns, weather systems, oral histories, agricultural legacies, and more. "We walked in with a complete tabula rasa," David explained. "We asked, 'What does this place want from us?'"

The first output was a map—massive, layered, and multidimensional—that represented the land's essence. From this, core values emerged. Initially seven, later condensed to five, these principles became Playa Viva's operating manual:

1. Use cleaner, more abundant, and more transparent energy, water, and waste streams.
2. Promote meaningful community.
3. Create transformational experiences.
4. Foster and generate biodiversity.
5. Establish a living legacy—thinking seven generations ahead.

These values proved indispensable. When discussions around guest room amenities arose—such as whether to install kitchenettes and refrigerators—David and his team asked: "Does this promote cleaner energy? Does it foster community?" The answer was no. Refrigerators consumed too much energy and isolated guests from communal meals. Yet the needs of families with babies still had to be met. The solution? "We got coolers and ice for breast milk," David said. "We navigated heated debates with our principles as the North Star."

Over the next decade, Playa Viva evolved into a model of ecological and social coevolution. "Coevolution was a term Bill Reed kept pushing on me," David said. "I began to see that the perimeter fence didn't define our boundaries. Our influence extended into villages, homes, supply chains, and consciousness." Employees brought regenerative practices home. Children started recycling. Farmers abandoned slash-and-burn techniques. "It's a two-way street," he emphasized. "We're learning from them as much as they learn from us."

They initiated a baseline impact study ten years into the project to assess shifts in community well-being, environmental health, and economic resilience. "That was something we should have done from the get-go," David admitted. It became clear that regeneration was not just about the land—it was about relationships, responsibility, and continuous listening.

Despite his deeply rooted vision for Playa Viva, David Leventhal increasingly sensed that the work unfolding on the shores of Juluchuca was part of a broader, yet unnamed movement. He often referred to himself and other pioneering hoteliers as "prisoners of paradise"—each building passion-driven projects in isolated corners of the world, often on remote coastlines or in wild mountain regions, deeply committed to place but disconnected from one another. That sense of isolation began to shift when he met me.

I was a New York–based creative strategist and media entrepreneur, exploring the intersection of storytelling, sustainability, and design. My work in travel journalism and content production had taken me around the world, seeking out destinations that embodied purpose and integrity. When I arrived at Playa Viva, it wasn't just to write a story—it was to witness something that transcended tourism. I was deeply moved by what David was building, but I also saw the potential for a much bigger narrative.

Our meeting was both serendipitous and catalytic. During our conversation about Playa Viva's ten-year regenerative journey, David shared the full arc of the project—from engaging anthropologists and permaculturists, to hosting design charrettes, working through community tensions, and navigating the challenges of coevolution. As I listened, I felt a powerful realization emerge: What if Playa Viva wasn't the end of the story, but the beginning of a much larger collective?

That question became the seed for what would grow into Regenerative Travel—a global platform and movement dedicated to uniting hotels, travelers, and changemakers around a shared commitment to regeneration as the future of tourism.

We began shaping the vision together with clarity and purpose. My background in journalism, branding, and community-building aligned naturally with David's deep experience in regenerative development. Through our collaboration, the foundation for Regenerative Travel was established—not as a concept, but as a concrete movement with the ambition to transform the travel industry from the ground up.

From the outset, we recognized that tourism needed a radical shift. Our shared vision was to build a platform that would unite hotels around the world committed to regeneration—destinations where tourism contributes to the healing of people, place, and planet. As David once said, "What Fogo Island has done, allowing the property to become the patrimony of the community, is something we aspire to. I don't want Playa Viva to belong to me or my family—I want it to belong to Juluchuca."

We built Regenerative Travel to be far more than a booking site. We designed it as a global alliance, a storytelling engine, an educational hub, and a strategic framework for the future of hospitality. From the very beginning, we attracted properties like Hamanasi in Belize and Tranquilo Bay in Panama—each offering excellence in areas such as conservation, culture, or wellness, yet all united by a shared regenerative ethos.

Together, David and I defined our mission: to support hospitality leaders in creating meaningful community, designing transformative guest experiences, and generating measurable positive impact—socially, environmentally, and economically. Our team has now developed a standards framework, built a global media platform, launched a Learning Series, and convened international summits to mobilize the industry around regenerative principles.

We faced challenges—as any pioneering initiative does. David has spoken openly about our early assumptions: "We thought, 'If we build it they will come.' But regeneration requires more than infrastructure—it demands long-term investment in relationships, community, and systems thinking." The lessons were critical. We refined our impact strategies, strengthened our financial model, and expanded our capacity to drive change at scale.

Today, Regenerative Travel continues to expand globally, guided by one essential question: Not what we can take from a place, but what we can give back to it. That philosophy is not aspirational—it is operational.

It all began with a single conversation on the Pacific coast of Mexico, between a hotelier and a strategist—David Leventhal and myself—who shared a belief that travel, when done with intention, could become one of the most powerful tools for regeneration on Earth.

Embracing the Regenerative Journey

The journey from sustainability to regeneration is not just a change in practices; it's a change in mindset, a transformation in how we see ourselves and our role in the world. As Bill Reed, Anna Pollock, and David Leventhal have shown us, this journey is about more than just minimizing harm—it's about actively contributing to the renewal and revitalization of the places we visit and the communities we engage with.

Regenerative travel challenges us to move beyond the traditional metrics of success—economic growth, visitor numbers, efficiency—and to embrace a more holistic, integrated approach. It asks us to consider the long-term history and future potential of the places we travel to, to engage deeply with the land and its people, and to continuously adapt and evolve as we learn and grow.

This is the promise of regenerative tourism: Not just to sustain, but to heal; not just to maintain, but to enrich. It is a call to action for travelers, businesses, and communities alike to join in this transformative movement and to build a future where travel is a force for regeneration—a future where we all become gardeners of the Earth, cultivating abundance and thriving together.

The Urgency of Regeneration

Regenerative tourism has evolved into a powerful movement that calls upon every stakeholder in the travel industry—from hoteliers and tour operators to travelers—to reimagine their interaction with the world. The sustainability of travel's future is contingent on our willingness to move beyond traditional sustainability practices and adopt a regenerative approach, one that actively contributes to the planet's health and the well-being of its inhabitants.

This approach isn't confined to the preservation of what already exists; it seeks to build a more sustainable and thriving future for coming generations. Through regenerative travel, we have the potential to counteract environmental degradation, support flourishing communities, and create travel experiences that resonate deeply and leave a lasting, positive impact.

To realize this regenerative future, there is a necessary shift where regenerative travel becomes the norm within the industry. By partnering with independent hospitality providers, our efforts are focused on driving this transformation, with a strong emphasis on achieving measurable regenerative outcomes. As a company, our aim is to provide travelers with the tools and insights needed to make their journeys more mindful and regenerative, facilitated through our membership program.

It is essential that both travelers and industry professionals have access to resources that enhance their understanding of the powerful impact regenerative principles can have. We are committed to fostering a global community that engages in collaboration, education, and meaningful dialogue about living a life anchored in regeneration.

As we look ahead, it's crucial to recognize that the decisions we make—whether as travelers, leaders in the industry, or global citizens—have the potential to shape the world. Embracing regeneration should be more than just a practice; it should become an integral part of how we live our lives.

In the next chapter, we will explore practical examples of regenerative tourism in action, highlighting the businesses, communities, and destinations that are leading the way. We will see how these principles are being applied on the ground and discover the innovative approaches that are redefining what it means to travel with purpose and impact.

Notes

1 United Nations World Tourism Organization. www.unwto.org (archived at https://perma.cc/P8WQ-8DXY)
2 Brundtland Commission. Our common future, Brundtland Commission, 1987.

3 Intergovernmental Panel on Climate Change (IPCC) (2021) *Climate Change 2021: The physical science basis. Contribution of Working Group I to the Sixth Assessment Report of the Intergovernmental Panel on Climate Change*, Cambridge University Press, Cambridge and New York. www.ipcc.ch/report/ar6/wg1 (archived at https://perma.cc/D9JY-KDYM)
4 P Hawken (ed) (2017) *Drawdown: The most comprehensive plan ever proposed to reverse global warming*, Penguin Books, New York.

The Interconnected Pillars of Regenerative Tourism

02

In an era marked by environmental degradation, cultural homogenization, and social inequality, the travel industry stands at a critical juncture. Traditional tourism models, often characterized by mass consumption and the exploitation of natural and cultural resources, have proven unsustainable and detrimental to both destinations and their inhabitants. The urgent need for a paradigm shift has given rise to the concept of regenerative travel—a holistic approach that seeks not only to minimize harm but to actively improve and revitalize the places we visit.

Regenerative travel transcends conventional sustainability by emphasizing restoration, renewal, and the flourishing of ecosystems, communities, and cultures. It recognizes that travel, when approached thoughtfully and responsibly, can be a powerful force for good. This chapter explores the foundational pillars of regenerative travel, providing a comprehensive overview of the principles and practices that underpin this transformative movement.

Figure 2.1 represents the interconnected nature of regenerative tourism through five core elements essential to regenerative systems: Ecological restoration, holistic well-being, economic viability, community empowerment, community empowerment, and capacity-building for cultural resilience.

Figure 2.1 The interconnected pillars of regenerative tourism

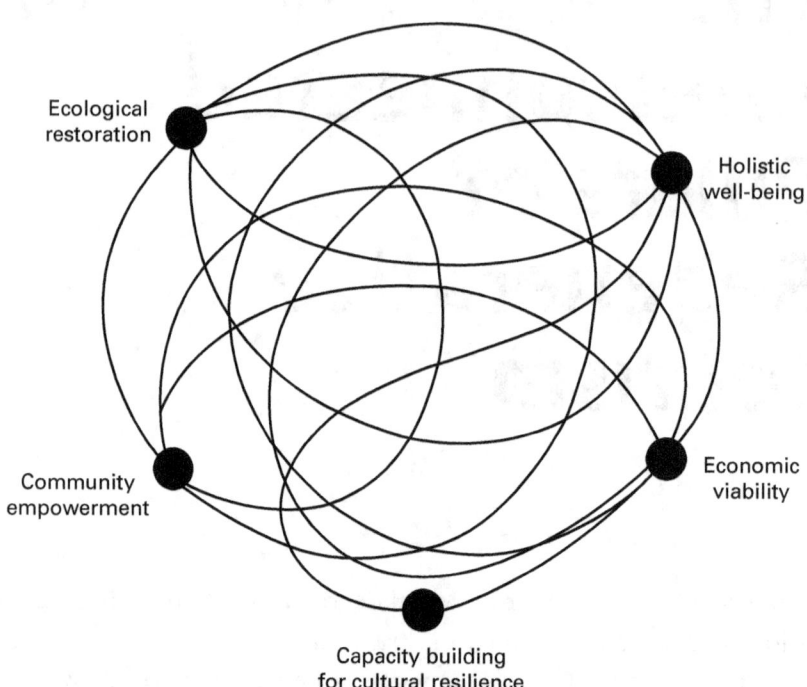

SOURCE Amanda Ho/Regenerative Travel and Bill Reed/Regenesis Group (2025) The interconnected pillars of regenerative tourism [Chart]. In *Regenerative Tourism and Hospitality: Building a resilient and positive impact-led travel industry.*

Rather than existing in a hierarchy or sequence, these elements operate concurrently, each influencing and reinforcing the others. For instance, community empowerment can both precede and result from ecological restoration or holistic well-being initiatives. The networked design highlights that meaningful, lasting change emerges from the dynamic interplay between these elements, where progress in one area strengthens the whole.

Capacity-Building for Cultural Resilience

Capacity-building is the process of strengthening the skills, resources, and agency of communities to lead their own cultural, social, and economic development. In the context of regenerative travel, it is the foundation upon which long-term cultural vitality, ecological stewardship, and community well-being are built.

Rather than preserving culture for tourism or repackaging it for external consumption, regenerative travel focuses on empowering communities to sustain and evolve their own traditions, practices, and knowledge systems. This means investing in education, leadership, infrastructure, and storytelling—enabling local people to make informed decisions about how tourism engages with their culture, land, and values.

Culture is a living, adaptive system. But its ability to evolve with integrity requires communities to have the capacity to shape that evolution from within. As articulated by Berkes and Folke,[1] resilience in social-ecological systems—including cultures—relies on the ability to absorb disturbances without losing core identity. In the context of tourism, this means creating experiences that respect and sustain cultural expression rather than dilute or appropriate it. That strength doesn't come from external recognition alone, but from community-led systems of governance, intergenerational learning, and economic self-determination.

Through capacity-building, regenerative tourism shifts the power dynamic. It centers local leadership in shaping tourism narratives, designing experiences, and defining what cultural exchange looks like. This requires a departure from passive observation to deeper engagement—what educator Paulo Freire might describe as a dialogic process, where both traveler and host are transformed through mutual exchange.[2]

The impacts of tourism on cultural resilience can be profound—both positive and negative. Mass tourism, with its emphasis on scale and standardization, often leads to cultural commodification. When traditions are packaged for entertainment without context, they risk being emptied of meaning. UNESCO warned in 2017 that unchecked tourism development can lead to the erosion of intangible cultural heritage and homogenization of cultural landscapes.[3] Conversely, regenerative travel presents an opportunity to counteract these trends by valuing cultural depth over spectacle.

Regenerative travel, therefore, is not just about respecting culture—it's about enabling communities to thrive. It begins by investing in local capacity, so that tourism serves as a platform for empowerment, not exploitation.

How Regenerative Travel Can Foster Cultural Resilience

Numerous examples illustrate how regenerative travel can foster cultural resilience. In Japan, the Kodo Cultural Immersion program offers travelers the chance to participate in tea ceremonies, calligraphy, and other traditional arts, guided by local artisans. These workshops serve not only to educate travelers but also to sustain the livelihoods of cultural bearers, ensuring the intergenerational transmission of knowledge. Similarly, in Mali, the *Festival au Désert* elevates traditional Tuareg music and art. Despite political instability, the festival has continued—sometimes in exile—demonstrating how cultural celebration can persist as an act of resistance and identity preservation.[4]

Heritage conservation projects also play a vital role. The restoration of Angkor Wat in Cambodia, undertaken through international partnerships and UNESCO oversight, is a powerful example of cultural resilience at scale. These efforts have ensured that the site remains both a spiritual center for Cambodians and an educational experience for visitors, helping to bridge past and present.[5]

Indigenous-led tourism ventures are among the most effective models for enhancing cultural resilience. In Australia, Aboriginal Cultural Tours offer insight into the Dreamtime stories, land stewardship practices, and ancient knowledge systems of the Ngarrindjeri people. These experiences, led by Aboriginal guides, allow visitors to engage with living cultures on their own terms, reinforcing community pride while challenging colonial narratives.[6]

In conclusion, cultural resilience is not about freezing traditions in time but about enabling them to adapt, renew, and thrive in the face of change. Regenerative travel supports this by shifting tourism from a transactional encounter to a transformational relationship—one that honors the dignity, voice, and cultural continuity of host communities. As the tourism industry seeks more ethical and sustainable pathways, fostering cultural resilience must remain at the heart of regenerative practice.

Promoting Capacity-Building Through Regenerative Travel: Benefits and Integration Strategies

In a globalized world where cultural homogenization poses a growing threat to traditional identities and knowledge systems, regenerative travel offers an alternative model that uplifts and sustains cultural resilience. Defined as the capacity of cultures to adapt, endure, and evolve while maintaining core values and practices, capacity-building is central to ensuring that communities can assert and celebrate their heritage amidst external pressures.[7] Regenerative travel not only recognizes this dynamic nature of culture but actively supports its continuation by embedding respectful cultural engagement into tourism practices.

One of the most significant benefits of promoting capacity-building through travel is the preservation and revitalization of heritage. Globalization, urbanization, and the commodification of culture have contributed to the erosion of traditional knowledge and practices. According to UNESCO, intangible cultural heritage—such as language, music, rituals, and craftsmanship—is particularly vulnerable.[8] Tourism, when aligned with community-led goals, can serve as a tool for safeguarding these elements. Initiatives that support living cultural traditions, rather than reducing them to performances for tourist consumption, play a crucial role in ensuring their transmission to future generations.[9]

Cultural tourism also brings economic opportunities that can further incentivize preservation efforts. When cultural practitioners such as artisans, musicians, and elders receive income from sharing their heritage through workshops, performances, or guided experiences, the economic value of culture becomes evident and aligned with its social value. Studies show that cultural tourism contributes significantly to local economies, particularly in rural and Indigenous communities where other forms of economic development may be limited.[10] For example, Indigenous tourism ventures in Australia and Canada have demonstrated how community-owned cultural enterprises can support both livelihoods and the continuity of traditions.[11]

Beyond economics, social empowerment is a key benefit of fostering cultural resilience through travel. When community members see their traditions acknowledged and respected by visitors, it can enhance pride and strengthen collective identity. This validation counters historical narratives of marginalization, supporting cultural renewal and community cohesion.

Travelers, too, benefit profoundly from engaging in culturally immersive experiences. Enriched travel experiences rooted in authentic cultural exchange offer deeper understanding, empathy, and appreciation for human diversity. Rather than viewing culture as a spectacle, regenerative travel encourages participation in context-rich, respectful engagements that lead to personal growth and expanded worldviews. These experiences leave lasting impressions and often inspire travelers to adopt more conscious and inclusive lifestyles beyond their journey.

To effectively support capacity-building, tourism stakeholders must move beyond good intentions to adopt practices grounded in respect, collaboration, and reciprocity to create cultural resilience. This begins with a commitment to cultural sensitivity. Travelers should take the time to understand the historical and social context of the places they visit, including learning about customs, taboos, and the legacy of colonialism or displacement that may affect cultural dynamics. Education initiatives, whether through pre-trip orientations or interpretive content, can prepare travelers for more meaningful and ethical interactions.[12]

Tourism providers should also actively support authentic cultural expressions, avoiding exploitative or performative representations. This means working with communities to co-create experiences that reflect genuine cultural narratives and practices. For instance, the Cultural Immersion Program in Japan's Kodo region offers hands-on learning in traditional arts led by local masters, with the dual goal of educating visitors and sustaining endangered practices.

Equally important is the need to collaborate with cultural custodians. Elders, artists, and spiritual leaders must be involved in the design and delivery of tourism products to ensure that cultural representation is accurate, consent-based, and aligned with community values. This participatory approach not only increases the authenticity of experiences but also ensures community ownership and control over cultural knowledge.

Finally, regenerative travel can contribute to long-term cultural preservation efforts. Supporting initiatives such as language revitalization, youth apprenticeship programs, and craft cooperatives, helps sustain cultural practices beyond the tourism encounter. Organizations like the Endangered Language Fund and Cultural Survival have demonstrated how partnerships with tourism enterprises can amplify cultural preservation goals while providing educational opportunities for travelers.

In conclusion, integrating cultural resilience into travel practices enhances tourism's ability to serve as a force for good. By centering community agency, respecting cultural integrity, and fostering transformative experiences for travelers, regenerative tourism contributes to a more inclusive and equitable future. In doing so, it safeguards the rich tapestry of human culture—not as a relic of the past, but as a living, evolving force capable of informing and inspiring future generations.

Ecological Restoration

At the heart of regenerative travel lies a profound commitment to ecological restoration. This pillar emphasizes the active healing and enhancement of natural environments that have been degraded by human activities. Unlike traditional conservation efforts that focus on preserving existing conditions, ecological restoration seeks to return ecosystems to their original, thriving states, promoting biodiversity and resilience against environmental challenges such as climate change.

Ecological restoration involves a range of practices, including reforestation, wetland rehabilitation, soil regeneration, and the reintroduction of native species. These efforts not only repair past damage but also create healthier and more robust ecosystems capable of supporting diverse life forms and providing essential services such as clean air, water, and fertile soil.

The Role of Travel in Ecological Restoration

Tourism, as one of the largest and fastest-growing global industries, exerts considerable pressure on ecosystems through its reliance on transportation, accommodation, and recreational infrastructure. These activities often contribute to environmental degradation, including deforestation, carbon emissions, water pollution, and habitat loss.[13] While sustainable tourism has sought to minimize such harm, regenerative travel represents a more ambitious paradigm—one that not only avoids negative impacts but actively restores ecological health and biodiversity.

Ecological restoration in the context of travel refers to the process of assisting in the recovery of ecosystems that have been degraded or destroyed, with the travel experience itself serving as a vehicle for environmental repair. Regenerative tourism embeds this ethos into the travel lifecycle, engaging tourists directly in restoration activities, funding conservation efforts, and creating mutually beneficial relationships between travelers, host communities, and natural systems.[14]

Reforestation efforts are among the most prominent examples of ecological restoration in tourism. Organizations like Eden Reforestation Projects have partnered with eco-lodges and tour operators to plant millions of trees across countries such as Madagascar, Nepal, and Mozambique. These projects not only mitigate the effects of deforestation and climate change but also generate employment and promote local environmental stewardship. Tourists are often invited to take part in tree-planting activities, making their participation a meaningful contribution to both ecological and social regeneration.

Marine ecosystems are also benefiting from regenerative travel practices, particularly in coral reef environments that have been heavily impacted by climate change and mass tourism. In Australia, the Great Barrier Reef Restoration Program involves visitors in coral propagation and monitoring under the supervision of marine scientists. These experiences enhance awareness while providing critical support to reef ecosystems that sustain marine biodiversity and local livelihoods. Such initiatives reflect the growing integration of citizen science into tourism, empowering travelers to become active participants in conservation.

Another vital area is the restoration of wildlife habitats. Safari tourism, particularly in African countries, increasingly supports landscape rehabilitation through collaborations with conservation organizations.

The African Wildlife Foundation, for example, works with community conservancies and tourism operators to restore savannahs and wetlands, thereby improving conditions for threatened species while enhancing the long-term viability of ecotourism.[15] These projects demonstrate how tourism can be aligned with habitat preservation when designed thoughtfully and inclusively.

Agricultural regeneration also plays a central role in the ecological restoration movement within tourism. Agrotourism initiatives, especially those grounded in regenerative agriculture and permaculture, allow travelers to engage in soil restoration, composting, and organic farming. In Italy, the Agriturismo network offers immersive experiences on family-run farms, where tourists can learn about sustainable food systems and contribute to the renewal of degraded agricultural land.[16] These experiences provide education while reinforcing the links between food, ecology, and community resilience.

The benefits of ecological restoration in tourism extend beyond the immediate environmental impacts. Restored landscapes enhance biodiversity, strengthen ecosystem services such as water filtration and carbon sequestration, and improve resilience to climate-related disruptions.[17] Economically, such initiatives generate jobs, support local enterprises, and diversify income sources in rural and conservation-dependent regions. On a psychological level, travelers who engage in regenerative practices often report heightened emotional well-being and a deeper sense of connection to place.[18]

To scale these benefits, the tourism industry must adopt a more active role in promoting ecological restoration. This involves prioritizing travel experiences that contribute to restoration outcomes, supporting businesses with verifiable environmental commitments, and choosing low-impact transportation options where possible. Carbon offsetting, though not a complete solution, can supplement broader mitigation strategies when linked to credible and verifiable restoration projects.[19] Furthermore, travelers can amplify the regenerative message by sharing their experiences and advocating for greater environmental responsibility within their communities and networks.

Ultimately, regenerative travel reframes the role of the tourist from passive consumer to active steward. When ecological restoration is embedded into the design and delivery of travel experiences, tourism becomes a powerful force for healing the planet. This transformative shift challenges the industry to go beyond sustainability—to reimagine tourism as a tool not just for exploration, but for regeneration.

Holistic Well-Being in Regenerative Travel

Holistic well-being refers to the comprehensive harmony of physical, mental, emotional, spiritual, and environmental health. It recognizes the intrinsic interconnectedness of these dimensions, asserting that true wellness cannot exist in isolation. In the context of regenerative travel, holistic well-being emerges as a foundational pillar that guides tourism experiences toward nurturing not only the individual traveler but also the host communities and the ecosystems they inhabit. This approach contrasts sharply with conventional tourism models that often prioritize escapism or economic gain over personal, social, and ecological harmony.

Understanding holistic well-being requires a systems-thinking perspective, acknowledging that individual wellness is inextricably linked to the health of broader social and ecological systems.[20] Regenerative travel emphasizes this interdependence, creating conditions in which all forms of life can flourish. It champions travel as a practice that can heal, awaken, and reconnect—serving as a conduit for personal transformation, cultural exchange, and environmental stewardship.

Travel inherently offers individuals the opportunity to step outside the habitual and into the liminal. It invites disconnection from everyday stressors and fosters reconnection with self, nature, and others. Regenerative travel harnesses these possibilities by cultivating experiences designed to support mindfulness, healing, and reflection. Destinations and travel providers that prioritize holistic well-being intentionally design offerings that create space for introspection, reconnection, and renewal—qualities that are essential in an increasingly fast-paced and fragmented world.[21] One of the most tangible expressions of holistic well-being in regenerative travel is found in wellness retreats. These retreats integrate activities such as yoga, meditation, traditional healing practices, and nutritional education to provide comprehensive rejuvenation.

Nature immersion is another powerful vehicle for holistic well-being. Time spent in wild, biodiverse settings has been shown to reduce cortisol levels, lower blood pressure, and improve mood and cognition.[22] Experiences such as forest bathing—or *shinrin-yoku*—invite travelers to slow down and engage sensorially with the natural world. In Chile's Patagonia National Park, for instance, immersive hiking experiences promote not only appreciation of remote ecosystems but also emotional grounding and mental clarity. These moments of presence in nature reinforce a reciprocal relationship with the Earth and often inspire lasting commitments to environmental protection.

Mindful travel practices further support holistic well-being by encouraging intentionality and depth of experience. The slow travel movement, for instance, promotes spending extended time in fewer places to cultivate deeper connections with local cultures and environments. This approach reduces the psychological and ecological toll of high-paced tourism while enhancing personal fulfillment.[23] Mindfulness can also be cultivated through daily practices such as journaling, meditating, or observing the rhythms of a place, allowing travelers to engage more meaningfully with their surroundings.

Regenerative travel also encompasses the wellness of host communities. Community health initiatives embedded in tourism—such as infrastructure development, clean water access, and healthcare support—are vital to fostering resilience and equity. Programs like Pack for a Purpose empower travelers to bring much-needed medical and educational supplies to their destinations, directly contributing to the health and well-being of local populations.[24] These initiatives demonstrate that traveler well-being is intertwined with the dignity and vitality of host communities.

The benefits of focusing on holistic well-being in travel are manifold. On a personal level, travelers often report reduced stress, improved physical health, and greater mental clarity when engaging in regenerative travel experiences. For communities, tourism that contributes to health and education builds social cohesion and long-term resilience. Environmentally, travelers who foster deeper relationships with nature are more likely to adopt conservation behaviors and support ecological restoration. Culturally and spiritually, engaging with diverse wellness traditions expands worldviews, fosters empathy, and cultivates mutual respect across cultural boundaries.[25]

Integrating holistic well-being into tourism practices calls for an intentional shift from extractive models toward ones that prioritize regeneration and reciprocity. This can be achieved by choosing destinations that align with ethical and sustainable principles, incorporating mindfulness practices into the travel experience, respecting local rhythms and ecosystems, and supporting community-led wellness initiatives. By doing so, regenerative travel becomes not merely a means of escape or exploration, but a catalyst for transformation.

Ultimately, embracing holistic well-being in travel allows tourism to fulfill its highest potential: to be a force that heals, uplifts, and connects. It nurtures not just the individual body and mind, but the broader communities and landscapes that sustain us all.

Economic Viability

For regenerative travel to be sustainable and scalable, it must be economically viable. This pillar focuses on creating and maintaining tourism models that are financially sustainable while delivering social and environmental benefits. Economic viability ensures that regenerative practices can be effectively implemented and sustained over time, providing consistent value to all stakeholders involved.

Reimagining the Travel Value Supply Chain: The Case for Regenerative and Inclusive Models

The travel industry is a complex ecosystem, often described as a value supply chain, where various interconnected players—from airlines and hotels to tour operators and local communities—work together to create the experiences that define global tourism. Traditionally, this supply chain has been designed to maximize efficiency and profit, often at the expense of the environment, local cultures, and even the well-being of those who provide the services. However, the global crises of recent years, including the Covid-19 pandemic and the growing impacts of climate change, have highlighted the urgent need to rethink this model.

Economic Viability as a Cornerstone of Regenerative Travel

Economic viability plays a foundational role in ensuring that regenerative travel not only delivers environmental and social benefits but also operates sustainably and effectively within the realities of the global market. Far from being at odds with regenerative outcomes, financial success can reinforce and sustain these goals when aligned with ethical principles and long-term vision. In regenerative tourism, profitability and purpose are not mutually exclusive. Rather, they are mutually reinforcing—a dynamic that encourages innovation, stakeholder alignment, and resilient growth across destinations and business models.

Regenerative travel demands a rethinking of traditional tourism economics. Instead of maximizing short-term returns through high-volume, low-cost approaches, regenerative tourism focuses on value-driven experiences that generate deep and lasting benefits for both visitors and host communities. Economic viability, in this context, involves creating and sustaining business models that are profitable while also delivering measurable positive outcomes for people and the planet.[26]

One such example of economic viability in action is Six Senses Hotels Resorts Spas. Known for its luxury accommodations, Six Senses has embedded sustainability, wellness, and community engagement into the core of its business model. From using renewable energy and banning single-use plastics to investing in local development initiatives, the company demonstrates that high-end tourism can generate significant financial returns while remaining deeply regenerative in practice.[27] By proving that luxury and sustainability can coexist, Six Senses sets a powerful precedent for economic viability in the regenerative tourism sector.

Another vehicle for fostering economic viability is impact investment. This form of investment channels capital into projects that yield measurable social and environmental benefits alongside financial returns. Funds such as the Global Sustainable Tourism Partnership have focused on identifying and supporting tourism ventures committed to regenerative principles, helping scale models that prioritize equity, conservation, and cultural integrity.[28] Through this alignment of capital with purpose, impact investment accelerates innovation and bridges the gap between profitability and planetary stewardship.

Local communities have also leveraged regenerative tourism to build diversified income streams that strengthen their economic resilience. For instance, a community-run eco-lodge may combine overnight accommodation with guided nature walks, traditional handicraft markets, and cultural workshops. Such diversification reduces dependency on a single revenue source while allowing communities to retain control over how their culture and environment are shared.[29] This model not only boosts financial stability but ensures broader distribution of benefits, fostering more inclusive prosperity.

Public–private partnerships also illustrate how collaborative governance can underpin economic viability in regenerative travel. The development of the Monteverde Cloud Forest Reserve in Costa Rica, for example, was made possible through cooperative efforts between NGOs, local communities, private investors, and the government. This initiative has generated sustained income from ecotourism while preserving one of the world's most biodiverse cloud forest ecosystems.[30] Such partnerships exemplify the value of multi-stakeholder collaboration in creating tourism models that are both profitable and protective of natural and cultural assets.

The benefits of embedding economic viability in regenerative travel are manifold. First, sustainable growth is made possible when businesses and initiatives are financially self-sufficient, allowing them to continue and scale their operations without dependency on external subsidies. This financial durability ensures that regenerative principles are implemented consistently and can expand to broader contexts over time.[31]

Second, economically viable tourism directly contributes to community prosperity. When tourism is structured to provide dignified employment, stimulate local entrepreneurship, and support inclusive economies, it becomes a driver of development and poverty alleviation. According to the United Nations World Tourism Organization, tourism accounts for one in ten jobs globally, and regenerative tourism can ensure that these jobs are rooted in fairness, equity, and community well-being.[32]

Furthermore, economic success breeds investor confidence, which in turn attracts further capital for innovation and expansion. Demonstrated profitability helps convince stakeholders that regenerative tourism is not merely a niche ideal but a competitive and scalable model. As conscious consumerism rises, businesses that align with regenerative values also gain a competitive advantage in the marketplace, appealing to travelers seeking meaningful, ethical experiences.[33]

To integrate economic viability into regenerative travel, both travelers and industry actors have essential roles to play. Travelers can support regenerative businesses by choosing services and destinations that uphold sustainability and social equity while demonstrating operational excellence. At the industry level, there must be a shift away from volume-driven growth toward value-based models, where quality, intimacy, and local enrichment take precedence.

Moreover, stakeholders should foster innovation by investing in technologies and practices that reduce environmental impact and increase operational efficiency. This includes everything from low-impact infrastructure and digital storytelling platforms to circular economy initiatives and carbon accounting tools. Crucially, regenerative travel businesses must measure and communicate their impact, using robust frameworks to assess economic, environmental, and social outcomes. Transparent reporting not only builds trust with customers and investors but also informs adaptive management and continuous improvement.[34]

In conclusion, grounding regenerative travel in economic viability ensures that its values are not only aspirational but actionable and enduring. By proving that profitability and purpose can go hand in hand, regenerative travel sets a new standard for what responsible tourism can achieve—sustaining people, planet, and prosperity in harmony.

Understanding the Traditional Travel Value Supply Chain

The travel value supply chain comprises all the interconnected stages that collectively deliver a travel experience—from initial planning and booking to on-the-ground service delivery. At its base are suppliers such as airlines, hotels, transportation services, food and beverage providers, and tour operators who offer the primary components of a trip. These elements are distributed and marketed by travel agencies, online booking platforms, and promotional firms that connect suppliers to consumers. Local service providers, including guides, drivers, and hospitality workers, then engage directly with travelers to bring the experience to life. The end consumers are the travelers themselves. However, an often overlooked but critical part of the supply chain is the host community, those who live in the destinations being visited. While these communities shoulder many of tourism's environmental and social burdens, they frequently receive minimal benefit from the industry.

Traditional tourism models prioritize efficiency, high-volume visitor numbers, and profit margins. This has led to a tourism economy dominated by mass travel, where the focus lies more on scale than on sustainability or meaningful experiences. As a result, many destinations have experienced environmental degradation, economic inequity, cultural commodification, and social displacement. Such extractive models have created systems in which the value generated by tourism is disproportionately absorbed by global intermediaries, while local ecosystems and cultures bear the long-term costs.

In response to these challenges, regenerative travel has emerged as a new framework that reimagines tourism as a healing and reciprocal practice. Rather than simply reducing harm, regenerative tourism seeks to leave destinations and communities better off than they were before. This model views tourism as a means of contributing to ecological restoration, cultural preservation, social equity, and inclusive economic development.

Environmental stewardship is one of the foundational principles of regenerative tourism. This involves not just minimizing ecological footprints but actively participating in the restoration of natural ecosystems. Regenerative tourism supports practices such as reforestation, habitat rehabilitation, carbon offsetting, and resource conservation within tourism infrastructure. Hotels and travel providers are increasingly expected to reduce waste, conserve water, and transition to renewable energy sources as part of their operational models.

Another key component is cultural respect and preservation. Regenerative travel emphasizes the value of protecting intangible cultural heritage and supporting community-based narratives. This means working with local artisans, respecting sacred traditions, and ensuring that tourism does not commodify or misrepresent cultures for the sake of profit. Empowering communities to tell their own stories ensures that cultural exchange remains authentic and rooted in mutual respect.

Economic equity is equally vital in regenerative travel. One of the major critiques of traditional tourism is its tendency to cause economic leakage, where profits made in a destination flow back to international corporations rather than staying within local economies. Regenerative tourism models aim to reverse this trend by promoting local procurement, supporting small and medium-sized enterprises, and ensuring fair wages and ethical labor practices throughout the supply chain.

Finally, regenerative travel embraces social inclusion by prioritizing the voices and needs of historically marginalized groups, including indigenous peoples, women, and persons with disabilities. This involves creating inclusive hiring practices, co-developing tourism initiatives with local communities, and ensuring that travel experiences do not exacerbate existing social inequities.

In conclusion, the regenerative travel model offers a transformative alternative to the dominant extractive tourism paradigm. It calls for a fundamental restructuring of the travel value supply chain, one that centers the health of people, places, and the planet. By actively involving all stakeholders—from travelers and operators to local residents and ecosystems—regenerative tourism creates pathways for tourism to become a force of renewal rather than depletion.

Community Empowerment

Community empowerment stands as a mainstay of the regenerative tourism pillars, emphasizing the importance of involving and uplifting local populations in tourism development and operations. This approach recognizes that sustainable and meaningful travel experiences are deeply interconnected with the well-being and prosperity of host communities. Empowering communities involves providing them with the resources, opportunities, and authority to actively participate in and benefit from tourism. It encompasses economic empowerment through job creation and fair wages, social empowerment through education and skill development, and political empowerment through inclusive decision-making processes.

Traditional tourism models have often failed to deliver meaningful benefits to the communities in which they operate. Instead, such models frequently exacerbate inequalities, leading to economic leakage, cultural commodification, and the marginalization of local voices. Much of the revenue generated by mass tourism flows to international operators and investors, bypassing the people who live in the destinations being marketed. This dynamic can deepen social disparities and foster resentment among residents who feel excluded from the decision-making processes that shape their own environments. In response to these limitations, regenerative travel presents an alternative paradigm—one that places community empowerment at its core.

Regenerative travel reorients tourism around the principle of reciprocity, seeking to restore and uplift the social and ecological systems on which travel depends. Central to this is the belief that communities must not only benefit from tourism but must have control over how tourism is designed, implemented, and experienced. When local people are positioned as active agents rather than passive recipients, tourism becomes a tool for self-determination and long-term resilience.[35]

One of the most effective strategies for achieving community empowerment through tourism is the development of community-based tourism (CBT). These initiatives are owned and managed by local residents and emphasize the importance of authentic cultural exchange. For instance, the Mae Kampong Village in northern Thailand has become a model for CBT. Visitors are hosted in homestays and invited to participate in daily routines such as cooking, farming, and weaving. This approach not only generates direct income for community members but also reinforces local pride and cultural continuity.[36]

Fair trade tourism is another important model that advances community empowerment. This approach ensures that economic benefits are equitably shared among all stakeholders, particularly those who have been historically marginalized. In South Africa, Fair Trade Tourism (FTT) certifies tourism enterprises that adhere to ethical labor practices, fair wages, and community reinvestment. By holding businesses accountable to transparent social standards, FTT empowers communities and enhances their bargaining power within the tourism value chain.[37]

Social enterprises also offer powerful mechanisms for linking travel with community development. These businesses reinvest profits into programs that address local challenges, such as education, healthcare, and job training. A notable example is the Sala Bai Hotel School in Cambodia, which trains disadvantaged youth in hospitality and culinary arts. Graduates of the program gain employment in high-end hotels and restaurants, while visitors to the school's training restaurant receive high-quality service and insight into Cambodia's development challenges. This model demonstrates how tourism can serve as a platform for inclusive growth and skill-building.[38]

Participatory planning and governance are equally vital to fostering community empowerment. Rather than imposing tourism development from the top down, regenerative models emphasize inclusive processes where community members actively shape policy and practice. The Waitangi Treaty Grounds in Aotearoa New Zealand exemplifies this approach. Managed in partnership with the local Māori community, the site honors the principles of the Treaty of Waitangi and ensures that tourism aligns with indigenous values. Visitors learn about New Zealand's foundational history through the voices of Māori guides, while revenues are reinvested into cultural preservation and community well-being.[39]

The outcomes of community-empowered tourism are manifold. Economically, communities gain resilience through diverse income streams, local ownership, and reduced reliance on external actors. Tourism becomes a driver of entrepreneurship and a buffer against economic shocks.[40] Socially, such models promote equity by involving all segments of the population—women, youth, and marginalized groups—in decision-making and benefit-sharing. Cultural empowerment also follows when communities are given the agency to define how their stories and traditions are shared with the world. This results in more authentic and sustainable representations, while also enriching the experiences of travelers who gain deeper insight into local ways of life.

To support community empowerment, travelers and tourism stakeholders must make conscious choices. This involves prioritizing locally owned accommodations, tour operators, and restaurants, and seeking out opportunities to engage respectfully with host communities. Ethical travel requires asking questions, listening to community voices, and contributing resources—whether financial, technical, or social—toward locally identified needs. It also means advocating for transparency and accountability in the travel industry, ensuring that businesses are not only claiming to do good but are demonstrating real, measurable impacts on the ground.

When community empowerment becomes the foundation of tourism, the travel experience is transformed. It becomes not merely a leisure activity but a means of fostering equity, resilience, and mutual understanding. Regenerative travel, by centering local voices and redistributing power, offers a model through which tourism can fulfill its potential as a force for social and economic transformation.

Steps Toward Regenerative Travel

The call to rethink the travel value supply chain and adopt more regenerative and inclusive models is not just a moral imperative; it is a practical necessity. The disruptions caused by the Covid-19 pandemic have shown how fragile the traditional tourism model is, with its reliance on mass travel and its focus on profit over sustainability. As the industry rebuilds, there is an opportunity to create a more resilient, responsible, and equitable system.

Furthermore, as travelers become more aware of the environmental and social impacts of their journeys, they are increasingly seeking out experiences that align with their values. The rise of conscious consumerism means that businesses that adopt regenerative and inclusive practices are likely to attract a growing segment of the market.

Reimagining the travel value supply chain to focus on regeneration and inclusivity is not just a trend—it is the future of tourism. By prioritizing environmental stewardship, cultural respect, economic equity, and social inclusion, the travel industry can play a crucial role in building a more sustainable and just world. This shift will require collaboration, innovation, and a commitment to long-term thinking, but the rewards—for travelers, communities, and the planet—will be profound.

Education and Awareness

The foundation of regenerative travel lies in education. Empowering travelers with knowledge allows them to make informed, responsible decisions. This includes access to guides on sustainable destinations, tips for reducing environmental impact, and real-life examples of successful regenerative initiatives. Equally important is industry training—providing tourism professionals with the tools to adopt and implement regenerative practices through certifications, workshops, and knowledge-sharing platforms. Local communities must also be engaged in this learning process, deepening their understanding of the cultural and ecological value of their land and how tourism can become a force for renewal.

Making Conscious Travel Choices

Mindful decision-making is central to regenerative travel. This begins with selecting destinations and experiences that embody regenerative principles—places where community well-being and environmental stewardship are prioritized. Transportation choices also play a role; travelers are encouraged to choose lower-impact options like trains or carpools and to offset emissions for necessary flights. Consumption habits matter too—supporting local economies through ethical purchases, reducing waste, and conserving resources can significantly shift the tourism footprint toward regeneration.

Engaging in Regenerative Experiences

Regenerative travel is not a passive activity. It involves hands-on engagement in meaningful, community-led projects. Participatory tourism, such as environmental restoration or cultural preservation efforts, allows travelers to give back while learning from local knowledge. Educational exchanges—such as learning traditional crafts, organic farming methods, or conservation practices—provide deeper insight into regenerative lifestyles. At the heart of this is mindful interaction: approaching each experience with humility, respect, and a sincere desire to contribute positively.

Creating Post-Trip Engagement and Advocacy

The regenerative journey doesn't end when the trip does. In fact, what happens afterward is just as important. Travelers are encouraged to share their experiences and insights, using storytelling and social media to inspire others. Continued support for the communities and initiatives they've encountered—whether through donations, partnerships, or return visits—fosters long-term impact. Moreover, travelers can use their voices to advocate for industry and policy changes, pushing for more equitable, sustainable models of tourism at home and abroad.

Collaborative Efforts for Systemic Change

True regeneration cannot happen in isolation. It demands cooperation across all levels of society. Multi-stakeholder partnerships—among governments, businesses, non-governmental organizations (NGOs), and local communities—can pool resources, coordinate efforts, and amplify outcomes. Policy development is another vital lever for change. Incentivizing regenerative practices, protecting cultural and ecological assets, and supporting fair, inclusive development are essential components of systemic transformation. Research and innovation, too, play a critical role in understanding what works, what doesn't, and how best to scale impact. Global networks and forums offer spaces for knowledge exchange and collective action, strengthening the movement from the grassroots to the global stage.

Embracing a Regenerative Mindset

Ultimately, regenerative travel is anchored in a mindset—a way of seeing and being in the world. It requires holistic thinking, recognizing the interconnectedness of social, ecological, and economic systems. It values adaptability and resilience, acknowledging that change is constant and necessary. Empathy and respect guide all interactions, placing human and planetary dignity at the forefront. Above all, it is driven by purpose: A commitment to leaving each place better than we found it, and to traveling not just for leisure, but for learning, healing, and connection.

The pillars of regenerative travel—ecological restoration, community empowerment, cultural resilience, holistic well-being, and economic viability—provide a comprehensive framework for reimagining and transforming the travel industry. By integrating these principles into our travel experiences and industry practices, we can harness the power of tourism as a force for positive change, contributing to the healing and flourishing of our planet and its diverse inhabitants.

This journey toward regeneration is not only necessary in the face of pressing global challenges but also offers profound opportunities for personal growth, meaningful connections, and sustainable prosperity. As travelers, businesses, and communities embrace this transformative approach, we move closer to realizing a future where travel enriches lives, revitalizes environments, and fosters a more equitable and harmonious world.

In the chapters that follow, we will delve deeper into each of these pillars, exploring practical strategies, inspiring case studies, and actionable insights that illuminate the path forward.

Key Takeaways

The five interconnected pillars:

- Cultural resilience, ecological restoration, holistic well-being, economic viability, and community empowerment work together, not in hierarchy.
- Progress in one area strengthens the entire regenerative system.

Cultural resilience through capacity-building:

- Communities lead their own cultural development rather than performing for tourists.
- Examples: Japan's Kodo immersion programs, Aboriginal-led tours in Australia.
- Shifts power from external operators to local cultural stewards.

Ecological restoration as active healing:

- Goes beyond conservation to actively restore degraded ecosystems.
- Tourists participate in reforestation, coral restoration, and habitat rehabilitation.
- Transforms travelers from consumers into environmental stewards.

Holistic well-being integration:

- Connects individual wellness with community and ecosystem health.
- Includes wellness retreats, nature immersion, and slow travel approaches.
- Benefits both travelers and host communities through health initiatives.

Economic viability as foundation:

- Proves profitability and purpose reinforce each other in regenerative models.
- Focus on value-driven experiences over high-volume tourism.
- Examples: Six Senses Hotels, impact investment funds, public–private partnerships.

Community empowerment as core:

- Local communities control and benefit from tourism development.
- Community-based tourism, fair trade practices, and participatory planning.
- Ensures economic benefits stay within local economies.

Implementation pathway:

- Education provides foundation for conscious travel choices.
- Hands-on engagement through participatory tourism creates real impact.
- Post-trip advocacy extends influence beyond individual journeys.
- Multi-stakeholder collaboration enables systemic industry transformation.

Notes

1 F Berkes and C Folke (1998) *Linking Social and Ecological Systems: Management practices and social mechanisms for building resilience*, Cambridge University Press, Cambridge.
2 P Freire (2000/1968) *Pedagogy of the Oppressed*, 30th anniversary edn, trans M B Ramos, Continuum, London.
3 United Nations Educational, Scientific and Cultural Organization (UNESCO). Sustainable tourism and cultural heritage, UNESCO, 2017. whc.unesco.org (archived at https://perma.cc/7S72-USV4)
4 T Oakes. Cultural strategies of development: Implications for community-based cultural tourism in China, *Tourism Geographies*, 2016, 8 (4), 425–43.
5 UNESCO. Safeguarding the Angkor site, 2013. whc.unesco.org/en/list/668/ (archived at https://perma.cc/M2VH-R4LD)
6 T Hinch and R Butler (2007) *Tourism and Indigenous Peoples: Issues and implications*, Butterworth-Heinemann, London.
7 F Berkes and C Folke (1998) *Linking Social and Ecological Systems: Management practices and social mechanisms for building resilience*, Cambridge University Press, Cambridge.
8 United Nations Educational, Scientific and Cultural Organization (UNESCO). Sustainable tourism and cultural heritage, UNESCO, 2017. whc.unesco.org (archived at https://perma.cc/7S72-USV4)
9 United Nations Educational, Scientific and Cultural Organization (UNESCO). Safeguarding the Angkor site, UNESCO, 2013. whc.unesco.org/en/list/668/ (archived at https://perma.cc/M2VH-R4LD)
10 Organisation for Economic Co-operation and Development (2009) The impact of culture on tourism, OECD Publishing. https://doi.org/10.1787/9789264040731-en (archived at https://perma.cc/THL6-2TG2)

11 T Hinch and R Butler (2007) *Tourism and Indigenous Peoples: Issues and implications*, Butterworth-Heinemann, London.
12 N Salazar, 2012. Community-based cultural tourism: issues, threats and opportunities, *Journal of Sustainable Tourism*, 20 (1), 9–22. https://doi.org/10.1080/09669582.2011.596279 (archived at https://perma.cc/B2X2-3G2S), ResearchGate+2ojs.jdss.org.pk+2.
13 S Gössling and C M Hall (2006) *Tourism and Global Environmental Change: Ecological, social, economic and political interrelationships*, Routledge, London.
14 R Bellato and M Hughes. Regenerative tourism: Beyond sustainable tourism towards nature restoration, *Tourism Recreation Research*, 2021, 46 (2), 245–57.
15 African Wildlife Foundation. Conservation through tourism, 2023. www.awf.org (archived at https://perma.cc/WAU4-F7MS)
16 S Gössling and C M Hall (2006) *Tourism and Global Environmental Change: Ecological, social, economic and political interrelationships*, Routledge, London.
17 J Aronson, S J Milton and J N Blignaut (2007) *Restoring Natural Capital: Science, business, and practice*, Island Press, Washington, DC.
18 L White. Mindful travel: The role of mindfulness in tourism, *Annals of Tourism Research*, 2015, 53, 1–19.
19 S Becken and J E Hay (2007) *Tourism and Climate Change: Risks and opportunities*, Channel View Publications, Bristol.
20 F Capra and P L Luisi (2014) *The Systems View of Life: A unifying vision*, Cambridge University Press, Cambridge.
21 L White. Mindful travel: The role of mindfulness in tourism, *Annals of Tourism Research*, 2015, 53, 1–19.
22 Q Li. Effect of forest bathing trips on human immune function, *Environmental Health and Preventive Medicine*, 2010, 15 (1), 9–17.
23 S Fullagar, K Markwell and E Wilson (2012) *Slow Tourism: Experiences and mobilities*, Channel View Publications, Bristol.
24 www.packforapurpose.org (archived at https://perma.cc/MNR2-LAW3)
25 M Smith and L Puczkó (2009) *Health and Wellness Tourism*, Butterworth-Heinemann, Oxford.
26 A Pollock (2019) *The Conscious Travel Manifesto: A call to action for regenerative tourism*, Conscious Travel, Stockport.
27 Six Senses. Sustainability overview, 2023. www.sixsenses.com/en/about-us/sustainability

28 United Nations Environment Programme (UNEP). Sustainable tourism investment guidelines, UNEP, 2020.
29 H Goodwin (2016) *Responsible Tourism: Using tourism for sustainable development*, Goodfellow Publishers, Oxford.
30 M Honey (2008) *Ecotourism and Sustainable Development: Who owns paradise?* Island Press, Washington, DC.
31 S F McCool and K Bosak (eds) (2016) *Reframing Sustainable Tourism*, Springer, New York.
32 United Nations World Tourism Organization (UNWTO). Tourism and jobs: A better future for all, UNWTO, 2018.
33 P H Ray and Anderson (2000) *The Cultural Creatives: How 50 million people are changing the world*, Three Rivers Press, New York.
34 United Nations Environment Programme (UNEP). Sustainable tourism investment guidelines, UNEP, 2020.
35 R Bellato and M Hughes. Regenerative tourism: Beyond sustainable tourism towards nature restoration, *Tourism Recreation Research*, 2021, 46 (2), 245–57.
36 N Kontogeorgopoulos. Community-based ecotourism in Phuket and Ao Phangnga, Thailand: Partial victories and bittersweet remedies, *Journal of Sustainable Tourism*, 2005, 13 (1), 4–23.
37 H Goodwin (2008) *Tourism, Local Economic Development, and Poverty Reduction*, Channel View Publications, Bristol.
38 Sala Bai. Sala Bai Hotel School: Training for a better future, Sala Bai, 2024. www.salabai.com (archived at https://perma.cc/72EL-5C64)
39 Te Puni Kōkiri. Realising Māori tourism potential, Te Puni Kōkiri, 2015. www.tpk.govt.nz/en/a-matou-mohiotanga/business-and-economics/realising-maori-tourism-potential (archived at https://perma.cc/4ZYJ-H8VL)
40 C Ashley, C Boyd and H Goodwin (2001) *Pro-Poor Tourism Strategies: Making tourism work for the poor*, Overseas Development Institute, London.

Capacity-Building in Tourism

03

Capacity-building stands as the foundational element of regenerative tourism, equipping communities with the tools, skills, and systems they need to lead their own development while maintaining control over their cultural and environmental assets. It is through intentional investment in education, training, leadership development, and institutional strengthening that communities are empowered to thrive in the face of change.

In the context of regenerative tourism, capacity-building ensures that communities are not passive recipients of tourism but active shapers of it. By cultivating local expertise, strengthening governance, and fostering inclusive participation, capacity-building enables communities to harness tourism as a platform for innovation, pride, and economic opportunity. It supports the development of locally rooted solutions that reflect the unique identity and needs of each place.

Capacity-building informs every layer of regenerative practice. It supports holistic well-being by enabling community members to access meaningful livelihoods, education, and health resources. It guides ecological restoration by empowering local stewards to apply traditional and scientific knowledge in conservation. It underpins economic viability by building resilient, community-led business models that generate long-term benefits.

Most importantly, capacity-building ensures that tourism serves as a tool for empowerment, rather than extraction. It shifts the focus from short-term gains to long-term resilience, cultivating the conditions for communities to adapt, lead, and thrive on their own terms.

Figure 3.1 A regenerative model for capacity-building in tourism

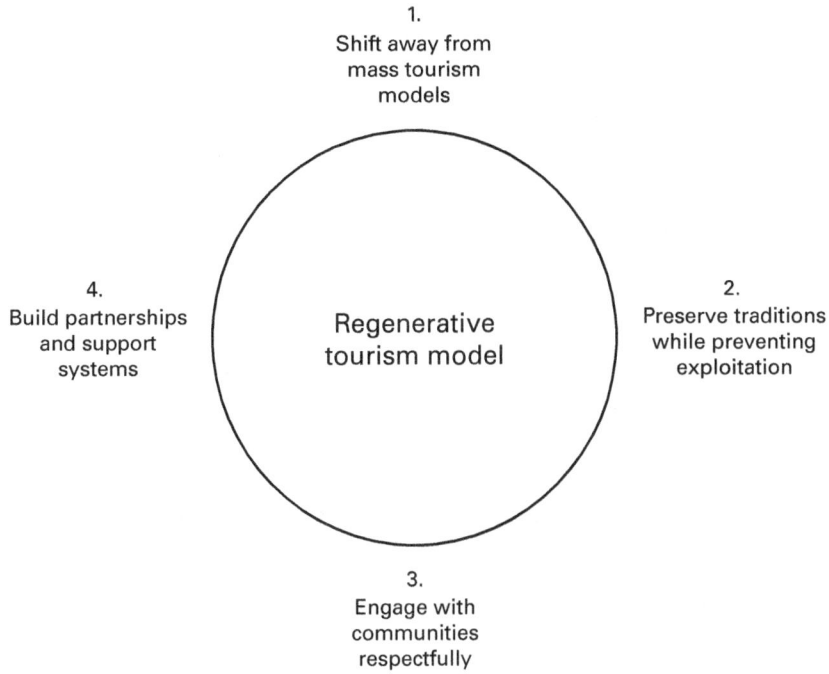

SOURCE Amanda Ho/Regenerative Travel (2025) The regenerative tourism circle [Chart]. In *Regenerative Tourism and Hospitality: Building a resilient and positive impact-led travel industry.*

Regenerative tourism transforms the industry into a catalyst for equity, sustainability, and self-determination. By prioritizing capacity-building, it creates a model where tourism supports the ongoing empowerment of host communities, enriches the experiences of travelers, and safeguards the ecological and cultural wealth of destinations for future generations (Figure 3.1).

1 Shift away from mass tourism models: This emphasizes the transition from high-volume, low-value tourism to sustainable, high-quality models that prioritize mutual benefits for visitors and locals. Central to this shift is the role of strong, inclusive governance frameworks, which empower communities, ensure equitable benefit-sharing, and safeguard cultural and environmental resources.

2 Preserve traditions while preventing exploitation: This theme focuses on supporting the authentic evolution of cultural practices while avoiding the commodification or misuse of traditions for tourism purposes.

3 Engage with communities respectfully and with intention: This emphasizes the importance of meaningful and respectful interactions with host communities, ensuring their voices, needs, and aspirations are central to tourism development.

4 Build partnerships and support systems: This strategy emphasizes the importance of collaboration among stakeholders—communities, governments, and private sector entities—to create robust networks that support sustainable tourism and community resilience.

Shift Away from Mass Tourism Models

The 20th century brought rapid technological progress that further democratized tourism. The advent of commercial aviation in the mid-century made long-distance travel viable for the middle class. Airlines like Pan Am introduced the world to the golden age of air travel, while budget carriers like Ryanair and easyJet, emerging in the late 20th century, made international flights affordable to millions.[1]

Simultaneously, tourism infrastructure expanded globally. Iconic developments such as Mediterranean resorts, Disney theme parks, and luxury hotels catered to the growing appetite for leisure travel. High-speed trains, such as Japan's Shinkansen in the 1960s, and mega cruise ships further diversified travel options, increasing accessibility and affordability.

Economic globalization also played a pivotal role. Trade agreements, international corporations, and the emergence of a global middle class, particularly in Asia, fueled a dramatic increase in tourism. By the late 20th century, travel was no longer a privilege but an expectation for millions worldwide, supported by cheap package tours and competitive pricing from travel agencies.

Media and the Cultural Push for Travel

The media's portrayal of travel as a desirable and aspirational activity significantly contributed to the growth of mass tourism. During the post-war boom of the 1950s and 1960s, travel advertisements in magazines, films, and television romanticized exotic destinations. With the rise of social media in the 2000s, platforms like Instagram amplified this trend, showcasing idyllic locations and encouraging "bucket list" tourism. This created a culture of consumption around travel, where experiencing popular destinations became a status symbol.

Governments also played a role in promoting tourism through policies like open skies agreements, which reduced restrictions on international aviation routes, and visa-free travel arrangements. For many countries, tourism became a cornerstone of their economic development strategy, incentivizing the growth of the industry.

The mass tourism model, long predicated on maximizing visitor numbers and economic gains, has reached a critical inflection point. By prioritizing high volume and low value, this approach has often disregarded the long-term health of destinations, communities, and ecosystems. Its consequences—overtourism, environmental degradation, and cultural erosion—have created an urgent need for a transformative shift. Regenerative tourism offers a promising alternative, focusing on mutual benefit and sustainable practices that protect and uplift both local communities and visitors. By emphasizing quality over quantity, regenerative tourism fosters meaningful connections, cultural preservation, and ecological stewardship.

Overtourism: Destinations Under Pressure

Overtourism epitomizes the unsustainable nature of mass tourism, with destinations like Venice, Barcelona, and Machu Picchu serving as cautionary tales. Venice, which receives over 20 million visitors annually, has seen its infrastructure strained to the breaking point. The influx has driven up living costs, forcing local residents out of the city and contributing to depopulation. UNESCO has flagged the city's cultural and architectural heritage as being at risk from such unsustainable tourism levels.[2]

Similarly, Machu Picchu's fragile archaeological sites have suffered from excessive foot traffic, prompting authorities to introduce strict visitor caps and timed entry slots to mitigate damage. These measures aim to preserve the site's historical integrity while addressing the challenges of high tourist demand.[3] Such examples highlight the urgent need for destination management strategies that balance visitor numbers with preservation efforts.

Environmental Degradation: The Toll of Unchecked Growth

The mass tourism model exerts immense pressure on natural environments, resulting in pollution, habitat loss, and resource depletion. Thailand's Maya Bay, immortalized in the movie *The Beach*, became a stark example of environmental degradation. Overrun by tourists, the bay's coral reefs suffered severe bleaching due to excessive snorkeling and boat traffic. In 2018, the Thai government temporarily closed the bay to allow its ecosystems to recover, a move praised by environmental advocates.[4]

Coastal and island destinations often face additional pressures, such as severe water shortages caused by high demand from hotels and resorts. The World Bank has documented cases where tourism-driven water usage has left local communities struggling to access sufficient supplies for daily needs, highlighting the resource inequities exacerbated by mass tourism.[5]

Cultural Exploitation: Commodification of Traditions

Cultural exploitation is another adverse consequence of mass tourism. Indigenous dances, crafts, and ceremonies are often altered to cater to tourist preferences, stripping them of their original meaning and significance. This commodification not only erodes cultural authenticity but also diminishes the value of traditions for the communities that practice them. According to the *Stanford Social Innovation Review*, sustainable tourism initiatives must engage local communities as custodians of their heritage, ensuring that cultural expressions are preserved in their authentic forms while benefiting the people who sustain them.[6]

Regenerative tourism seeks to address these challenges by shifting the focus from high-volume, profit-driven models to sustainable practices that enhance the well-being of destinations. By reducing overtourism, protecting natural ecosystems, and empowering communities to preserve their cultural heritage, regenerative tourism offers a path forward. This approach not only addresses the limitations of mass tourism but also ensures the long-term viability and appeal of destinations.

Governance Frameworks for Resilience

Regenerative tourism acknowledges that resilient communities are the foundation of sustainable tourism. In this context, resilience refers to the capacity of communities to adapt, thrive, and retain their cultural integrity amidst external pressures such as mass tourism, climate change, and economic volatility. This resilience is nurtured through respectful engagement, co-creation, and the empowerment of communities to lead tourism initiatives.

As Dr. Sue Snyman, Director of Research at the School of Wildlife Conservation at the African Leadership University, notes, "Protected areas are heavily dependent on communities seeing the value of the protected areas, because if they don't see a value, they have no incentive to conserve." This highlights the importance of aligning tourism development with local priorities, cultural values, and ecological needs to ensure community support for conservation efforts and discourage unsustainable practices such as poaching or land degradation.

A successful governance framework for community-led tourism recognizes that one-size-fits-all solutions are ineffective. Each community has distinct cultural, economic, and environmental contexts that must inform the design of tourism initiatives. Sue emphasizes the importance of tailoring solutions, stating, "It's not about imposing the same cookie-cutter solution but designing options that can be tailored to specific communities."

Tailoring solutions requires an understanding of local power dynamics, governance structures, and community priorities. Stakeholders must engage in local power mapping to identify key leaders and decision-makers, whether they are traditional leaders, democratically elected officials, or other influential figures. This approach ensures projects align with local values and fosters trust among community members. For instance, in Namibia, an NGO once provided solar panels to a Himba community but failed to recognize their immediate need for water access. The solar panels were repurposed to collect water, highlighting the necessity of aligning solutions with actual community needs.

Community-led tourism is a core principle of regenerative tourism, as externally imposed projects often fail to address local needs and aspirations. When communities are actively involved in decision-making from the outset, they gain a sense of ownership and pride, fostering their ability to respond to challenges and build sustainable futures.

The Role of Policy and Governance

Effective governance frameworks and supportive policies are critical for empowering communities to engage meaningfully in tourism and conservation efforts. Policies must grant communities land-use rights, property rights, and mechanisms for benefiting directly from natural resources. As Sue emphasizes, "You cannot have a wildlife economy without good policy and legislation... it has to start at a government level."

While Kenya and Tanzania are often cited as prominent examples of wildlife economies, it is essential to note significant challenges in both countries, including issues of centralized wildlife ownership, inconsistent benefit-sharing, corruption, and elite capture.[7] Despite isolated successful projects, the broader enabling environment in East Africa still needs improvement to ensure equitable community benefits. For instance, Kenya has lost approximately 60 percent of its wildlife over the past 35 years due to habitat loss, policy gaps, and lack of inclusive frameworks, prompting new policy initiatives aimed at overtourism and sustainability in areas like Amboseli National Park.[8]

By contrast, Southern Africa and countries like Uganda and Rwanda offer stronger examples of community-based natural resource management and more structured benefit-sharing mechanisms. In Uganda, the Uganda Wildlife Authority allocates 20 percent of national park entry fees to surrounding communities, funding projects such as schools, healthcare, and infrastructure.[9] Similarly, Rwanda directs a percentage of tourism revenue from parks like Volcanoes National Park into community development, financing water systems, roads, and livelihood programs that reduce dependency on park resources.[10]

These examples demonstrate how policy frameworks can integrate conservation goals with socio-economic development, fostering local support for biodiversity protection.

Diversification for Resilience

The Covid-19 pandemic exposed the vulnerabilities of communities reliant solely on tourism. In Kenya, conservancies heavily dependent on tourism revenue experienced severe economic distress when travel halted. Conversely, countries and communities with diversified wildlife economies fared better. For instance, Tanzania integrates sustainable agriculture, livestock ranching, beekeeping, and carbon credits alongside tourism to create multiple revenue streams and greater resilience.[11]

Sue highlights that while tourism remains a critical pillar of the wildlife economy, it must be complemented by alternative livelihoods to ensure community resilience. Kenya's Ewaso Conservancy, for example, blends tourism with livestock grazing, wildlife estates, and beekeeping, diversifying income and buffering communities against tourism market fluctuations.[12]

In Uganda, communities around Bwindi Impenetrable National Park participate in revenue sharing from gorilla tourism and supplement their incomes through tea farming, beekeeping, and handicraft sales.[13] Similarly, Rwanda has promoted community enterprises in agriculture and handicrafts linked to tourism, enhancing economic stability and conservation outcomes.[14]

Diversification not only increases financial security but also strengthens community engagement in conservation, as people see tangible, multifaceted benefits from protecting wildlife and ecosystems.

Engaging Communities: A "Hand Up, Not a Handout"

True empowerment involves equipping communities with skills, knowledge, and resources. Sue stresses the importance of capacity-building, enabling communities to participate effectively in tourism enterprises, manage natural resources, and negotiate equitable partnerships. Training in business management, financial literacy, conservation, and hospitality fosters economic independence and cultural pride.

Engagement must be genuine and respectful. As Sue states, "Tourism should be engaging very clearly with communities in what they need... it's critical to have that engagement." Listening to communities ensures that tourism initiatives reflect local values and priorities, leading to sustainable and culturally relevant outcomes.

Revenue-sharing agreements, transparent governance structures, and community trusts ensure benefits are distributed equitably. For instance, Rwanda's tourism revenue-sharing scheme has funded over 800 community projects since 2005, ranging from water systems to schools.[15] In Uganda, revenue from gorilla permits helps finance education, healthcare, and infrastructure, fostering goodwill and support for conservation among local people.[16]

Beyond economic gains, tourism offers intangible benefits, including cultural pride and recognition of environmental services. Many communities value protected areas not only for income but for spiritual significance and ecosystem services, such as water security and climate regulation. Recognizing these intangible benefits is crucial for building long-term community support for conservation efforts.

Managing Overtourism Through Policy: The Kenya Example

Kenya provides an instructive case study in addressing overtourism while attempting to build community resilience. The Maasai Mara National Reserve draws significant global attention, especially during the Great Migration, resulting in congestion, habitat degradation, and wildlife stress. To manage these pressures, Kenya increased park fees effective from January 2024, with non-residents now paying up to $200 per adult per day during peak seasons.[17]

Higher fees are intended to reduce overcrowding, fund conservation efforts, and contribute to community projects. While concerns remain that these price hikes could deter budget-conscious travelers, proponents argue that the strategy targets eco-conscious tourists willing to invest in sustainable experiences, aligning with a high-value, low-impact tourism model.

Beyond park fees, Kenya has developed community-led conservancies, such as the Naboisho Conservancy, which limit visitor numbers and vehicles, offering exclusive, low-impact experiences. Revenue from park fees and eco-lodges is shared among local Maasai landowners, funding essential services like schools and healthcare. However, despite such initiatives, significant challenges remain in Kenya regarding equitable benefit-sharing and consistent governance frameworks.

Diversifying Economic Opportunities

Kenya's model demonstrates how innovative governance and community-led conservation can transform tourism into a tool for socioeconomic development. Initiatives like Naboisho Conservancy showcase the power of equitable revenue-sharing and active community engagement. Local Maasai landowners play a central role in managing tourism, ensuring cultural values and priorities shape tourism experiences.

Recognizing the risks of overreliance on tourism, Kenya and other East African nations are exploring integrated models combining tourism with livestock farming, beekeeping, sustainable agriculture, and carbon projects.[18] Similarly, Rwanda and Uganda have successfully diversified local economies around national parks, strengthening both livelihoods and conservation outcomes. While Kenya's experiences offer valuable lessons, the ultimate success of wildlife economies across Africa hinges on robust governance, equitable benefit-sharing, genuine community engagement, and diversified livelihoods. Southern Africa, Uganda, and Rwanda provide important examples of how policy frameworks can balance conservation goals with tangible community benefits, offering pathways for a truly regenerative tourism model.

Bhutan: A Real World Example of High-Value, Low-Impact Tourism

Bhutan's approach to tourism offers a globally admired blueprint for sustainable and regenerative practices. While many nations chase high visitor numbers to fuel short-term economic gains, Bhutan has chosen to prioritize the well-being of its people, the preservation of its culture, and the protection of its environment. Its "High Value, Low Impact" policy, implemented in 1974 when the country first opened its borders to international tourism, exemplifies how carefully managed tourism can benefit both locals and visitors alike.[19]

Essential to Bhutan's tourism model is the Sustainable Development Fee (SDF), currently set at $200 per person per day. This fee covers accommodation, meals, and a licensed guide, ensuring a seamless experience for travelers while directly funding essential national priorities.

KEY GOALS OF THE SUSTAINABLE DEVELOPMENT FEE

- Limit visitor numbers: The SDF positions tourism as a premium experience, controlling visitor inflow and preventing overcrowding that could strain infrastructure and degrade the environment.[20]
- Revenue for social programs: Proceeds from the fee are invested in free healthcare, education, and Bhutan's commitment to remaining carbon-negative.[21]
- Sustainable infrastructure: The SDF also supports eco-friendly facilities, waste management systems, and renewable energy projects.[22]

This model ensures that tourism directly benefits Bhutan's citizens while fostering an elevated experience for visitors.

Safeguarding Cultural Integrity

Safeguarding cultural integrity is fundamental to Bhutan's tourism strategy, which positions the country's rich traditions, spiritual heritage, and societal values as its greatest assets. To protect and celebrate this cultural wealth, the Bhutanese government enforces measures such as requiring all international visitors to travel with licensed Bhutanese guides, who provide cultural insights and ensure adherence to local customs and practices. Tourists are also encouraged to respect local norms, including modest dress and appropriate conduct at sacred sites. Furthermore, tourism revenues help sustain significant cultural events like the annual Paro Tsechu, ensuring that such festivals remain authentic community practices rather than performances altered to cater to tourist expectations. These policies help preserve Bhutan's cultural identity and prevent the commodification often seen in mass tourism destinations.[23]

Environmental Stewardship: A Carbon-Negative Commitment

Equally important is Bhutan's environmental stewardship, underpinned by its unique status as the world's only carbon-negative nation, absorbing more carbon dioxide than it emits.[24] Tourism plays a significant role in maintaining this balance, as over 70 percent of Bhutan's land remains under forest cover, with tourism revenues supporting reforestation and wildlife conservation initiatives. Proceeds from Bhutan's Sustainable Development Fee also contribute to renewable energy projects, especially hydropower, which supplies clean domestic energy and generates revenue through exports. Bhutan enforces strict waste management and recycling policies, particularly in tourist areas, to preserve its pristine landscapes for future generations. Through strategic alignment of tourism revenue with ecological goals, Bhutan protects its natural beauty and biodiversity.[25]

Economic Impact on Local Communities

Economically, Bhutan's tourism model aims to ensure that benefits flow directly to local communities, in contrast to mass tourism models where profits often accrue to international corporations.[26] Employment opportunities in guiding, hospitality, and traditional crafts contribute to widespread economic benefits and help sustain local livelihoods. Community-based tourism initiatives, such as rural homestays, foster meaningful interactions between visitors and local families, generating direct income and facilitating cultural exchange. Additionally, tourism revenues significantly contribute to public services like free healthcare and education, ensuring that all Bhutanese citizens—not only those working in the tourism sector—share in the sector's prosperity.

Challenges and Ongoing Efforts

Despite its success, Bhutan's tourism model faces challenges. The Covid-19 pandemic severely disrupted global travel, significantly affecting Bhutan's tourism revenue and prompting the country to reevaluate its strategy.[27] In response, Bhutan has invested in digital promotion and efforts to attract high-value travelers who align with its sustainability ethos. The country is also exploring diversified tourism offerings, including wellness retreats, adventure tourism, and agro-tourism, to broaden its appeal while remaining committed to its core principles. Furthermore, Bhutan is considering flexible pricing models for the SDF to address concerns over high costs for repeat visitors and regional tourists while preserving its high-value, low-impact approach.

A Model for Regenerative Tourism

Bhutan's tourism approach demonstrates that economic development can coexist with cultural integrity and environmental stewardship. By emphasizing quality over quantity, Bhutan has established a tourism framework that preserves cultural heritage, safeguards natural resources, and distributes economic benefits equitably among its population. For nations grappling with the negative effects of mass tourism, Bhutan offers a compelling case study in regenerative tourism, showing how intentional policies can place local communities and ecological health at the core of development, transforming travel into a force for mutual benefit and lasting positive change.

Preserve Traditions While Preventing Exploitation

Cultural traditions are the living expressions of a community's history, identity, and way of life. They embody values, knowledge, and practices passed down through generations, forming the backbone of collective identity. However, the rapid pace of globalization and mass tourism often places these traditions at risk, either by commodifying them or eroding their authenticity. Supporting the evolution of traditions is not about freezing them in time but empowering communities to protect and adapt their cultural heritage in ways that remain relevant and meaningful to them.

Empowering local communities to protect and guide the evolution of their traditions is central to regenerative travel. By involving community members as custodians of their cultural heritage, we respect their agency and ensure that any adaptations are in harmony with their values.

Education and awareness play a vital role in preserving intangible cultural heritage by creating platforms for knowledge-sharing both within communities and with the wider public, fostering pride and deeper understanding of cultural practices. Equally important is economic support, which involves offering fair compensation to traditional artisans, performers, and cultural guides, ensuring their skills are valued and sustained for future generations. Additionally, policy advocacy is essential, as it requires collaboration with local governments and organizations to implement policies that protect and promote intangible cultural heritage.

Traditions are ever-changing, shaped by the experiences and needs of the people who practice them. Supporting the evolution of traditions allows communities to balance preserving their cultural roots with adapting to modern challenges and opportunities. This approach ensures that cultural practices remain vibrant and integral to daily life rather than being relegated to performances staged for tourist consumption.

Gentrification: A Threat to Cultural Heritage and Community Integrity

Gentrification, often fueled by mass tourism and unchecked development, poses a significant threat to cultural traditions and the integrity of local communities. While increased economic activity and visibility can bring opportunities, they often come at the cost of displacing local populations, commodifying culture, and eroding authenticity. This process undermines the unique identity of a community, replacing its rich cultural heritage with superficial experiences designed primarily for tourists. According to a study published in *Tourism Geographies*, the rapid influx of tourism dollars into local economies often leads to rising property values, loss of affordable housing, and cultural dislocation.[28]

Cultural practices that were once deeply rooted in daily life risk being reduced to performances tailored to tourists. These staged experiences often strip traditions of their original meaning and value to the community.[29] Simultaneously, rising real estate prices and living costs, driven by luxury developments and short-term rentals, force long-standing residents to move away. This displacement weakens the community's social fabric and disrupts the intergenerational transmission of cultural knowledge.[30] In the pursuit of broader tourist appeal, some communities dilute their unique traditions to create more universally recognizable experiences, erasing the distinctiveness of local cultures and replacing diversity with a globalized sameness.[31]

Regenerative tourism offers a framework to counteract the negative effects of gentrification by prioritizing the well-being of local communities and preserving their cultural heritage. Actively involving communities in tourism planning ensures that development aligns with their needs and values, empowering residents to have a voice in how tourism affects their lives.[32] Community-owned enterprises, such as cooperatives and locally managed guesthouses, help retain economic benefits within the community and reduce the influence of external developers.[33]

Supporting the natural evolution of cultural traditions ensures they remain meaningful and relevant while preserving their roots. This approach prevents traditions from being frozen in time for external consumption and instead fosters pride and resilience among community members.[34] Educating tourists about the intrinsic value of these traditions further enhances their appreciation for cultural authenticity. Transparent economic models, like Fogo Island Inn's Economic Nutrition label, also play a vital role by educating tourists on the impact of their spending and promoting responsible economic engagement.

Policy advocacy and protection are critical in addressing the structural issues underlying gentrification. Policies that limit unsustainable development and short-term rentals, such as zoning laws and cultural preservation grants, can help maintain community integrity. Collaboration between governments, NGOs, and local communities to safeguard cultural heritage ensures that tourism serves the interests of residents first and foremost.

Regenerative tourism emphasizes that development should benefit communities without displacing or marginalizing them. By prioritizing cultural integrity and community well-being, this approach ensures that traditions evolve naturally and local identities remain vibrant and authentic. Research has shown that thoughtful travel can empower communities, strengthen resilience, and preserve cultural heritage.

Gentrification does not have to be an inevitable consequence of tourism. Through sustainable, community-led initiatives, regenerative travel can transform tourism into a force for cultural preservation rather than cultural erasure. Gentrification, driven by tourism, has significantly impacted cities like Lisbon, Barcelona, and regions like Bali, Indonesia. These destinations illustrate the challenges of balancing tourism growth with the preservation of local communities and cultural heritage.

Lisbon, Portugal

Lisbon has experienced significant gentrification due to its rapid rise as a global tourist destination. Historic neighborhoods such as Alfama have become hotspots for short-term rental platforms like Airbnb, driving up property prices and displacing long-term residents. This "touristification" has transformed once-residential areas into tourist-centric locales, eroding the traditional character and social cohesion of these neighborhoods.[35]

To combat these issues, Lisbon City Council introduced the "Return to the Neighborhood" program. This initiative aims to reclaim vacant municipal housing and provide affordable living options for residents impacted by rising rents. The program represents an effort to restore Lisbon's social fabric while addressing the adverse effects of mass tourism.[36]

Barcelona, Spain

Barcelona, a top European destination, has faced intense gentrification in districts such as the Gothic Quarter and Barceloneta. The rise of short-term rentals has driven up housing costs, leading to the displacement of locals and transforming these neighborhoods into tourist hubs. This has sparked anti-tourism sentiment, with residents staging protests to demand stricter regulations on tourist accommodations.[37]

In response, Barcelona's government announced plans to ban all holiday apartment rentals by 2028, aiming to revoke over 10,000 licenses. This policy seeks to curb the housing crisis and improve the livability of the city for its residents.[38] These measures, combined with sustainable tourism strategies, reflect a broader effort to balance the city's tourism economy with the needs of its population.

Bali, Indonesia

Bali's reputation as a tropical paradise has attracted millions of visitors annually, leading to widespread gentrification. Areas like Canggu and Ubud have been transformed by the construction of luxury resorts and tourist facilities, often funded by foreign investments. This development has displaced local communities and marginalized Balinese traditions, with cultural practices increasingly commodified for tourist consumption.[39]

The environmental impact of Bali's tourism boom has been severe, with increased pollution and resource depletion. For example, water shortages have become common due to the high demands of tourist facilities. These challenges the need for sustainable tourism practices that prioritize environmental preservation and local well-being. Scholars argue that Bali's experience serves as a wake-up call for addressing overtourism and its consequences.[40]

The cases of Lisbon, Barcelona, and Bali highlight the complex relationship between tourism and gentrification. Each destination demonstrates the importance of policies that balance economic benefits with the preservation of local communities and cultural authenticity.

Empowering Communities as Custodians: Lessons from Global Communities

While policies and regulations like Lisbon's housing programs, Barcelona's rental restrictions, and Bali's sustainable tourism initiatives are essential in addressing the impacts of gentrification, another powerful approach lies in empowering local communities as custodians of their cultural heritage. This strategy focuses on fostering pride, preserving traditions, and creating sustainable livelihoods that allow communities to thrive without external exploitation or loss of identity.

Preserving cultural traditions while preventing exploitation is a delicate balance that communities worldwide must navigate. This process involves safeguarding intangible heritage while addressing the pressures of commercialization, globalization, and cultural appropriation. Below are examples from diverse regions illustrating effective strategies to preserve traditions and maintain cultural integrity.

Sumba Island: Celebrating the Tradition of Ikat Weaving

Karaja Sumba is an initiative in Indonesia's West Sumba region that intertwines cultural preservation with economic empowerment. By safeguarding the ancient art of ikat weaving, Karaja Sumba not only ensures the continuity of a rich tradition but also uplifts the lives of nearly 190 women across 18 villages. This initiative highlights how cultural heritage can be preserved through grassroots efforts that empower local artisans, offering them fair compensation and opportunities to achieve financial independence. The impact of Karaja Sumba extends beyond weaving as the financial independence gained through their work enables these women to break free from violence, educate their children, and contribute to their community's prosperity.

Nepal: Safeguarding Intangible Cultural Heritage

Nepal, a country with over 100 ethnic groups and 92 languages, has been proactive in preserving its intangible cultural heritage. Efforts include documenting traditional practices and ensuring their transmission to future generations. By focusing on cultural preservation, Nepal promotes diversity and fosters mutual respect among communities. These initiatives align with UNESCO's framework for safeguarding intangible cultural heritage, demonstrating how preservation contributes to humanity's broader cultural development.

China: Meishan Cultural Park

In Hunan Province, China, the Meishan Cultural Park was created to preserve the region's Meishan culture while boosting the local economy. The park replicates traditional Meishan neighborhoods, providing visitors with an authentic cultural experience. By combining cultural preservation with regional development, the initiative highlights the importance of community participation in safeguarding heritage.

Malaysia: Kadazandusun Penampang Community

The Kadazandusun Penampang community in Sabah, Malaysia, have undertaken significant efforts to document and promote their traditional cultural expressions. This proactive approach ensures the survival and growth of their cultural identity. The community-driven preservation emphasizes the importance of indigenous peoples leading their cultural revitalization initiatives.

Greenland: Revitalizing Inuit Drum Dancing

In Greenland, efforts to revive the traditional Inuit practice of *qilaatersorneq* (drum dancing and singing) are ongoing. After its decline during Danish colonization, cultural advocates have sought UNESCO's support to protect and reinvigorate this heritage. The initiative emphasizes the importance of cultural revival in maintaining identity and preventing exploitation of indigenous traditions.

Empowering local communities to act as custodians of their heritage is the cornerstone of sustainable preservation. This involves fostering pride through education, providing fair economic opportunities, and advocating for supportive policies. By addressing the challenges of modernization and commercialization, communities can ensure that their traditions remain vibrant, relevant, and integral to their daily lives.

Ultimately, cultural preservation succeeds when it respects the values of the people it serves, enabling traditions to thrive while fostering dignity, equality, and resilience. These efforts remind us that safeguarding heritage is not only about protecting the past but also about shaping a future where cultural diversity is celebrated as a cornerstone of our shared humanity.

Engage with Communities Respectfully and with Intention

Tourism has the power to transform economies, preserve cultural heritage, and protect natural ecosystems, but when not approached thoughtfully, it can disrupt local lives, erode cultural identity, and exploit resources. To truly regenerate and uplift, tourism must prioritize engagement with communities in ways that honor their voices, respect their autonomy, and deliver tangible benefits.

Respectful community engagement ensures that local people are not only participants but leaders in shaping how their destinations evolve. When communities are included as co-creators in tourism initiatives, their insights and aspirations guide the development of experiences that reflect their unique identities and needs. This approach helps foster deeper connections between visitors and hosts, creating travel experiences that are both enriching and transformative.

By engaging with communities respectfully, regenerative tourism addresses systemic imbalances, prioritizes long-term well-being over short-term profit, and ensures that tourism serves as a tool for empowerment rather than exploitation. In doing so, it paves the way for a more inclusive and resilient future, where travel is not only a journey for the visitor but a source of pride, prosperity, and preservation for the host.

The Story of NIHI

On the remote island of Sumba, Indonesia, NIHI stands today as one of the world's most celebrated eco-luxury resorts. Its success is rooted in a story of vision, resilience, and collaboration—beginning with its origins as Nihiwatu Resort in 1988. This remarkable journey was shaped by the determination of its founder, Claude Graves and his wife, Petra Graves, whose respectful partnership with the local community turned an ambitious dream into an inspiring reality. Graves's story demonstrates how trust, humility, and collaboration can preserve cultural identity while fostering social and economic resilience.

Graves's journey began with a personal dilemma. As an avid American surfer married to a wife who valued comfort and tranquility, he found it difficult to locate destinations that met both their needs. "There is no place I can go and take her where she can be relaxed, and I can surf," he lamented. This challenge inspired Graves and his wife to imagine a retreat that would blend untouched natural beauty with cultural depth and world-class amenities. Their vision was clear: a place respectful of its surroundings, offering meaningful experiences for visitors and tangible benefits for local communities.

Their search took them across the globe, from the Philippines to Africa and finally Indonesia, where they discovered Sumba Island. The remote island's tribal heritage and pristine landscapes captivated them. "We walked the entire coastline for weeks," Graves recalled. "When we finally found this spot, it was almost exactly what we had imagined."

On Sumba, the rhythm of life is set by the ancient Marapu belief system, a spiritual connection that ties the living to their ancestors and the natural world. In the villages of Sumba, towering Uma Mbatangu houses reach toward the heavens, their thatched roofs a testament to craftsmanship honed over generations.

Engaging with Communities Respectfully

Sumba's isolation and unique cultural heritage presented both an opportunity and a challenge. The Sumbanese community, unfamiliar with outsiders, initially viewed Graves and his wife with suspicion. "We were the first foreign people they had seen since World War II," Graves recounted. "Villagers would cry or run away when they saw us."

Understanding that trust could not be rushed, Graves adopted an approach rooted in respect and patience. For three years, he and his wife lived simply among the Sumbanese, immersing themselves in local customs and daily life. They fished, fetched water, and observed the rhythms of village life, slowly building connections. "We would go three, four days a week, dressed up, just to talk to the guys in the village," Graves shared. These conversations began as casual exchanges but evolved into deeper discussions about the community's future. "When we started talking about their children and grandchildren—their legacy—everything shifted," he explained.

One pivotal moment came when Graves decided to bring local elders to Bali to help them visualize his vision for a resort. It was their first time leaving Sumba, and the chaotic tourism of Kuta in Bali was an eye-opener. "When they saw the crowds and the trash, they told me, 'We don't want that here,'" Graves recalled. This shared understanding solidified their commitment to preserving Sumba's cultural identity while embracing tourism as a tool for empowerment.

Building Trust Through Action

Graves's respect for the community extended beyond words. He involved the Sumbanese people in every step of the resort's development, prioritizing local employment and ensuring that decisions aligned with their values. Negotiating land agreements, a process complicated by the lack of formal titles, required patience and cultural sensitivity. "We had to wait for everyone to agree they wanted to sell the land," Graves said. "It was a long process, but we respected their traditions and took our time."

Graves also addressed the community's immediate needs to demonstrate his commitment. During the dry season, he and his team dug wells to provide water and shared their daily catch of fish with villagers. These tangible acts of support helped foster trust that the project was as much about uplifting the community as it was about building a resort.

Over time, the Sumbanese community began to see Graves's vision as their own. This mutual understanding gave rise to the Sumba Foundation, a philanthropic initiative designed to address the island's most pressing challenges. "The resort creates the economy that supports the foundation," Graves explained.

The foundation's work has been transformative. Healthcare has improved significantly, with five clinics providing treatment for malaria, tuberculosis, and other diseases, as well as maternal care and vaccinations. Education has also flourished, with scholarships enabling over 80 students to attend universities across Indonesia. Many of these graduates return to Sumba as skilled professionals in fields like nursing, teaching, and hotel management. Additionally, sustainable water systems have been implemented in remote villages, reducing illness and freeing up time for economic and educational pursuits. Programs addressing malnutrition have provided healthy meals to schoolchildren while educating families about nutrition.

Today, NIHI is under new ownership, and the Sumba Foundation still stand as a global model for tourism that respects and uplifts local communities. Graves's approach—listening, learning, and collaborating—ensured that the resort not only succeeded economically but also contributed to the cultural and social resilience of the Sumbanese people.

"When you go into places like this, the main priority should be making an impact, not making money," Graves emphasized. His story illustrates how tourism, when thoughtfully executed, can empower communities, preserve cultural heritage, and create lasting change. Graves's journey is a testament to the power of partnerships built on mutual respect and shared values. It serves as an inspiring reminder that success is best measured not just by profits, but by the positive legacy we leave behind.

Tourism, at its best, is a transformative exchange that fosters understanding, cultural appreciation, and economic development. For tourism to be truly sustainable and regenerative, it must create a symbiotic relationship where both the host communities and visitors gain meaningful benefits. This principle is vital for ensuring long-term viability, reducing negative impacts, and fostering positive social, economic, and environmental outcomes.

Build Partnerships and Support Systems

Regenerative tourism emphasizes a holistic approach to tourism development, focusing on restoring and enhancing ecosystems, cultures, and communities. Central to its success are collaborative partnerships and proactive policy advocacy, which together safeguard cultural heritage and promote sustainability. These efforts ensure tourism serves as a regenerative force, leaving destinations better than they were found.

Regenerative tourism thrives on collaboration across sectors, bringing together stakeholders from tourism, conservation, agriculture, local government, and community organizations. This holistic approach recognizes that the challenges faced by communities and conservation areas are interconnected and cannot be addressed in isolation. Dr. Sue Snyman, Director of Research at the School of Wildlife Conservation at the African Leadership University, highlights the importance of cross-sectoral collaboration, stating, "The wildlife economy is cross-sectoral... collaboration and partnerships are critical."

Partnerships with NGOs, private sector companies, and academic institutions can provide communities with access to resources, expertise, and support that they might not otherwise have. For example, NGOs can offer training and capacity-building programs, while private sector partners can provide market access and investment opportunities. Collaborative efforts ensure that tourism and conservation initiatives are integrated into broader community development plans, creating synergies that amplify their impact.

Partnerships in Regenerative Tourism: Cross-Sector Collaboration

Collaborative partnerships involve local communities, governments, NGOs, and private sectors working together to create sustainable tourism models. These alliances are critical for resource-sharing, capacity-building, and protecting cultural heritage.

KEY COMPONENTS OF COLLABORATIVE PARTNERSHIPS

1 **Community empowerment and involvement**
- Involving local communities in tourism planning ensures that development aligns with their cultural values and needs. This participatory approach fosters ownership and responsibility toward cultural preservation.
- *Example:* In Guatemala, indigenous weaving cooperatives partner with tourism operators to host workshops and tours. This model preserves cultural heritage while providing economic opportunities for artisans.[41]

2 **Training and capacity-building**
- Partnerships often include programs that train local residents in sustainable tourism practices, equipping them to offer authentic and eco-conscious experiences.
- *Example:* The Tiaki Promise in New Zealand brings together local iwi (tribes), the government, and businesses to instill Maori cultural values in tourism. This initiative educates visitors on respecting the environment and culture while promoting local traditions.[42]

3 **Resource sharing and financial support**
- Collaborative efforts include sharing financial and technical resources to support cultural preservation.
- *Example:* The Fogo Island Inn in Canada reinvests profits into the Shorefast Foundation, funding initiatives that protect local heritage and promote economic resilience.[43]

4 **Co-management of resources**
- Communities co-manage natural and cultural resources to ensure their sustainable use.
- *Example:* In Kenya, the Maasai collaborate with tourism operators to manage protected areas, ensuring cultural preservation and direct economic benefits from tourism.

Policy Advocacy in Regenerative Tourism

Policy advocacy ensures the implementation of frameworks that protect cultural and natural resources while promoting sustainable tourism development. Resilient communities leverage their voice to influence policies that prioritize conservation, cultural preservation, and equitable development.

KEY AREAS OF POLICY ADVOCACY

1 Heritage conservation policies
- Advocacy efforts push for legal protections of cultural heritage sites to mitigate the negative impacts of overtourism.
- *Example:* Bhutan's "High Value, Low Volume" policy limits the number of tourists and enforces cultural immersion requirements, ensuring sustainable tourism that protects its unique heritage.[44]

2 Overtourism mitigation
- Policies regulate tourist activities to prevent the degradation of fragile ecosystems and cultural sites.
- *Example:* Venice has restricted cruise ships from entering its lagoon, protecting its historic canals and reducing environmental stress.[45]

3 Community rights and equity
- Advocacy ensures local communities benefit equitably from tourism revenues.
- *Example:* In Norway, Sami communities successfully lobbied for policies recognizing their rights to co-manage natural resources, leading to tourism that respects and benefits indigenous traditions.

4 Climate action and sustainability
- Tourism stakeholders advocate for policies addressing climate change, such as renewable energy use and waste reduction.
- *Example:* The Maldives banned single-use plastics and adopted renewable energy to align tourism with its climate goals.[46]

The Synergy Between Collaborative Partnerships and Policy Advocacy

Collaborative partnerships serve as a crucial foundation for effective policy advocacy in regenerative tourism, creating a powerful synergy that drives meaningful change. When diverse stakeholders—such as governments, scientists, communities, and tourism operators—come together, they generate evidence-based examples of successful regenerative practices. These real-world initiatives provide compelling proof that sustainable tourism is not only viable but also beneficial for ecosystems, economies, and local communities. Such demonstrable successes lend credibility and weight to advocacy efforts, enabling stakeholders to influence policy decisions with concrete data and visible outcomes.

Conversely, well-designed policies play an equally vital role in strengthening partnerships. Policy frameworks can create an enabling environment by offering financial support, legal protections, and institutional backing for regenerative tourism initiatives. These supportive measures help partnerships thrive by reducing barriers to implementation, attracting investment, and ensuring long-term sustainability. The reciprocal relationship between partnerships and policy underscores how collaborative action and systemic change go hand in hand.

A compelling example of this synergy can be seen in the management of Australia's Great Barrier Reef. The Reef 2050 Plan exemplifies a multi-stakeholder partnership in which the Australian government, local communities, scientists, and tourism operators work together to protect one of the world's most iconic ecosystems. Through this collaborative framework, stakeholders have successfully advocated for stricter water quality regulations and measures to reduce carbon emissions, both of which are critical for mitigating environmental damage to the reef. The combined force of partnership-driven initiatives and effective advocacy has led to tangible improvements in reef health while supporting sustainable tourism that continues to benefit local communities and the national economy.

This interconnected approach demonstrates that neither partnerships nor policies alone are sufficient to drive regenerative change at scale. Instead, it is the synergy between collaborative action and policy advocacy that creates lasting impact, ensuring that tourism can evolve into a force for environmental stewardship and social resilience.

Challenges and Opportunities

Balancing conservation with economic growth presents significant challenges, often leading to conflicting interests among stakeholders who may prioritize short-term financial gains over long-term environmental sustainability. Even when policies supporting conservation are in place, weak enforcement can undermine advocacy efforts, leaving ecosystems and cultural heritage vulnerable to ongoing degradation.

Despite these challenges, there are notable opportunities for progress. Successful models such as Bhutan's high-value, low-impact tourism policies and Kenya's innovative co-management practices serve as inspiring examples for other destinations aiming to integrate conservation with economic development. Additionally, technological innovations like GIS mapping and AI analytics offer powerful tools to enhance resource management and support cultural preservation, opening new pathways for sustainable and regenerative tourism practices.

Building Strong Partnerships: The Datai Pledge as a Model

Collaborative partnerships and policy advocacy are essential pillars of regenerative tourism, enabling destinations to preserve their cultural and natural heritage while fostering community resilience. By pooling resources, advocating for supportive policies, and involving local communities in decision-making, regenerative tourism creates a sustainable and equitable model that benefits both people and the planet.

Situated on the pristine shores of Datai Bay, The Datai Langkawi sits on Langkawi, an archipelago of 99 islands in Malaysia, a UNESCO Global Geopark renowned for its dramatic landscapes, from emerald rainforests teeming with wildlife to crystal-clear waters that shelter vibrant coral reefs. This natural wonderland is steeped in myth and history, with ancient legends woven into its mountains, rivers, and seas.

Guided by a profound respect for the environment and a commitment to giving back to the community, the resort's ethos is deeply rooted in the philosophy of living in harmony with nature. It is within this context that The Datai Pledge was born—a transformative sustainability initiative that weaves together conservation, cultural preservation, and community empowerment. Through this visionary program, The Datai Langkawi is not only redefining the future of luxury hospitality but also inspiring a global movement to safeguard the planet's most cherished destinations.

The Datai Langkawi exemplifies how regenerative tourism thrives on the foundation of strong, multi-stakeholder partnerships through its sustainability initiative, known as The Datai Pledge, serving as a blueprint for how to collaborate across communities, NGOs, researchers, artisans, and sustainability enterprises can lead to a thriving, balanced ecosystem of tourism, conservation, and cultural resilience. This pledge, integrated into the resort's operations since its renovation in 2018, has become a cornerstone of its commitment to sustainability.

Funded through guest contributions, corporate revenue, and dedicated fundraising activities, The Datai Pledge has generated MYR 2.3 million to date, enabling it to drive impactful initiatives across its four pillars: Pure for the Future, Wildlife for the Future, Fish for the Future, and Youth for the Future.

At the heart of The Datai Pledge lies its community partnerships, which are pivotal in fostering resilience and empowerment. Collaborations with grassroots organizations like Geng Bersih Kampung (GBK) have facilitated the creation of educational spaces that teach underprivileged children about sustainability and biodiversity. These efforts are complemented by initiatives with social enterprises such as The Kanshalife Project, which transforms resort waste into reusable products like candles and ottoman cushions, reducing landfill contributions while creating jobs for marginalized groups.

Scientific research and conservation are equally integral to The Datai Pledge. Partnerships with organizations such as MareCet, a marine mammal research NGO, have enabled significant strides in marine biodiversity conservation. The Datai Langkawi supports MareCet's research on the Indo-Pacific humpback dolphin and fosters guest engagement through programs like "A Day Out with Dolphin Researchers." Additionally, collaborations with Reef Check Malaysia help monitor and regenerate coral reefs, ensuring the sustainability of marine ecosystems in Datai Bay.

Beyond environmental efforts, The Datai Pledge actively celebrates and preserves cultural heritage. Through partnerships with local artisans, the resort organizes in-residence workshops on crafts like batik printing and glass-blowing, enriching the guest experience while providing artisans with a global platform. These initiatives not only enhance cultural appreciation but also support the local economy.

By integrating conservation into its operations and fostering meaningful partnerships, The Datai Langkawi provides a replicable model for other destinations aiming to balance growth with ecological and social stewardship.

How Partnerships Advance Regenerative Tourism

The success of The Datai Pledge lies in its deep integration of partnerships across every facet of its regenerative tourism model. By collaborating with a diverse network of stakeholders, The Datai Langkawi has built a comprehensive system that simultaneously benefits people, nature, and culture, positioning the resort as a leading example of how collective efforts can advance regenerative tourism principles.

The key to impact is the resort's commitment to integrated community engagement. Partnerships with organizations like GBK and Kanshalife ensure that initiatives are tailored to real community needs, addressing vital areas such as education, livelihood creation, and waste management. These collaborations foster a strong sense of ownership among local communities, empowering them to become active participants in the regenerative process and ensuring that efforts have lasting impact.

Equally important is the resort's dedication to science-led conservation. Collaborations with organizations such as MareCet and Reef

Check Malaysia anchor conservation initiatives in rigorous scientific research and global best practices. Through these partnerships, The Datai Langkawi has been able to implement highly effective programs aimed at protecting biodiversity and preserving fragile marine ecosystems, contributing to both local ecological health and broader conservation goals.

Cultural and economic sustainability also play a significant role in The Datai's partnership approach. Collaborations with local artisans help preserve traditional crafts by integrating them into the guest experience. Workshops led by skilled craftspeople not only educate visitors about Langkawi's rich cultural heritage but also generate meaningful economic opportunities for artisans, ensuring that cultural preservation and economic development go hand in hand.

Furthermore, The Datai Langkawi has embraced circular economy principles through strategic partnerships with organizations such as Kanshalife and Nurture Knots. These collaborations focus on waste management and upcycling, transforming discarded materials into valuable products. This innovative approach not only reduces the resort's environmental footprint but also creates new income streams for marginalized groups, further demonstrating how sustainability can drive positive social and economic change.

The impact of The Datai Pledge's partnership-driven model has been profound, yielding measurable benefits on both local and global scales. Initiatives such as the placement of artificial reefs, dolphin research programs, and coral reef restoration projects have led to significant improvements in Langkawi's marine biodiversity. Meanwhile, community-focused programs like permaculture education and waste upcycling have provided new economic opportunities and fostered a culture of environmental stewardship among local residents.

These concerted efforts have also garnered global recognition. The Datai Pledge's innovative and holistic approach has earned prestigious accolades, including EarthCheck and ASEAN Green Hotel certifications, solidifying The Datai Langkawi's reputation as a leader in regenerative tourism. Through its unwavering commitment to partnerships, The Datai Langkawi demonstrates how collaboration across sectors and communities can transform tourism into a force for ecological renewal, cultural preservation, and social empowerment.

The Datai Pledge demonstrates that strong partnerships are essential for regenerative tourism. By collaborating with communities, NGOs, artisans, and sustainability enterprises, The Datai Langkawi has created a holistic model that regenerates ecosystems, empowers local people, and preserves cultural heritage. This approach proves that tourism, when driven by collaboration and sustainability, can be a powerful force for good, benefiting not only visitors but also the communities and environments they engage with.

Key Takeaways

Capacity-building is foundational:

- Capacity-building lies at the core of regenerative tourism. It reflects a community's ability to strengthen its skills, knowledge, and systems in order to adapt, innovate, and thrive—while preserving its identity, traditions, and values.

Culture as a source of strength and innovation:

- Regenerative tourism recognizes cultural assets not as commodities but as sources of innovation, pride, and economic opportunity for communities.

Interconnected benefits:

- Cultural resilience strengthens holistic well-being, supports ecological conservation through indigenous knowledge, and fosters sustainable livelihoods linked to authentic cultural experiences.

Rejecting mass tourism's pitfalls:

- Mass tourism's high-volume, low-value model often leads to overtourism, cultural erosion, and environmental harm. Regenerative tourism instead prioritizes quality experiences that benefit both communities and visitors.

Risks of cultural commodification and gentrification:

- Without safeguards, tourism can exploit and commodify cultural traditions or drive gentrification, displacing communities and eroding authenticity.

Empowering communities as custodians:

- Communities should lead the preservation and evolution of their traditions. Authentic engagement, respect, and shared decision-making ensure tourism aligns with local values.

Economic models must be fair and transparent:

- Fair compensation, revenue sharing, and models like Fogo Island Inn's Economic Nutrition label help communities capture the true economic benefits of tourism.

Diversification builds resilience:

- Overreliance on tourism makes communities vulnerable. Regenerative models integrate other economic activities—like agriculture, crafts, or carbon credits—to ensure sustainable livelihoods.

Examples of effective cultural preservation:

- Real-world examples—from Bhutan's high-value tourism to Sumba's ikat weaving, Uganda's revenue sharing, and Greenland's drum dancing revival—illustrate how tourism can strengthen cultural resilience rather than undermine it.

Governance and policy are crucial:

- Robust governance, clear rights, and policy frameworks empower communities to benefit directly from tourism and to safeguard cultural heritage.

Collaboration drives success:

- Cross-sector partnerships among communities, governments, NGOs, and businesses amplify tourism's regenerative impact and support long-term cultural resilience.

Intangible benefits matter:

- Beyond economic gains, tourism contributes to cultural pride, environmental stewardship, and the preservation of spiritual and social values.

A vision for regenerative tourism:

- Ultimately, regenerative tourism is about creating a travel model that enriches visitors while empowering communities, preserving cultural heritage, and sustaining ecosystems for future generations.

Notes

1 A Graham, A Papatheodorou and P Forsyth (2010) *Aviation and Tourism: Implications for leisure travel*, Ashgate, Aldershot.
2 United Nations Educational, Scientific and Cultural Organization (UNESCO). Venice and its lagoon, UNESCO, 2023. whc.unesco.org/en/list/394/ (archived at https://perma.cc/89RM-WYP2)
3 United Nations Educational, Scientific and Cultural Organization (UNESCO). Historic sanctuary of Machu Picchu, UNESCO, 2023. whc.unesco.org/en/list/274/ (archived at https://perma.cc/5CRW-33GQ)
4 BBC News. Thailand's Maya Bay to close until 2021 to let it recover from tourists, BBC News, 2018. www.bbc.com/news/world-asia-45717650 (archived at https://perma.cc/3EN2-B4M3)
5 World Bank (2017) *Tourism and Water: Interactions, impacts and challenges*, World Bank, Washington, DC.
6 *Stanford Social Innovation Review*. Sustainable tourism: Preserving culture and supporting communities, 2018, *Stanford Social Innovation Review*.
7 African Leadership University (2019) *State of the Wildlife Economy in Africa: Emerging opportunities and challenges*, ALU School of Wildlife Conservation, Kigali. https://sowc.alueducation.com/ (archived at https://perma.cc/TE62-V5XN)
8 Kenya Wildlife Conservancies Association (KWCA). The state of wildlife conservancies in Kenya report 2022, KWCA, 2022. kwcakenya.com (archived at https://perma.cc/FWA2-A4SG)
9 Uganda Wildlife Authority. Revenue sharing programme overview, UWA, 2023. www.ugandawildlife.org (archived at https://perma.cc/ENZ5-PKDR)
10 Rwanda Development Board. Tourism revenue sharing program report, RDB, 2022. rdb.rw/tourism-revenue-sharing/ (archived at https://perma.cc/J88J-QFXF)
11 African Leadership University (2019) *State of the Wildlife Economy in Africa: Emerging opportunities and challenges*, ALU School of Wildlife Conservation, Kigali. https://sowc.alueducation.com/ (archived at https://perma.cc/TE62-V5XN)
12 Kenya Wildlife Conservancies Association (KWCA). The state of wildlife conservancies in Kenya report 2022, KWCA, 2022. kwcakenya.com (archived at https://perma.cc/LC2B-UU2T)
13 Uganda Wildlife Authority. Revenue sharing programme overview, UWA, 2023. www.ugandawildlife.org (archived at https://perma.cc/ENZ5-PKDR)

14 Rwanda Development Board. Tourism revenue sharing program report, RDB, 2022. rdb.rw/tourism-revenue-sharing/ (archived at https://perma.cc/J88J-QFXF)

15 Rwanda Development Board. Tourism revenue sharing program report, RDB, 2022. rdb.rw/tourism-revenue-sharing/ (archived at https://perma.cc/J88J-QFXF)

16 Uganda Wildlife Authority. Revenue sharing programme overview, UWA, 2023. www.ugandawildlife.org (archived at https://perma.cc/ENZ5-PKDR)

17 Kenya Wildlife Conservancies Association (KWCA). The state of wildlife conservancies in Kenya report 2022, KWCA, 2022. kwcakenya.com (archived at https://perma.cc/LC2B-UU2T)

18 African Leadership University (2019) *State of the Wildlife Economy in Africa: Emerging opportunities and challenges*, ALU School of Wildlife Conservation, Kigali. https://sowc.alueducation.com/ (archived at https://perma.cc/TE62-V5XN)

19 Tourism Council of Bhutan. 2024 Bhutan tourism policy and sustainable development fee, Tourism Council of Bhutan, 2024.

20 World Tourism Organization (UNWTO). 2022 Overtourism: Solutions for sustainable management, UNWTO, 2022.

21 Tourism Council of Bhutan. 2024 Bhutan tourism policy and sustainable development fee, Tourism Council of Bhutan, 2024.

22 United Nations Environment Programme (UNEP). 2020 environmental impacts of tourism, UNEP, 2020.

23 Marvellous Bhutan. Tourism policy of Bhutan 2021, Marvellous Bhutan Travel, 2021. www.marvellousbhutan.com/tourism-policy-2021 (archived at https://perma.cc/LMB2-NAYE)

24 United Nations Development Programme (UNDP) (2021) *Bhutan's Second Nationally Determined Contribution to the UNFCCC*, UNDP, Thimphu. www.undp.org/bhutan/publications (archived at https://perma.cc/64HN-4V87)

25 WWF Bhutan (2020) *Bhutan for Life: Conservation and sustainable financing for Bhutan's protected areas*, WWF Bhutan, Thimphu. www.wwfbhutan.org.bt/ (archived at https://perma.cc/UH78-42SE)

26 D Gurung and K Seeland. Ecotourism in Bhutan: Extending its benefits to rural communities, *Annals of Tourism Research*, 2008 35 (2), 489–508.

27 Asian Development Bank (ADB) (2022) *Asian Development Outlook 2022*, Bhutan country chapter, ADB, Manila. www.adb.org/publications/asian-development-outlook-2022 (archived at https://perma.cc/2MJT-SNFN)

28 K F Gotham (2005) *Tourism Gentrification: The case of New Orleans' Vieux Carré (French Quarter)*, Tourism Geographies, New York.
29 United Nations Educational, Scientific and Cultural Organization (UNESCO). Cultural tourism and sustainable development, UNESCO, 2021.
30 A P Russo and A Scarnato. Heritage and urban regeneration: Towards creative tourism, *Journal of Cultural Heritage Management and Sustainable Development*, 2018.
31 ICOMOS (2019) *Cultural Heritage and Tourism: Managing the impacts of mass tourism*, ICOMOS.
32 H Goodwin (2011) *Taking Responsibility for Tourism*, Goodfellow Publishers, Oxford.
33 J Mitchell and C Ashley (2010) *Tourism and Poverty Reduction: Pathways to prosperity*, ODI, London.
34 United Nations Educational, Scientific and Cultural Organization (UNESCO). Cultural tourism and sustainable development, UNESCO, 2021.
35 J Sequera and J Nofre. Touristification, transnational gentrification and urban change in Lisbon, JSTOR, 2020. www.jstor.org/stable/26959626 (archived at https://perma.cc/28CY-FTLD)
36 *The Portugal Daily*. Lisbon's plan to combat gentrification and mass tourism, *The Portugal Daily*, 2024.
37 A Syed. Why protesters are squirting water at tourists in Barcelona, Time, 2024. time.com/6995756/barcelona-protesters-water-pistols-tourists/ (archived at https://perma.cc/H2LA-QF2M)
38 J Faus. Barcelona plans to shut all holiday apartments by 2028, Reuters, 2022. www.reuters.com/world/europe/top-tourist-destination-barcelona-plans-shut-all-holiday-apartments-by-2028-2024-06-21/ (archived at https://perma.cc/M4EK-7RB2)
39 I Wayan Suyadnya. Tourism gentrification in Bali, Indonesia: A wake-up call for overtourism, *Masyarakat: Journal Sosiologi*, 2022. www.researchgate.net/publication/359946999_Tourism_Gentrification_in_Bali_Indonesia_A_Wake-up_Call_for_Overtourism (archived at https://perma.cc/5W5Q-KG5R)
40 UI ScholarHub. Socio-spatial inequalities in Bali's tourism development, UI ScholarHub, 2022.
41 Regenera Luxury. Indigenous collaboration in regenerative tourism, Regenera Luxury, nd. regenera.luxury (archived at https://perma.cc/J8LE-A6CY)

42 Mize.Tech. Regenerative tourism examples and principles, Mize.Tech, nd.
43 Sustainable Jungle. Regenerative travel practices, Sustainable Jungle, nd. www.sustainablejungle.com (archived at https://perma.cc/DX7Z-77D3)
44 Mize.Tech. Regenerative tourism examples and principles, Mize.Tech, nd.
45 Time. Venice and sustainable tourism, Time, nd.
46 Hotelier Middle East. Maldives climate goals, Hotelier Middle East, nd. www.hoteliermiddleeast.com (archived at https://perma.cc/CMN4-RL4U)

Ecological Restoration

04

Conservation and Biodiversity

Ecosystems form the foundation of life on Earth, providing essential services such as clean air, water, fertile soil, and a stable climate. These services are not just ecological luxuries; they are critical to human survival and well-being. Ecosystems regulate the air we breathe, filter and replenish the water we drink, and sustain the agricultural systems that feed us. They also help mitigate climate change, buffer against natural disasters, and support cultural and recreational activities that enrich human life.[1] However, decades of human activity—including deforestation, industrial pollution, overfishing, urbanization, and unsustainable agricultural practices—have led to widespread ecosystem degradation. This ongoing damage threatens biodiversity, disrupts natural cycles, and jeopardizes the health and prosperity of communities and economies worldwide.

The scale of this degradation is staggering. According to the Intergovernmental Science-Policy Platform on Biodiversity and Ecosystem Services (IPBES), approximately 75 percent of the Earth's land surface has been significantly altered, and nearly a million species face extinction due to habitat loss, climate change, and pollution.[2] These disruptions erode the resilience of ecosystems, diminishing their ability to provide essential services such as carbon storage, flood control and water purification. Vulnerable populations, particularly in low-income regions, withstand the worst of these impacts, facing heightened risks of food insecurity, water scarcity, and economic instability.

Regenerating ecosystems is critical to reversing these trends and fostering a thriving, balanced world. Ecosystem regeneration involves actively restoring degraded environments to a state of health and resilience. This can include reforestation projects, wetland restoration, soil regeneration through sustainable farming practices, and reintroducing native species to damaged habitats. The objective is not merely to halt degradation but to rebuild ecosystems that are more robust and adaptive in the face of future environmental challenges.

One of the most urgent reasons for ecosystem regeneration is its potential to combat climate change. Forests, wetlands, and marine ecosystems act as powerful carbon sinks, capturing and storing vast amounts of carbon dioxide. Research by the International Union for Conservation of Nature (IUCN) highlights that restoring 350 million hectares of degraded land globally could sequester up to 1.7 gigatons of carbon dioxide annually.[3] Additionally, regenerated ecosystems help mitigate the effects of climate change by regulating local temperatures, preventing soil erosion, and buffering against extreme weather events such as hurricanes and floods.

Ecosystem regeneration also enhances food and water security. Regenerative agricultural practices, which prioritize soil health and biodiversity, can increase crop yields while reducing dependence on chemical fertilizers and pesticides. Similarly, restoring watersheds and wetlands improves water filtration, ensuring access to clean water for millions of people.[4] These efforts contribute directly to achieving the United Nations Sustainable Development Goals (SDGs), particularly those related to hunger, clean water, and climate action.

Furthermore, regenerating ecosystems supports local communities by creating sustainable economic opportunities, such as eco-tourism, regenerative farming, and sustainable forestry. It fosters a renewed sense of stewardship, reconnecting people to the natural world and encouraging long-term conservation efforts.

In the face of escalating environmental challenges, regenerating ecosystems is not just an ecological necessity—it is a moral imperative and a pathway to a more sustainable and equitable future. By restoring the Earth's natural systems, humanity can ensure a resilient planet that supports biodiversity, sustains economies, and nurtures communities for generations to come.

Rewilding and Restoring Ecosystem Health and Biodiversity

Ecological restoration is a critical response to the damage caused by overexploitation, pollution, and land-use changes. By replenishing soil health, re-establishing native vegetation, and managing invasive species, restoration efforts create biodiverse ecosystems that are more resilient, adaptable, and capable of supporting life. Healthy ecosystems inherently regenerate, fostering biodiversity and essential ecosystem services that benefit both human well-being and the environment.

Restoration serves as the cornerstone of regenerative tourism—a foundation upon which all other initiatives depend. It provides the resources, habitats, and conditions necessary for sustainable efforts to take root and flourish. Beyond merely preserving what remains, restoration actively rebuilds degraded environments, creating ecosystems that are stronger and better equipped to withstand future challenges. Destinations like Matetsi Victoria Falls exemplify this principle, showcasing how comprehensive rewilding and habitat rehabilitation can transform damaged landscapes into thriving ecosystems. These efforts not only safeguard biodiversity but also create sustainable tourism opportunities that strengthen local economies and empower communities.

Rewilding Matetsi Private Game Reserve

Spanning an impressive 136,000 acres in Zimbabwe, Matetsi Private Game Reserve exemplifies the transformative power of ecological restoration. Before its rejuvenation, the reserve had suffered extensive degradation due to decades of poaching, illegal hunting, and overuse. Wildlife populations had plummeted, habitats were fragmented, and biodiversity faced significant threats. In response to this ecological crisis, the Gardiner family, owners of Matetsi Victoria Falls, launched an ambitious rewilding initiative aimed at rehabilitating the land, reintroducing wildlife, and creating a vibrant ecosystem that would support biodiversity and sustainable tourism.

Key to the restoration process was the formation of the Amaganyane team, a dedicated anti-poaching unit tasked with protecting the reserve's wildlife from illegal activities. Working in tandem with a conservation team, the project also focused on developing critical infrastructure, including an expansive road network, solar-powered boreholes for water security, and a robust radio communications system to support coordinated conservation efforts. These foundational measures set the stage for rewilding efforts that have yielded extraordinary results. Within six years, the reserve witnessed the return of large herds of elephants and buffalo, alongside thriving populations of lions, leopards, and over 400 bird and mammal species. This transformation demonstrates the profound potential of ecological restoration when pursued with foresight, commitment, and strategic planning.

Restoring Habitats and Biodiversity

A critical component of Matetsi's success has been its focused efforts on habitat restoration. The reserve, previously scarred by agricultural overuse and hunting, has undergone a carefully managed rehabilitation process to support a wide array of flora and fauna. Key to this transformation has been the installation of solar-powered boreholes, which provide reliable water sources, fostering vegetation growth and sustaining wildlife populations.

This restoration work has reestablished the natural balance of the reserve's ecosystems, turning it into a leading example of rehabilitated teak forests and grasslands. Situated within the Kavango-Zambezi Transfrontier Conservation Area (KAZA)—the world's largest cross-border conservation initiative—Matetsi's flourishing ecosystems now serve as an integral part of a broader network that spans five countries. By aligning its efforts with this regional conservation vision, Matetsi contributes to a vast interconnected wilderness that allows wildlife to roam freely across borders, amplifying the impact of its rewilding efforts.

Through its commitment to ecological restoration, Matetsi Private Game Reserve highlights how degraded environments can not only be revived but also become thriving natural havens that benefit biodiversity, local communities, and the tourism economy. Its story serves as a powerful model for the foundational role restoration plays in the broader pursuit of regenerative tourism.

The reserve's location within KAZA—spanning five countries and nearly twice the size of the United Kingdom—adds another layer of ecological significance. KAZA is the world's largest transboundary conservation area, allowing wildlife to roam freely across vast landscapes unimpeded by fences. Matetsi's efforts contribute to this monumental conservation initiative by ensuring that its corner of the ecosystem thrives as part of a larger interconnected whole.

The success of Matetsi's rewilding and conservation efforts is evident in the flourishing biodiversity and the return of iconic species to the reserve. Looking ahead, Matetsi's long-term vision includes further investments in conservation and community development. Plans to expand the lodge's facilities will prioritize sustainability and continue to integrate local partnerships. By reinvesting profits into the reserve and its surrounding communities, Matetsi aims to ensure that its positive impact endures for generations.

Through its rewilding efforts, the property has transformed a once-degraded landscape into a thriving ecosystem that supports biodiversity, benefits local communities, and provides unforgettable experiences for guests. By prioritizing conservation and biodiversity, Matetsi not only safeguards the natural environment but also sets a standard for sustainable travel, proving that tourism can be a force for regeneration and renewal.

Enhancing Climate Resilience and Carbon Sequestration

Restored ecosystems are essential in enhancing climate resilience, enabling both natural and human communities to better adapt to and withstand the escalating impacts of climate change. These ecosystems act as natural buffers against extreme weather events, stabilize the environment, and provide vital services that mitigate climate risks.

One of the most effective examples is mangrove restoration, which serves as a natural shield for coastal areas. Mangroves reduce the energy of storm surges, mitigate erosion, and prevent saltwater intrusion into freshwater systems. Research shows that healthy mangrove forests can reduce wave height by up to 66 percent, significantly diminishing the destructive power of storms and protecting human and natural communities alike.[5] In addition, mangroves play a critical role in carbon sequestration, capturing and storing up to four times more carbon per hectare than terrestrial forests.[6] These attributes make mangrove restoration a cornerstone of climate resilience strategies in coastal areas.

Similarly, wetland restoration is crucial in managing water-related climate impacts. Wetlands function as natural sponges, absorbing and storing excess rainfall, which reduces runoff and the severity of downstream flooding. During drought periods, wetlands slowly release stored water, maintaining groundwater levels and ensuring a steady supply for agriculture and drinking water.[7] Additionally, wetlands improve water quality by filtering pollutants, supporting biodiversity, and sustaining the health of surrounding ecosystems.[8]

In arid and semi-arid regions, grassland restoration combats desertification while enhancing climate resilience. Grasslands stabilize soils, reduce erosion, and improve water infiltration, mitigating the impacts of prolonged droughts. Restoring native grasses and adopting sustainable grazing practices can significantly enhance the capacity of these ecosystems to support wildlife and agriculture. Grassland ecosystems also act as carbon sinks, storing significant amounts of organic carbon in their soils, further contributing to climate mitigation efforts.

Beyond immediate climate impacts, restored ecosystems contribute to long-term adaptation by maintaining ecological balance and providing essential ecosystem services. For instance, healthy forests regulate local and regional climates by influencing precipitation patterns and reducing surface temperatures. Restored river basins and watersheds ensure consistent water flow, supporting agriculture and hydroelectric power generation, even in the face of unpredictable weather patterns.

By prioritizing ecological restoration, tourism and hospitality, operators can play a pivotal role in enhancing climate resilience. These efforts ensure that natural systems are better equipped to buffer against climate extremes while supporting the communities and economies that rely on them. As climate change accelerates, investing in restoration and regeneration is not just a moral imperative but a practical strategy for safeguarding both people and the planet.

This holistic approach was vividly demonstrated in early 2024 when EMBOO, a pioneering regenerative lodge in Kenya's Maasai Mara, faced unprecedented floods caused by a combination of El Niño, climate change, and upstream changes to the landscape, including overgrazing, deforestation, previous droughts, and unplanned developments.

"When we stood amidst the destruction, it was heartbreaking," reflects Valery Super, Co-founder of EMBOO. "This lodge was not just our home but a testament to what regenerative tourism could achieve. It was a place of joy, dreams, and innovation for our guests and our team. Even in the devastation, we got a major motivation—that all our past efforts to drive sustainability within the industry and beyond are essential—and we took it as an opportunity to build back better."

The flooding served as a stark reminder of the vulnerability of even the most sustainable operations to the forces of climate change. Loïc Amado, Co-founder of AMBOO, explains: "We've always believed in the power of regenerative tourism to combat climate change." "And this disaster showed us that we were on the right track. Over the years we had learned so much and this was a chance to rebuild while embracing even more sustainable technology and innovation." With that vision in mind, the founders embarked on an ambitious journey to reconstruct EMBOO with a heightened focus on climate adaptation, sustainability, and innovation.

Rebuilding Stronger: A Climate-Resilient Lodge

The reconstruction of EMBOO became a masterclass in adaptive design. Every aspect of the lodge was reimagined to ensure it could withstand future extreme weather events. Elevated platforms were introduced for guest rooms and communal spaces to reduce vulnerability to flooding. Resilient, locally sourced, and reclaimed materials replaced what had been lost, blending durability with environmental harmony. Enhanced water management systems, including expanded wetlands and lagoons, were implemented to mitigate flooding while supporting local biodiversity.

"We didn't just rebuild a lodge; we built a model for the future," Valery emphasizes. "Every choice we made—whether it was the materials we used or the elevation of our structures—was about ensuring longevity and harmony with the environment."

The floods also reinforced EMBOO's commitment to carbon neutrality. The lodge rebuilt its solar energy systems, which power all operations, including its fleet of electric safari vehicles. These vehicles not only eliminate harmful emissions but also allow guests to experience silent safaris, preserving the tranquility of the Maasai Mara. "Our electric vehicles are more than a technological innovation," Loïc notes. "They symbolize the quiet revolution we need in tourism—a way to immerse yourself in nature, while reducing our footprint."

Community Empowerment: Building Resilience Together

The 2024 floods were not just a disaster for EMBOO; they disrupted the entire Maasai Mara community. Recognizing this shared vulnerability, the lodge expanded its efforts to empower local residents. The Innovation Hub, a cornerstone of EMBOO's community engagement, began offering trainings on flood mitigation, sustainable agriculture, and water management. "This wasn't just about rebuilding our lodge. It was about rebuilding together with our community. We had a team of over 100 people working with lots of passion and coordination to reenvision, recreate and reopen Emboo within only seven weeks! Emboo guides, chefs, admin, housekeepers, management… supported by more local talent joined forces to dig trenches, clean up mud, and create magic. Guests are also helping to regenerate the ecosystem by planting indigenous trees that help prevent soil erosion," Valery shares.

Regeneration and the Circular Economy

The flooding reinforced the interconnectedness of ecosystems and human activity, leading EMBOO to double down on its regenerative practices. Damaged habitats were restored with expanded wetlands and rewilding initiatives, ensuring the lodge's surroundings could thrive.

The lodge also expanded its hydroponic farming operations, conserving water while providing fresh, organic produce. Wastewater treatment systems were upgraded to handle increased capacity, ensuring that every drop of water is recycled and reused. "We now operate with an even tighter loop," Valery says. "Our systems are not just sustainable; they're regenerative, giving back more than they take."

Scaling Impact: Advocacy and Education

EMBOO's journey has elevated its role as a global advocate for regenerative tourism. Through its Eco Tour, which shows guests behind the scenes, guests gain firsthand insights into the lodge's sustainable operations, learning practical ways to reduce their own environmental footprint. The Innovation Hub has become a resource for other tourism operators, offering consultancy services on adopting regenerative practices and building climate resilience.

The lodge has also deepened its partnerships with organizations like Kenya's Ministry of Tourism and Ecotourism Kenya, advocating for policies that support climate resilience across the region. Plans are underway to expand EMBOO's regenerative model across East Africa.

Reflecting on the journey, Loïc concludes, "The floods were a defining moment—not just for us, but for the entire tourism industry. They tested our resilience, but they also deepened our commitment to combating climate change. Now, more than ever, we're determined to create a model for regenerative tourism that can withstand the challenges of the future."

EMBOO's story serves as both an inspiration and a call to action. Its response to adversity demonstrates that with innovation, collaboration, and unwavering commitment, it is possible to build a future where tourism regenerates the planet rather than depleting it. As Valery puts it, "This isn't just our journey; it's a shared mission to prove that tourism, when done right, can heal the world."

Restoration projects such as reforestation, wetland recovery, and grassland rehabilitation are vital in combating climate change. These efforts enhance carbon sequestration, regulate temperatures, and create natural buffers against climate impacts like flooding and drought. By ensuring long-term stability and resilience, they protect both ecosystems and the communities that depend on them. Once restoration takes root, the interconnectedness of systems—land, wildlife, and people—becomes increasingly apparent. Healthy ecosystems not only provide critical services such as clean water, fertile soil, and habitats for wildlife but also support thriving communities and sustainable tourism opportunities.

The Role of Ecosystems in Carbon Sequestration

Carbon sequestration, the process of capturing and storing atmospheric carbon dioxide (CO_2), is essential for mitigating climate change and reducing greenhouse gas concentrations. Healthy ecosystems—forests, grasslands, wetlands, and oceans—are nature's most effective carbon sinks, absorbing significant amounts of CO_2 and locking it away in biomass and soils. In the context of regenerative tourism and hospitality, integrating carbon sequestration strategies through ecological restoration is not only environmentally beneficial but also economically and socially advantageous.

Forests: The Powerhouses of Carbon Storage

Forests are among the most effective carbon sinks on the planet, storing an estimated 45 percent of terrestrial carbon in biomass and soils.[9] Trees absorb CO_2 through photosynthesis, converting it into organic carbon stored in wood, leaves, and roots. Forest restoration, particularly through reforestation and afforestation projects, can significantly enhance carbon sequestration. For example, the Bonn Challenge, a global effort to restore 350 million hectares of degraded land by 2030, has the potential to sequester up to 1.7 gigatons of CO_2 annually.[10] In regenerative tourism, reforestation initiatives are becoming a common practice. Projects like the Valle Sagrado Verde initiative in Peru involve planting native trees to restore ecosystems while engaging local communities. These efforts not only capture carbon but also improve biodiversity and create sustainable livelihoods.

Wetlands: Carbon-Rich Ecosystems

Wetlands, including peatlands, mangroves, and salt marshes, are some of the most efficient carbon sinks. Peatlands, for example, cover just 3 percent of the Earth's surface but store twice as much carbon as all the world's forests combined.[11] Mangroves sequester up to four times more carbon per hectare than terrestrial forests, storing carbon in their dense root systems and underlying sediments.[12] Restoring these ecosystems is critical, as their degradation can release significant amounts of stored carbon back into the atmosphere. Regenerative tourism destinations like Playa Viva in Mexico and Tranquilo Bay in Panama support mangrove restoration as part of their climate action strategies. By enhancing mangrove ecosystems, these initiatives not only sequester carbon but also protect coastal areas from storm surges and erosion, creating a dual benefit of mitigation and adaptation.

Grasslands: An Overlooked Carbon Sink

Grasslands are often undervalued for their carbon sequestration potential. These ecosystems store carbon primarily in their soils, with deep-rooted grasses contributing to long-term carbon storage. Restoring degraded grasslands through sustainable grazing practices, native grass planting, and soil management can increase their carbon sequestration capacity.[13]

In semi-arid regions, such as parts of Africa and South America, regenerative tourism projects often include grassland restoration to combat desertification and enhance ecosystem health. These initiatives create habitats for wildlife, stabilize soil, and provide carbon offsets.

Regenerative tourism and hospitality businesses are increasingly embracing carbon sequestration as a critical component of their operations, actively contributing to climate solutions rather than merely reducing harm. Resorts like Matetsi Victoria Falls in Zimbabwe exemplify this approach by integrating reforestation initiatives that plant native trees, offsetting their carbon footprint while simultaneously enhancing local biodiversity.[14] Such efforts align tourism operations with ecological restoration goals, reinforcing the industry's potential to play a pivotal role in mitigating climate change.

Beyond reforestation, soil carbon sequestration also offers significant opportunities for regenerative tourism. Soil, a major reservoir of organic carbon, has the capacity to sequester 2–3 gigatons of CO_2 annually through improved land management practices.[15] Practices like minimizing tillage, planting cover crops, and implementing crop rotation are increasingly adopted by regenerative destinations, not only enhancing carbon storage in soils but also supporting local food systems and improving resilience to drought and erosion. These methods exemplify how regenerative tourism can strengthen the productivity and sustainability of agricultural systems, benefiting both the environment and local communities.

Coastal ecosystems, often referred to as "blue carbon" systems, also play a vital role in carbon sequestration. Mangroves, seagrasses, and tidal marshes capture CO_2 and store it in sediments, where it can remain sequestered for centuries if undisturbed.[16] Restoring these ecosystems delivers immediate and long-term benefits by reducing atmospheric CO_2 levels while simultaneously supporting marine biodiversity, fisheries, and coastal resilience. For example, mangrove restoration projects not only serve as efficient carbon sinks but also protect shorelines from storm surges, reducing erosion and safeguarding communities that depend on these ecosystems.[17] These coastal restoration efforts highlight the interconnectedness of carbon sequestration with environmental, economic, and social benefits, establishing them as a cornerstone of regenerative tourism practices.

Investing in carbon sequestration through ecological restoration also yields significant economic and social returns, particularly in the context of regenerative tourism projects. Many initiatives actively involve local communities in restoration efforts, creating jobs, enhancing livelihoods, and fostering environmental stewardship. For instance, mangrove restoration projects often engage local fishers, who benefit from healthier ecosystems through improved fish stocks and increased storm protection.[18] Similarly, reforestation projects can generate income through carbon credit programs, providing financial incentives for maintaining restored landscapes. These initiatives enhance the ecological integrity of tourism destinations while also boosting their appeal through improved natural beauty and biodiversity. This, in turn, increases guest satisfaction and encourages more sustainable tourism practices.

The urgency of scaling carbon sequestration efforts is particularly pronounced as the world strives to meet the goals of the Paris Agreement. Regenerative tourism and hospitality offer a model for integrating carbon sequestration into broader ecological restoration efforts, showcasing how businesses can not only reduce their emissions but actively reverse climate impacts. Restoring forests, wetlands, and grasslands contributes to global climate solutions while enhancing the resilience, beauty, and economic viability of tourism destinations. This dual focus on climate action and ecological restoration positions regenerative tourism as a transformative force in addressing the challenges of climate change and building a sustainable future.

Reforestation: Restoring Biodiversity and Water Cycles

Ecological restoration within regenerative tourism highlights this deep interdependence. When ecosystems flourish, they create a ripple effect, fostering coexistence between humans and wildlife while enriching both community well-being and guest experiences. This holistic approach underpins regenerative tourism, where the health of each element reinforces the whole. A striking example is Playa Viva in Mexico, where the restoration of the Juluchuca microwatershed has rejuvenated the local ecosystem, empowered farmers, and enhanced tourism offerings, demonstrating how interconnected systems can thrive together.

Located along Mexico's Pacific coast near Juluchuca, Playa Viva is a living laboratory for regenerative tourism models. Co-founded by David Leventhal and his family in 2005, Playa Viva was built with a bold vision: to regenerate degraded landscapes, protect local ecosystems, and uplift the surrounding community while creating an unparalleled guest experience. This 86-hectare property integrates conservation, permaculture, and community-driven initiatives, setting a global standard for how tourism can drive systemic change.

Playa Viva's journey began with the purchase of a former coconut plantation that had suffered from years of ecological degradation.

Recognizing the urgent need for restoration, David and his team embraced a regenerative approach, allocating portions of the property to conservation, permaculture farming, and a low-impact hospitality venture. "We saw an opportunity to create something truly transformative," explains David. "Our mission was to restore the land and watersheds, support the local community, and show that tourism can be a powerful force for good."

From the start, Playa Viva adopted a whole-systems approach, focusing on the interconnectedness of ecosystems, economies, and communities. This philosophy has guided every aspect of the property's development, from its eco-conscious architectural design to its community engagement programs.

Permaculture lies at the heart of Playa Viva's ecological restoration efforts. Guided by experienced practitioners and local agriculturalists, the hotel's farm team works to regenerate soil health, improve water retention, and increase biodiversity. Techniques such as syntropic and biodynamic farming are used to cultivate nutrient-dense crops and sustainably raised animals. These practices not only provide fresh, organic ingredients for the hotel's farm-to-table restaurant but also serve as a training ground for local farmers.

> Permaculture is a sustainable design approach that mimics natural ecosystems to create self-sufficient systems for food production, living spaces, and community resilience, aiming to care for the Earth, people, and share resources fairly.

"Permaculture is about more than growing food," David emphasizes. "It's about designing systems that restore the land while building resilient communities. Our farm is both a resource and an education hub for the entire watershed."

Guests can explore these efforts firsthand through guided permaculture tours, learning about everything from agroforestry techniques to the importance of microbial-rich soils. Playa Viva also emphasizes long-term sustainability, planting over 100 clumping bamboo patches and tropical hardwoods that will provide resources for future generations.

One of Playa Viva's most ambitious projects is reforestation, which aims to reverse decades of deforestation caused by cattle ranching and unsustainable farming. The team has reintroduced native tree species to improve soil quality, sequester carbon, and rebuild natural habitats. These efforts are part of a broader agroforestry initiative designed to restore historic water cycles in the Juluchuca microwatershed.

"Our community now receives half the rainfall it did a generation ago," David notes. "By reforesting the landscape, we're not just improving soil and biodiversity—we're actively working to bring back the rains and support a more resilient ecosystem."

Playa Viva's reforestation work is deeply collaborative, involving local residents in tree planting and forest management. Guests are also invited to participate, planting trees during their stay and connecting directly with the restoration process.

Protecting Endangered Wildlife: La Tortuga Viva

Playa Viva is home to La Tortuga Viva (LTV), a sea turtle sanctuary founded in 2010 to protect endangered Olive Ridley, Green, and Leatherback turtles. Staffed by local volunteers from the community of Juluchuca, LTV patrols the beaches nightly, rescuing turtle eggs from predators and poachers and relocating them to a protected incubation area. Since its inception, the sanctuary has safely released over 450,000 baby turtles into the ocean.

"Protecting sea turtles is about more than saving a species—it's about restoring balance to the marine ecosystem," says David. "It's incredibly rewarding to see the community come together around this cause."

Playa Viva supports the sanctuary by providing funds for equipment and hosting fundraising efforts, ensuring the long-term viability of the program. Guests can witness turtle hatchings during their stay, offering a powerful reminder of the interconnectedness of tourism and conservation.

Scaling Impact: The ReSiMar Watershed Network

Playa Viva's work extends beyond its immediate property through its involvement with ReSiMar, an emergent regenerative watershed network. This initiative brings together practitioners, community leaders, and organizations to address systemic challenges across the Juluchuca microwatershed. ReSiMar focuses on five key areas: water culture, education, permaculture, fisheries, and ecosystem restoration, with cross-cutting themes like community governance and innovative finance.

"Playa Viva is just one piece of a much larger puzzle," David explains. "Through ReSiMar, we're scaling our impact and creating a model for holistic regeneration that can be replicated in other coastal watersheds."

Playa Viva's vision is rooted in balance—between people and the land, between economic opportunity and ecological preservation. This commitment is evident in every facet of the property, from its regenerative farming practices to its role as a community hub for education and engagement.

"Our goal is to create a culture where the health of the land and the well-being of the people are inseparable," says David. "Regeneration isn't just a buzzword—it's a way of life. And at Playa Viva, we're proud to be part of the movement showing what's possible when tourism is done right."

By integrating ecological restoration, community-driven initiatives, and sustainable tourism, Playa Viva offers a powerful example of how hospitality can transform not just landscapes but lives. It is a beacon of hope for Guerrero, for Mexico, and for the global regenerative tourism movement.

Wildlife Reintroduction and Biodiversity Conservation

The interconnected challenges of biodiversity loss and climate change represent two of the most significant environmental crises of the modern era. Wildlife reintroduction and biodiversity conservation are not only ethical imperatives but also strategic solutions for combating climate change. By restoring ecosystems, sequestering carbon, and enhancing climate resilience, these efforts align ecological health with global climate goals.

Biodiversity underpins the stability and functionality of ecosystems, which are essential for regulating the Earth's climate. Forests, wetlands, and marine ecosystems act as critical carbon sinks, absorbing significant amounts of carbon dioxide. A study published in *Nature* highlights that intact ecosystems can absorb up to 30 percent of anthropogenic carbon emissions annually, highlighting the importance of protecting and restoring biodiversity.[19]

Wildlife plays a crucial role in maintaining these ecosystems. For instance, herbivores like elephants facilitate forest regeneration by dispersing seeds, while predators regulate populations and prevent overgrazing. The reintroduction of wolves in Yellowstone National Park demonstrates how keystone species can restore trophic cascades, benefiting vegetation and increasing carbon storage in riparian areas.[20]

Wildlife Reintroduction: A Tool for Ecosystem Restoration

Wildlife reintroduction involves the deliberate release of species into their native habitats, often reversing local extinctions caused by habitat loss, hunting, or climate change. This practice revitalizes ecosystems, enhancing their capacity to adapt to and mitigate climate impacts.

One compelling example is the reintroduction of the European bison (Bison bonasus), which contributes to grassland biodiversity by preventing forest encroachment, thereby preserving carbon-storing grasslands. Similarly, beavers have been reintroduced to areas in the United States and Europe to restore wetlands, which act as natural water purifiers and carbon sinks while reducing flood risks.[21]

Healthy ecosystems not only sequester carbon but also bolster climate resilience by reducing the impacts of extreme weather events. Mangroves, coral reefs, and seagrass meadows—key biodiversity hotspots—protect coastal communities from storm surges while storing vast amounts of carbon. Studies reveal that mangroves alone can store up to 1,023 metric tons of carbon per hectare.[22]

Wildlife reintroduction enhances these ecosystem services. For example, the reintroduction of sea otters to kelp forest ecosystems has allowed these forests to thrive by controlling sea urchin populations, which destroy kelp. Thriving kelp forests sequester significant amounts of carbon while providing habitats for diverse marine life.[23]

While the benefits of wildlife reintroduction and biodiversity conservation are clear, these efforts face challenges such as habitat fragmentation, human–wildlife conflicts, and funding limitations. Effective solutions require interdisciplinary approaches, combining scientific research, community engagement, and policy support.

Governments and organizations must prioritize the integration of biodiversity conservation into climate policies. The Kunming-Montreal Global Biodiversity Framework, adopted at COP15 in 2022, provides a roadmap for restoring 30 percent of degraded ecosystems by 2030. Successful implementation of such initiatives requires collaboration between stakeholders, including local communities, whose traditional knowledge and stewardship are vital for sustainable conservation.

From Degradation to Thriving Wilderness: Phinda's Restoration Journey

Established in 1991 in the heart of KwaZulu-Natal, South Africa, the &Beyond Phinda Private Game Reserve stands as a testament to the transformative potential of ecological restoration within regenerative tourism. Once a landscape scarred by decades of pineapple farming, cattle grazing, and sisal production, Phinda has been restored to a thriving wilderness, showcasing how tourism, biodiversity conservation, and community empowerment can work in harmony. This ambitious project reflects a vision to rehabilitate degraded land, reintroduce wildlife, and create a sustainable model where conservation supports communities.

The original 13,076 hectares (32,311 acres) selected for Phinda were chosen for their ecological significance. This land, once teeming with life, had been stripped of its natural richness due to overuse and neglect. With a clear objective to restore the land's biodiversity and create a model for sustainable conservation, &Beyond embarked on a meticulous restoration journey. Through rewilding efforts, the reserve reintroduced large mammal species, including lions, cheetahs, elephants, and rhinos, that had been absent from the region for nearly a century. These reintroductions not only marked milestones for Phinda but also set new benchmarks for wildlife management and habitat restoration.

Phinda's wildlife reintroduction program represents one of its most celebrated achievements. The reserve pioneered innovative techniques to mix lions from different prides, creating one of South Africa's most genetically diverse populations. This population has since supported rewilding projects across Africa, including reversing a local extinction in Rwanda. Similarly, the reintroduction of cheetahs established one of Southern Africa's most significant populations, setting a precedent for the successful integration of this species into restored habitats. Phinda also became the first private reserve in South Africa to reintroduce elephants, starting with orphaned young and later expanding to breeding herds. Its rhino conservation efforts have been equally impactful, contributing to broader initiatives like the WWF/Ezemvelo KZN Wildlife Black Rhino Range Expansion Project.

Empowering Communities: A Regenerative Partnership

In 2007, Phinda deepened its commitment to ecological restoration by returning 9,085 hectares of land to the Makhasa and Mnqobokazi communities, the ancestral owners. These communities made the visionary decision to dedicate the land to conservation, forming the Munywana Conservancy in partnership with &Beyond and other private landowners. Today, the conservancy spans nearly 30,000 hectares and is officially recognized as a protected nature reserve. This collaborative effort highlights the importance of partnerships in achieving large-scale ecological restoration and sustainable land management.

Phinda's success is deeply intertwined with its commitment to the neighboring communities. In the early days, building trust with these communities was a challenging but essential process. Community member Gladys Zikhali recalls how initial skepticism gave way to belief in the reserve's potential. People were wary of the dangers associated with reintroducing wildlife, fearing harm to their livelihoods.

However, over time, they witnessed the tangible benefits brought by Phinda, including employment opportunities, education, and access to resources. The creation of Wild Impact (formerly Africa Foundation) facilitated the development of critical infrastructure, such as schools, clinics, and skills training programs, ensuring that conservation efforts directly benefited local residents.

Phinda's journey from degraded farmland to a flourishing wilderness offers a powerful model for the future of regenerative tourism. It demonstrates the immense potential of thoughtful stewardship and collaborative efforts, showing that when we care for the land, wildlife, and people, we create a future where all can thrive.

Revitalizing Essential Ecosystem Services

Ecosystem services—clean water, air purification, soil fertility, and pollination—are the lifeblood of human existence and the global economy. These natural systems underpin our well-being, provide the resources we depend on, and sustain countless industries. Yet, they are under significant threat from human activities, including deforestation, pollution, climate change, and unsustainable land use. The revitalization of these services through ecological restoration is essential not only for the health of our planet but also for ensuring the longevity of human development and economic sustainability.

The Foundation of Human Well-Being

Ecosystem services are indispensable to life on Earth. Clean water is essential for drinking, agriculture, and sanitation, while air purification ensures a breathable atmosphere by filtering pollutants and regulating atmospheric composition. Soil fertility enables food production and supports biodiversity, while pollination, driven by insects, birds, and other species, is crucial for the reproduction of crops and wild plants. According to the Food and Agriculture Organization (FAO), 75 percent of the world's food crops depend at least partially on pollinators, highlighting their irreplaceable role in food security.[24]

Without healthy ecosystems, these services falter, leading to dire consequences such as water scarcity, poor air quality, soil degradation, and a collapse in food systems. The World Resources Institute (WRI) reports that 25 percent of the world's land has already been degraded, with significant impacts on agricultural productivity and biodiversity.[25] For instance, the decline of pollinators like bees threatens global food security, as they contribute to the production of crops valued at over $235 billion annually.[26]

Supporting Economic Sustainability

The degradation of ecosystem services has far-reaching economic implications. Clean water, for example, is crucial for industries such as agriculture, energy, and manufacturing. Pollution or overuse of water resources can lead to increased costs for filtration and scarcity that disrupts supply chains. Similarly, healthy soils are essential for crop productivity, and their degradation leads to reduced agricultural yields and increased dependence on chemical fertilizers, which further harm the environment.[27]

Ecological restoration offers a path to reversing these losses. By restoring wetlands, reforesting degraded lands, and protecting pollinator habitats, we can safeguard the ecosystems that support industries ranging from tourism to agriculture. For example, ecotourism relies on the beauty and biodiversity of pristine environments, which are jeopardized when ecosystem services decline. A report from the United Nations Environment Programme (UNEP) emphasizes that nature-based solutions, such as reforestation and wetland restoration, can generate economic benefits by enhancing ecosystem services, including water purification and carbon sequestration.[28]

Catalyzing Regenerative Practices

Restoring ecosystem services provides a robust foundation for regenerative practices, which seek to replenish and enhance natural systems rather than merely sustaining them. In agriculture, regenerative practices such as crop rotation, agroforestry, and organic farming depend on fertile soils, adequate water supplies, and thriving pollinator populations—all of which are bolstered by ecological restoration. According to a report by the Rodale Institute, regenerative agriculture can increase soil carbon sequestration while improving crop yields and resilience to climate change.[29]

Similarly, in tourism, integrating regenerative principles involves protecting natural habitats, reducing carbon footprints, and supporting local communities, all of which are enhanced when ecosystems are healthy and functioning optimally. Restoration also fosters climate resilience by improving carbon sequestration and mitigating the impacts of extreme weather events. For instance, restored mangroves can absorb four times more carbon than terrestrial forests while protecting coastal communities from storms and flooding.[30]

Revitalizing essential ecosystem services is not merely an environmental issue; it is a societal and economic imperative. As global challenges like climate change, biodiversity loss, and water scarcity intensify, the need to restore and protect these systems has never been more urgent. Governments, businesses, and individuals must prioritize ecological restoration through policies, investments, and practices that value and sustain these critical services.

The restoration of ecosystem services offers a pathway to a healthier, more sustainable future. By safeguarding clean water, fresh air, fertile soils, and thriving pollination networks, we can create a foundation for regenerative practices that benefit both people and the planet. The urgency to act cannot be overstated—our well-being, economies, and collective future depend on these efforts.

A leading example of this vision is Ngalung Kalla Retreat on Indonesia's Sumba Island. Spanning 250 hectares, it stands as a beacon of ecological restoration and sustainable hospitality. Through regenerative practices, the retreat has revitalized critical ecosystem services, including water purification, soil fertility, air quality, and biodiversity, while fostering human well-being and long-term economic resilience. "Every decision we made, from planting trees to constructing buildings, was guided by the principles of regeneration," says Christian Sea, the retreat's founder. This ethos lies at the heart of Ngalung Kalla's mission to seamlessly integrate its operations with the natural environment.

Ngalung Kalla Retreat operates entirely off the grid, powered by solar energy and designed with sustainability at its core. Unlike typical resorts, there are no electric heating elements in the guest rooms—no electric tea kettles or hot water heaters—reflecting a deliberate choice to minimize energy use. Water throughout the retreat, apart from the bore pump for the well, flows purely by gravity, reducing reliance on electric pumps. The retreat also forgoes air conditioning. Instead, its open-air architecture, carefully chosen building materials, and strategic siting harness natural airflow to keep spaces comfortably cool, ensuring guests remain refreshed without the need for mechanical cooling systems.

Enhancing Water Systems for Long-Term Sustainability

Water, an essential ecosystem service, is carefully managed at Ngalung Kalla. Rainwater harvesting systems use expansive roof catchments to collect and store water during the wet season, while deep wells reaching 66 meters provide additional water during the dry months. The retreat uses approximately 10,000 liters daily, supporting agriculture, staff, guests, and other operational needs. "We measure every drop," Christian emphasizes. Techniques like mulching, drip irrigation, and minimizing evaporation from pools significantly enhance water efficiency.

The retreat's water management system not only sustains its own needs but also replenishes local groundwater reserves and reduces stress on community water resources. By demonstrating sustainable water stewardship, Ngalung Kalla serves as a model for addressing water scarcity in arid regions.

Restoring Soil Fertility with Regenerative Practices

Healthy soil is the foundation of agriculture, carbon storage, and water retention—key elements of ecosystem services. Ngalung Kalla has rehabilitated degraded land into a vibrant agroforestry system using permaculture techniques. Rows of nitrogen-fixing trees like Gliricidia are interplanted with food-bearing species such as jackfruit, mango, avocado, and breadfruit. Ground cover crops, including perennial peanuts, prevent soil erosion and enhance moisture retention.

The retreat's composting program transforms organic waste into nutrient-rich soil amendments, eliminating the need for chemical fertilizers. Christian highlights the sustainability of this approach: "Every part of the system supports another. Trees provide food, shade, and materials, while enriching the soil to grow even more." This restoration of soil fertility ensures climate-resilient crops and promotes sustainable food production.

Air Purification and Carbon Sequestration

Ngalung Kalla's reforestation efforts enhance air purification and carbon sequestration, stabilizing the microclimate. Endemic species, such as the Kesambi tree, play a vital role in maintaining air quality and creating habitats for native fauna. The increased tree cover not only purifies the air but also cools the landscape, mitigating the effects of extreme heat.

These efforts are complemented by a marine conservation program, which protects coral reefs and fish populations. A locally managed marine protected area enforces sustainable fishing practices, banning destructive methods like large-scale netting. Christian notes, "The coral is recovering, and fish are returning. This ensures food security for future generations and reinforces biodiversity."

Supporting Pollination and Wildlife Habitats

Pollination is an indispensable ecosystem service, vital for both agriculture and biodiversity. The retreat's food forests and flowering plants attract pollinators, including bees and birds, which boost crop productivity and aid in the natural regeneration of native flora. Habitat restoration initiatives, such as planting native trees and avoiding deforestation, have revitalized ecosystems for birds, small mammals, and other wildlife.

Through ongoing education and employment of local staff, Ngalung Kalla ensures these practices are adopted beyond the retreat's boundaries. Staff are trained in permaculture and organic farming, equipping them to replicate these methods in their own communities. "Our team learns not only how to grow food but how to sustain the environment that supports it," Christian explains.

Sustainable Architecture: Building with Nature

Ngalung Kalla's physical structures embody its commitment to sustainability. Buildings are constructed with natural, locally sourced materials, such as bamboo, teak, and limestone. Designs maximize airflow and natural light, reducing dependence on artificial cooling and heating systems. "Our structures blend into the landscape," Christian says. "They're designed to be both functional and harmonious with the environment."

Workshops on natural building techniques, such as cob construction and plastering, empower visitors and volunteers to implement these methods elsewhere. These hands-on courses are integral to the retreat's mission of spreading sustainable practices.

Ngalung Kalla Retreat exemplifies how revitalizing essential ecosystem services can create a sustainable foundation for industries like tourism and agriculture. By restoring clean water systems, enhancing soil fertility, purifying the air, protecting biodiversity, and fostering pollination, the retreat demonstrates the interconnectedness of natural processes. "Regeneration is happening in every way," Christian reflects. "The land is thriving, and so are the people who call it home."

Looking to the future, Christian envisions Ngalung Kalla as a model for regenerative practices worldwide. "We're proving that ecological restoration and economic success go hand in hand," he concludes. "Our work is just a seed—one that we hope inspires others to prioritize ecosystem services in their endeavors."

Supporting Livelihoods and Building Resilient Communities

Regeneration prioritizes equitable development by ensuring that restored ecosystems provide sustainable resources and meaningful opportunities for local communities. Initiatives such as regenerative agriculture and sustainable tourism create livelihoods that protect natural capital while fostering economic and social resilience. At its core, ecological restoration strengthens the bond between people and the natural world. By actively participating in restoration efforts, communities develop a sense of stewardship and shared responsibility for their environment. This renewed connection is essential for long-term success, inspiring collective action to protect and sustain natural systems.

Community-centered conservation becomes critical as ecosystems are restored and their interconnections recognized. For conservation efforts to succeed, local communities must see tangible value in these initiatives and benefit directly from their outcomes. Ecological restoration within regenerative tourism thrives when it is inclusive, engaging local people as active partners and stewards. Restored environments provide direct benefits such as employment, improved livelihoods, and enhanced access to resources, creating a virtuous cycle of ecological and social well-being. An exemplary model is El Albergue Ollantaytambo in Peru, where the Valle Sagrado Verde initiative involves more than 20 local communities in reforestation projects. These efforts not only enhance biodiversity but also build community resilience, demonstrating the transformative power of inclusive, community-driven restoration.

El Albergue Ollantaytambo, located in the heart of Peru's Sacred Valley, stands as a testament to the transformative power of conservation and community-focused tourism. Founded almost 50 years ago by Wendy Weeks and later expanded by her sons, Ishmael and Joaquín Randall, the property has evolved from a modest six-room backpacker lodge to a boutique hotel with 24 rooms, an organic farm, a café, a distillery, and a farm-to-table restaurant. Central to its mission is a commitment to preserving the Sacred Valley's fragile ecosystems and cultural heritage, a vision deeply rooted in the family's values and history.

United by their mother's vision and their own passion for sustainability, the brothers have since expanded the business while staying true to its roots. "For us, El Albergue is more than a hotel," says Joaquín. "It's a way to give back to the Sacred Valley, to honor the land and its people, and to inspire others to do the same."

Commitment to Ecological Restoration: Valle Sagrado Verde

At the heart of El Albergue's conservation efforts is Valle Sagrado Verde (VSV), an ambitious reforestation and conservation program established to protect and regenerate the Sacred Valley's native ecosystems. The hotel dedicates 1 percent of its net after-tax income to VSV, providing critical funding for projects such as community-led fire prevention, natural area regeneration, and the cultivation of native trees in an on-site nursery.

"Our vision with Valle Sagrado Verde is to create a self-sustaining cycle of regeneration," Joaquín explains. "We're not just planting trees; we're creating systems that allow communities to manage their natural resources more effectively and ensure the survival of native species."

The nursery, located on the hotel's three-acre organic farm, grows a variety of native trees, which are distributed to over 20 local communities for reforestation projects. Guests are encouraged to visit the nursery and participate in tree-planting activities as part of their stay, fostering a direct connection to the land and its restoration.

The farm at El Albergue is more than a source of fresh, organic produce for the hotel's restaurant, it's a living example of sustainable agriculture in action. The farm grows a diverse array of crops, from vegetables and herbs to coffee and quinoa, using organic methods that enrich the soil and reduce environmental impact. The farm also supplies ingredients for Destilería Andina, the hotel's distillery, which produces premium spirits using locally sourced products.

"Our farm is central to what we do," says Joaquín. "It's about more than just feeding our guests—it's about demonstrating that sustainable farming is possible and profitable in the Sacred Valley. We want to inspire local farmers to embrace organic practices and show them the benefits for both the land and their livelihoods."

The farm also serves as a community resource, offering educational tours and hosting the popular Pachamanca Farm Lunch, where guests can experience a traditional Andean meal cooked underground using hot stones.

In addition to its ecological restoration efforts, El Albergue dedicates 5 percent of its net after-tax income to cultural programs in Ollantaytambo, primarily through Asociación Kuska. This organization runs the Kuska School, a progressive educational initiative located on El Albergue's property, and a new community library. The hotel provides space and services for Kuska free of charge, enabling the school to thrive as a vital resource for local children.

"Education is the key to a sustainable future," Joaquín asserts. "Kuska School isn't just a school—it's a place where children learn to think critically, appreciate their culture, and understand the importance of conservation. It's deeply rewarding to see the impact it has on our community."

The hotel also engages with local artisans, purchasing handmade textiles, ceramics, and other crafts to stock its curio shop and support the regional economy.

Immersive Conservation Experiences for Guests

El Albergue offers a range of activities that connect guests to the Sacred Valley's natural and cultural heritage. Guided tours to the nearby Pumamarca ruins and the Choquechaka Conservation Area provide opportunities for hands-on participation in reforestation and conservation activities, such as forest management and tree planting. Visitors can also explore traditional Quechua communities and learn about age-old crafts like basket weaving and textile production.

"We want our guests to leave with a deeper understanding of this place," Joaquín explains. "It's not just about seeing the sights—it's about engaging with the land, the people, and the traditions that make the Sacred Valley so special."

Education and guest engagement stand as the culmination of restoration and conservation efforts, transforming travel into a platform for connection and advocacy. By educating guests and involving them in meaningful conservation activities, destinations can foster profound connections to nature while inspiring visitors to carry the message of restoration and sustainability beyond their stay. This engagement turns tourists into advocates, amplifying the impact of regenerative practices far beyond the destination itself.

Another example of this approach is Tranquilo Bay, located in the lush ecosystems of Bocas del Toro, Panama. At Tranquilo Bay, guest education is intricately woven into every aspect of the experience. Guided nature tours, birdwatching excursions, and interpretive hikes immerse guests in the region's rich biodiversity, revealing the delicate interconnections within the ecosystem. Visitors gain firsthand insights into the lodge's habitat enhancement projects, efforts to manage invasive species, and the critical role of conserving mangrove forests, coral reefs, and tropical rainforests. Each activity is designed not only to showcase the natural beauty of the area but also to foster a deeper understanding of the intricate balance required to sustain it.

For founders Renée and Jim Kimball, along with their long-time collaborator Jay Viola, the vision for Tranquilo Bay was clear from the outset: To heal and protect the land while creating a sustainable tourism model that uplifts local communities and wildlife. "For us, everything begins and ends with the land," explains Renée Kimball, owner and chief steward. "Without healthy ecosystems, nothing else is possible—not thriving communities, not abundant wildlife, not meaningful guest experiences."

The team at Tranquilo Bay emphasizes that guest engagement goes beyond observation. Visitors are invited to participate in conservation activities, monitoring wildlife, and contributing to data collection. These hands-on experiences create lasting impressions, empowering guests to become stewards of the environment long after they leave.

The Foundation: Building a Conservation Legacy

Tranquilo Bay's journey began over two decades ago, fueled by a shared passion for preservation. In 1999, Jim and Jay discovered a property on Isla Bastimentos, adjacent to the Bastimentos National Marine Park. What they saw was potential: a chance to regenerate degraded land, protect a unique ecological corridor, and build a sustainable business that could coexist harmoniously with nature. With Renée managing the planning and strategy from Houston, Texas, the team began transforming the property into a biodiversity refuge and a model for ecological restoration.

From an initial 19 acres, Tranquilo Bay has expanded its footprint to encompass over 200 acres, now operating as a private conservation reserve. "This wasn't about growth for the sake of growth," Kimball explains. "It was about ensuring that as much land as possible was safeguarded for the ecosystems and species that depend on it."

At Tranquilo Bay, ecological stewardship is a daily practice. The property's forests, wetlands, and coastline serve as a vital buffer to the 33,000-acre Bastimentos National Marine Park, helping to protect one of Panama's most biodiverse regions. Early efforts included planting native species in previously cleared or degraded areas, improving soil health, and enhancing habitats for local wildlife. "Our goal has always been to restore balance," Kimball shares. "Nature has an incredible ability to heal itself if we give it the space and support it needs."

Today, Tranquilo Bay boasts a thriving ecosystem that includes over 235 bird species identified on-site and more than 600 species observed during guided excursions. "Our bird list isn't just a point of pride—it's a barometer for the health of our environment," Kimball says. "When the number grows, it tells us that our restoration efforts are working."

The lodge's conservation principles extend to sustainable building practices. Less than 10 percent of the property has been developed, with structures designed to blend seamlessly into the landscape and minimize ecological disruption. Local hardwoods are used sparingly and only for decorative elements, ensuring that construction has a minimal environmental footprint. "Every decision we make is rooted in respect for the land," Kimball notes. "From how we build to how we manage waste, we're always thinking about long-term impacts."

Partnering with Local Communities for Conservation

Ecological restoration at Tranquilo Bay isn't limited to its own property. The lodge has partnered with local indigenous communities to establish a 500-acre municipal reserve that serves as both a sustainable resource for the community and a protective buffer for the marine park. "This reserve is a perfect example of what happens when conservation and community work together," Kimball explains. "It's not just about protecting land—it's about creating a system that benefits everyone."

The municipal reserve allows local communities to sustainably harvest palm leaves for traditional home construction while preserving critical habitats for wildlife. This dual-purpose approach ensures that ecological restoration efforts are both practical and culturally relevant.

The impact of Tranquilo Bay's ecological restoration efforts can be seen in the abundant wildlife that now calls the property home. From white-faced capuchins and sloths to rare birds and reptiles, the reserve is a vibrant ecosystem teeming with life. The lodge's naturalist guides, all deeply knowledgeable about the local environment, play a key role in fostering a connection between guests and the land. Guests are encouraged to join guided birding tours, kayaking excursions, and reforestation activities, immersing themselves in the region's ecological richness while contributing to its preservation. "We want our guests to leave not just inspired, but empowered to make a difference," Kimball emphasizes.

Tranquilo Bay's approach to ecological restoration is rooted in a long-term vision. The lodge is committed to maintaining its conservation reserve, expanding its partnerships with local communities, and refining its practices to meet the challenges of a changing climate. Water is sustainably sourced through rain catchment and reverse osmosis, and single-use plastics are strictly avoided. Restoration efforts continue, with a focus on the removal of invasive species and replanting of native flora on previously disturbed land.

"For us, regeneration is about thinking beyond our lifetime," Kimball says. "It's about creating systems that will thrive for generations to come."

Legacy of Regeneration: A Commitment to the Future

The enduring theme of ecological restoration in regenerative tourism is its focus on the long term. Restoration is not an immediate fix but a generational commitment, requiring patience, resilience, and a vision that extends far beyond the present. Destinations embracing this principle integrate sustainability into every facet of their operations, ensuring that the benefits of their efforts will resonate for decades to come. These destinations serve as living testaments to the regenerative power of tourism, illustrating that with purpose and principles, tourism can be a force for lasting change. Their legacies remind us that the seeds of today's restoration efforts will grow into thriving ecosystems and resilient communities for generations to follow.

Key Takeaways

Ecosystems as life-support systems:

- Ecosystems provide essential services like clean air, water, fertile soil, and climate regulation, critical for human survival and well-being.
- Over 75 percent of Earth's land surface has been significantly altered, placing one million species at risk of extinction.[31]
- Degradation threatens biodiversity, disrupts natural cycles, and impacts community health and economic stability.

The urgency of ecosystem restoration:

- Restoration aims to rebuild degraded ecosystems to a healthier, more resilient state.
- Techniques include reforestation, wetland recovery, soil regeneration, and wildlife reintroduction.
- Restored ecosystems are better able to adapt to environmental changes and provide critical services.

Climate change mitigation through restoration:

- Forests, wetlands, and marine systems act as powerful carbon sinks.
- Restoring 350 million hectares of degraded land could sequester up to 1.7 gigatons of CO_2 annually (IUCN).
- Healthy ecosystems regulate local climates, reduce erosion, and buffer extreme weather events.

Enhancing food and water security:

- Regenerative agriculture boosts soil health and yields while reducing chemicals.
- Restoring wetlands and watersheds improves water quality and availability.
- Restoration advances key SDGs, particularly those targeting hunger, clean water, and climate action.

Sustainable economic opportunities:

- Ecosystem restoration creates sustainable livelihoods in ecotourism, regenerative farming, and sustainable forestry.
- Projects like Matetsi Victoria Falls in Zimbabwe show how conservation can fuel economic growth and community resilience.
- Restoration fosters a sense of stewardship and cultural connection.

Rewilding and biodiversity conservation:

- Rewilding re-establishes native vegetation, controls invasive species, and restores wildlife populations.
- Matetsi's 136,000-acre reserve showcases successful rewilding with the return of elephants, lions, and over 400 other species.
- These efforts contribute to transboundary conservation areas like KAZA, amplifying biodiversity impact.

Restored ecosystems and climate resilience:

- Mangrove forests reduce storm impacts and sequester up to four times more carbon than terrestrial forests.
- Wetlands manage floods and droughts, improve water quality, and sustain biodiversity.
- Grassland restoration fights desertification and stores carbon in deep-rooted soils.

Innovative restoration models:

- EMBOO in Kenya rebuilt sustainably after devastating floods, integrating elevated architecture, wetlands, and renewable energy.
- Ngalung Kalla Retreat in Indonesia operates off-grid, uses gravity-fed water systems, and models sustainable design.
- Playa Viva in Mexico regenerates watersheds through permaculture and community engagement.

Wildlife reintroduction as ecosystem restoration:

- Wildlife reintroductions restore trophic cascades and ecosystem functions.

- Examples include reintroduced wolves in Yellowstone and European bison shaping grasslands.
- Wildlife presence boosts biodiversity and supports ecosystem services like carbon sequestration.

Regenerative tourism as a force for restoration:

- Tourism can fund and drive ecological restoration, transforming degraded land into thriving ecosystems and visitor experiences.
- Guest engagement turns tourists into advocates through hands-on conservation activities.
- Restoration enhances the natural beauty and biodiversity vital for sustainable tourism.

Revitalizing ecosystem services:

- Restoration protects essential services like pollination, water purification, air quality, and soil fertility.
- Healthy ecosystems support economies and industries, from agriculture to ecotourism.
- Initiatives like Valle Sagrado Verde in Peru show how tourism can fund reforestation and community resilience.

Community engagement and economic equity:

- Ecological restoration thrives on local involvement and community partnerships.
- Projects like El Albergue Ollantaytambo in Peru and Tranquilo Bay in Panama integrate education, conservation, and cultural preservation.
- Regenerative tourism empowers communities, ensuring economic benefits and ecosystem stewardship go hand in hand.

Long-term commitment and legacy:

- Ecological restoration is a generational endeavor, requiring sustained vision and dedication.
- Destinations embracing restoration create a legacy of thriving ecosystems, resilient communities, and sustainable economies.

- The future of tourism depends on regenerating natural systems rather than merely sustaining them.

Notes

1 Millennium Ecosystem Assessment (MEA) (2005) *Ecosystems and Human Well-Being: Synthesis*, Island Press, Washington, DC.
2 Intergovernmental Science-Policy Platform on Biodiversity and Ecosystem Services (IPBES) (2019) *Global Assessment Report on Biodiversity and Ecosystem Services*, Intergovernmental Science-Policy Platform on Biodiversity and Ecosystem Services, Bonn.
3 International Union for Conservation of Nature (IUCN) (2020) *The Bonn Challenge and Forest Landscape Restoration*, IUCN, Gland.
4 Food and Agriculture Organization (FAO) (2017) *The State of Food and Agriculture 2017: Leveraging food systems for inclusive rural transformation*, FAO, Rome.
5 C M Duarte, I J Losada, I E Hendriks, I Mazarrasa and N Marbà. The role of coastal plant communities for climate change mitigation and adaptation, *Nature Climate Change*, 2013, 3 (11), 961–68.
6 D M Alongi. Mangrove forests: Resilience, protection from tsunamis, and responses to global climate change. Estuarine, *Coastal and Shelf Science*, 2008, 76 (1), 1–13.
7 J B Zedler and S Kercher. Wetland resources: Status, trends, ecosystem services, and restorability, *Annual Review of Environment and Resources*, 2005, 30, 39–74.
8 W J Mitsch and J G Gosselink (2015) *Wetlands*, Wiley, Oxford.
9 Y Pan, R A Birdsey, J Fang, et al. A large and persistent carbon sink in the world's forests, *Science*, 2011, 333 (6045), 988–93.
10 J-F Bastin, Y Finegold, C Garcia, et al. The global tree restoration potential, *Science*, 2019, 365 (6448), 76–79.
11 H Joosten, M-L Tapio-Biström and S Tol (2016) *Peatlands: Guidance for climate action*, FAO, Rome.
12 D M Alongi. Mangrove forests: Resilience, protection from tsunamis, and responses to global climate change, *Estuarine, Coastal and Shelf Science*, 2008, 76 (1), 1–13.
13 R White, S Murray and M Rohweder (2000) *Pilot Analysis of Global Ecosystems: Grassland ecosystems*, World Resources Institute, Washington, DC.

14 Y Pan, R A Birdsey, J Fang, et al. A large and persistent carbon sink in the world's forests, *Science*, 2011, 333 (6045), 988–93.
15 R Lal. Soil carbon sequestration impacts on global climate change and food security, *Science*, 2004, 304 (5677), 1623–27.
16 C M Duarte, I J Losada, I E Hendriks, I Mazarrasa and N Marbà. The role of coastal plant communities for climate change mitigation and adaptation, *Nature Climate Change*, 2013, 3 (11), 961–68.
17 D M Alongi. Mangrove forests: Resilience, protection from tsunamis, and responses to global climate change, *Estuarine, Coastal and Shelf Science*, 2008, 76 (1), 1–13.
18 M Spalding, M Kainuma and L Collins (2014) *World Atlas of Mangroves*, Routledge, Abingdon.
19 B W Griscom, J Adams, P W Ellis, et al. Natural climate solutions, *Proceedings of the National Academy of Sciences*, 2017, 114 (44), 11645–50. doi.org/10.1073/pnas.1710465114 (archived at https://perma.cc/G2HA-NAZU)
20 W J Ripple and R L Beschta. Trophic cascades in Yellowstone: The first 15 years after wolf reintroduction, *Biological Conservation*, 2012, 145 (1), 205–13. doi.org/10.1016/j.biocon.2011.11.005 (archived at https://perma.cc/T9GH-FFVD)
21 A Puttock, H A Graham, A M Cunliffe, M Elliott and R E Brazier. Eurasian beaver activity increases water storage, attenuates flow, and mitigates diffuse pollution from intensively-managed grasslands, *Science of the Total Environment*, 2017, 576, 430–43. doi.org/10.1016/j.scitotenv.2016.10.122 (archived at https://perma.cc/8JR7-H499)
22 D C Donato, J B Kauffman, D Murdiyarso, S Kurnianto, M Stidham and M Kanninen. Mangroves among the most carbon-rich forests in the tropics, *Nature Geoscience*, 2011, 4 (5), 293–97. doi.org/10.1038/ngeo1123 (archived at https://perma.cc/U4PA-WDEA)
23 C C Wilmers, J A Estes, M Edwards, K L Laidre and B Konar. Do trophic cascades affect the storage and flux of atmospheric carbon? An analysis of sea otters and kelp forests, *Frontiers in Ecology and the Environment*, 2012, 10 (8), 409–15. doi.org/10.1890/110176 (archived at https://perma.cc/U6DK-P46K)
24 Food and Agriculture Organization (FAO). Pollinators vital to our food supply under threat, FAO, 2019. www.fao.org/newsroom/detail/Pollinators-vital-to-our-food-supply-under-threat/en (archived at https://perma.cc/7XJT-Q7J9)

25 World Resources Institute (WRI). The global land outlook, WRI, 2019. www.wri.org (archived at https://perma.cc/8UUG-3VZB)
26 Intergovernmental Science-Policy Platform on Biodiversity and Ecosystem Services (IPBES) (2016) *The Assessment Report on Pollinators, Pollination, and Food Production*, IPBES.
27 Food and Agriculture Organization (FAO). Pollinators vital to our food supply under threat, FAO, 2019. www.fao.org/newsroom/detail/Pollinators-vital-to-our-food-supply-under-threat/en (archived at https://perma.cc/AU9L-99WV)
28 United Nations Environment Programme (UNEP). Nature-based solutions for sustainable development, UNEP, 2021.
29 Rodale Institute. The promise of regenerative agriculture, Rodale Institute, 2020. rodaleinstitute.org (archived at https://perma.cc/678U-YFKF)
30 International Union for Conservation of Nature (IUCN). Mangroves and climate change, IUCN, 2021. iucn.org (archived at https://perma.cc/3KAX-9BN4)
31 Intergovernmental Science-Policy Platform on Biodiversity and Ecosystem Services, 2019. Global assessment report on biodiversity and ecosystem services of the Intergovernmental Science-Policy Platform on Biodiversity and Ecosystem Services (E. S. Brondízio, J. Settele, S. Díaz & H. T. Ngo, Eds.). Bonn, Germany: IPBES Secretariat. https://doi.org/10.5281/zenodo.3831673 (archived at https://perma.cc/2G8V-RGAM)

Holistic Well-Being

05

The Heart of Regenerative Tourism

Regeneration starts from within, as an intentional and integrated approach to life that nurtures harmony between ourselves, our communities, and the natural world. At its core, regeneration is about restoring balance, embracing wholeness, and fostering a deeper connection to the ecosystems that sustain us.

To regenerate is to live in alignment with the rhythms of nature, recognizing that our well-being is inseparably linked to the health of our environment. It invites us to slow down, to listen, and to reconnect with the innate wisdom of the Earth. This shift begins with individual mindfulness, cultivating practices that nourish the body, mind, and spirit, and extends outward to the collective, where communities can thrive in resilience and abundance.

An integrated approach to regeneration acknowledges the interdependence of all living systems. By returning to our roots—our connection to nature and the simple yet profound principles of care, reciprocity, and respect—we unlock the potential to create a world where flourishing is not limited to a few, but shared by all. Whether through restoring ecosystems, fostering cultural resilience, or championing equity, regeneration is both a personal and communal journey toward living well and living sustainably.

Regeneration and holistic well-being are deeply interconnected, as both emphasize a balanced, integrated approach to life that nurtures the individual, community, and environment. Regeneration recognizes that individual well-being cannot be separated from the health of the community and the environment. Holistic well-being similarly encompasses physical, mental, emotional, social, and spiritual health, all of which thrive when supported by a harmonious relationship with the natural world.

At the heart of this connection is a profound reconnection to nature. Regeneration begins with fostering a sense of belonging and grounding within the natural world, which is essential for mental and emotional well-being. Nature has a unique ability to heal and restore, offering benefits that align closely with the principles of holistic health. This shared foundation strengthens both individual and collective resilience, a key component of thriving systems.

Both regeneration and holistic well-being emphasize resilience and adaptation. Just as regeneration focuses on restoring ecosystems and cultural resilience, holistic well-being highlights the capacity to adapt, recover, and grow in the face of challenges. This mutual emphasis on resilience ensures sustainability, whether at the personal or communal level. They also share a systems-based approach, recognizing that health and vitality arise from the balance of interdependent elements—whether within the body, the community, or the environment.

Holistic Well-Being as a Pillar of Regenerative Tourism

Holistic well-being is the art of achieving harmony within oneself and with the surrounding world. It embraces the nurturing of every aspect of an individual's being—body, mind, emotions, and spirit—while honoring the intricate connections that unite them. Unlike conventional approaches to health that focus on eliminating illness, holistic well-being emphasizes a proactive journey toward balance, purpose, and fulfillment in all areas of life. This integrative perspective views health not as a static goal but as a dynamic, interconnected process that encompasses physical, emotional, mental, social, and spiritual dimensions.

Living in alignment with natural rhythms and values is another shared principle. For holistic well-being, this means nurturing practices that support the whole self, while regeneration involves making sustainable, life-affirming choices that benefit future generations. Both approaches seek to create conditions for mutual flourishing, where individuals thrive as their environments and communities do the same.

In today's fast-paced world, where isolated aspects of health such as physical fitness, career milestones, or mental clarity often take precedence, holistic well-being offers a broader and more integrated perspective. It invites individuals to tune into their bodies, embrace their emotions, nourish their minds, and connect with their deeper sense of purpose. Research has shown that practices such as mindfulness, regular physical activity, and fostering positive social connections significantly improve overall health and life satisfaction.[1] This multifaceted approach unlocks the potential for a richer, more meaningful existence by addressing the whole person rather than fragmented components of their life.

The cultivation of holistic well-being is transformative not only for individuals but also for the communities and systems they interact with. Studies have demonstrated that holistic practices can reduce stress, boost resilience, and enhance productivity, all while fostering a sense of connection and purpose.[2] By prioritizing care and intention across all dimensions of life, individuals can lead lives imbued with joy, vitality, and a deeper understanding of themselves and their relationships with others.

Holistic well-being is a cornerstone of regenerative tourism, shaping its philosophy and guiding its practices. Unlike conventional tourism models that prioritize short-term profits or narrow metrics like guest satisfaction, regenerative tourism adopts a systems-based approach. This perspective recognizes the profound interdependence between the well-being of employees, local communities, ecosystems, and travelers. It redefines success in tourism by seeking to restore and enhance the places and people involved, ensuring that all stakeholders thrive.

In regenerative tourism, employees flourish not merely when they are employed but when they are offered equitable opportunities for personal and professional growth. Research shows that workplaces that foster well-being and respect improve job satisfaction, retention, and productivity.[3] Similarly, communities benefit from partnerships that are not transactional but transformative, supporting their cultural heritage and long-term prosperity.

Ecosystems, too, must not only be preserved but actively regenerated. This principle aligns with findings from the United Nations Environment Programme, which emphasizes that sustainable tourism requires active investment in biodiversity restoration and resource conservation.[4] Healthy ecosystems ensure that tourism can continue to thrive while also contributing to climate resilience and biodiversity preservation.

This principle also extends to the guest experience, reimagining travelers as active participants rather than passive consumers. Guests are invited to engage in meaningful cultural exchanges, immersive wellness programs, and hands-on conservation and community projects. These experiences foster a deeper connection to the destinations they visit, transforming guests into advocates for environmental sustainability and cultural preservation. Research indicates that such transformative experiences enhance traveler satisfaction and inspire long-term stewardship of the places they visit.[5]

Regenerative tourism exemplifies the profound potential of holistic well-being when applied to global systems. By fostering interconnected health—of individuals, communities, and ecosystems—it offers a transformative path forward. This vision not only enhances the travel experience but also ensures that tourism becomes a force for good, benefiting people and the planet alike.

Figure 5.1 Holistic well-being in regenerative tourism

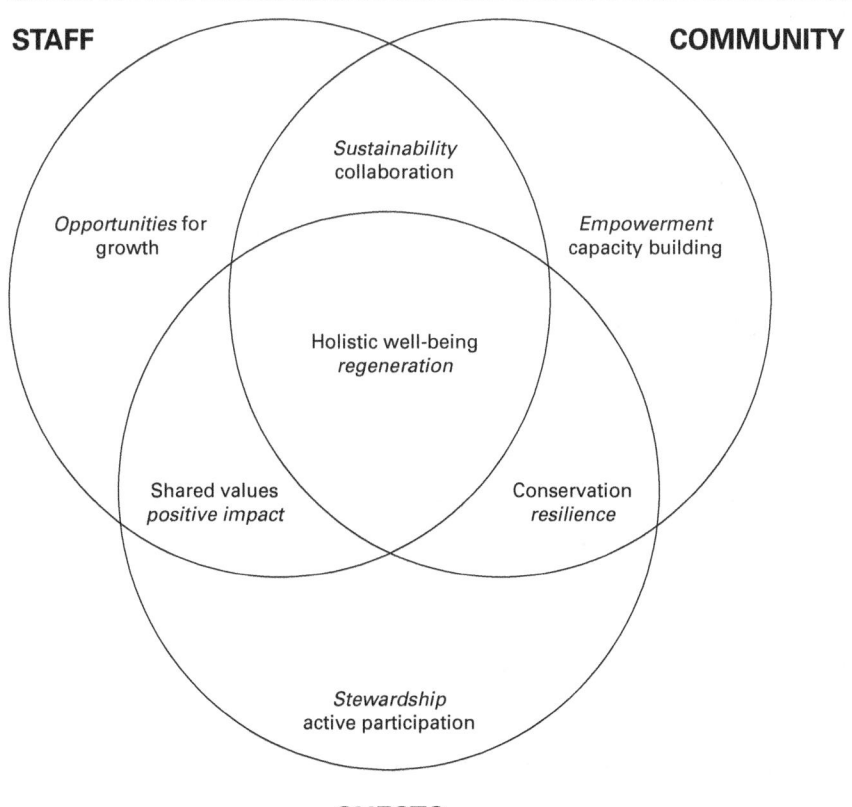

SOURCE Amanda Ho/Regenerative Travel (2025) Holistic well-being in regenerative tourism [Chart]. In *Regenerative Tourism and Hospitality: Building a resilient and positive impact-led travel industry*.

Structure

The Venn diagram consists of three overlapping circles, each representing one key element of holistic well-being in regenerative tourism: staff, community, and guests. The intersections of these circles highlight shared values, responsibilities, and outcomes, while the center, where all three overlap, represents the core principle of holistic regeneration.

Circle 1: Staff

Key focus:

- growth and development opportunities
- equitable treatment and respect
- secure and fulfilling employment

Themes unique to staff:

- employee empowerment and leadership development
- comprehensive health and well-being programs
- training to promote sustainability and cultural awareness

Circle 2: Community

Key focus:

- cultural preservation and pride
- economic opportunities and partnerships
- long-term social impact

Themes unique to community:

- community-led conservation efforts
- education and skill-building initiatives
- infrastructure development (e.g., schools, healthcare)

Circle 3: Guests

Key focus:

- transformative travel experiences
- participation in conservation and community projects
- deep cultural and environmental immersion

Themes unique to guests:

- opportunities for meaningful contribution
- wellness-focused travel programs
- authentic connections with local cultures

Overlaps

1 Staff + community:

- collaboration on conservation projects
- shared responsibility for preserving cultural heritage
- economic benefits derived from tourism partnerships

2 Staff + guests:

- exceptional guest service through empowered employees
- cultural and environmental education facilitated by staff
- mutual respect fostered through authentic interactions

3 Community + guests:

- direct guest involvement in community initiatives
- promotion of local crafts, cuisine, and traditions
- mutual benefit through responsible tourism practices

4 Core (staff + community + guests):

- holistic regeneration:
    - healthy ecosystems as the foundation of all efforts
    - collective well-being as a shared goal
    - active participation in restoring and sustaining destinations

The Symbiosis Between Communities and Conservation

Regenerative tourism recognizes that the well-being of one element of the system—whether it's staff, community, or the natural environment—directly influences the health of the whole. If employees feel secure and empowered, they provide exceptional service, enhancing guest satisfaction. When local communities are supported, they become stewards of the environment, ensuring the long-term viability of natural resources. This symbiosis creates a self-reinforcing cycle of prosperity that distinguishes regenerative tourism from conventional approaches.

Beks Ndlovu, founder and CEO of African Bush Camps (ABC), grew up surrounded by the raw beauty of Zimbabwe's wilderness. Born in the small town of Hwange, on the edge of the iconic national park that shares its name, he developed a deep love for Africa's landscapes and wildlife at an early age. That connection wasn't just a privilege, but a way of life.

"As a child, I was always out in the bush," Beks recalls. "My family had a small garden, and we would often see elephants and other animals passing through. I didn't realize then how extraordinary it was—it was just home."

This intimate bond with nature shaped the man Beks would become. In his early twenties, he began his career as a safari guide, leading travelers through Hwange National Park and sharing the magic of Africa's wilderness. His natural charisma, deep knowledge, and storytelling ability quickly earned him recognition as one of the most promising young guides in the region.

However, as Beks introduced visitors to the wonders of Africa, he became increasingly aware of the fragile balance between the wildlife he loved and the people who called these areas home. Many communities living near national parks struggled with poverty, limited access to education, and human–wildlife conflict. These challenges often made conservation feel like an abstract luxury.

"It became clear to me that conservation wasn't just about protecting animals," Beks explains. "It was about people. If the local communities didn't see the value in conservation, if they didn't feel like they were part of the equation, we would never achieve lasting success."

This realization planted the seeds of African Bush Camps. Beks envisioned a new kind of safari experience—one that celebrated Africa's beauty while empowering its people and ensuring the sustainability of its wildlife. In 2006, he founded African Bush Camps, opening the first camp in Zimbabwe's Hwange National Park.

"I wanted to create something that was deeply connected to the land and its people," Beks says. "Something that would show the world that luxury and sustainability could go hand in hand."

At ABC, this philosophy is not an abstract ideal but a tangible framework that informs every decision. From fostering staff empowerment to uplifting local communities and conserving Africa's wilderness, ABC creates a self-reinforcing cycle of prosperity that sets it apart from conventional tourism models. "True conservation begins with people," Beks asserts. "When communities see the value of preserving their environment and wildlife, they become its fiercest protectors."

"Our mission," says Beks, "is simple yet profound: Sharing and conserving Africa together. Every camp we build, every experience we create, and every project we support is aimed at achieving that vision. It's not just about offering a great safari—it's about creating a meaningful impact."

Community-Driven Conservation: The Foundation of ABC

Central to ABC's work is the African Bush Camps Foundation (ABCF), a non-profit arm established to uplift local communities and support conservation efforts around the camps. The foundation operates on three pillars: education, community empowerment, and conservation, which Beks describes as "intricately connected."

With every guest night at an ABC camp, $10 is directed to the Foundation, funding transformative projects across key communities like Khwai, Mola, and Dete. The Foundation's work ranges from building preschools and providing educational materials to supporting community gardens and mitigating human–wildlife conflict.

"In Khwai, we refurbished and built part of the pre-school, installed a jungle gym, and fenced the school to keep elephants out," Beks explains. "We're now working on a kitchen and ablution block, ensuring the school is safe and functional for the children and teachers. These may seem like small steps, but they're monumental for the communities we serve."

The Khwai Community Concession, where Khwai Leadwood and Khwai Lediba camps are located, is an area steeped in history and culture. The Khwai people, a Bushmen tribe, were relocated in the 1970s from what is now Moremi National Park. Today, the Foundation works closely with the Khwai community to address challenges like education gaps, unemployment, and human–wildlife conflict.

"True conservation starts with people," Beks asserts. "When communities see the value of preserving their environment and wildlife, they become its fiercest protectors. That's why our projects always begin with listening to the community and working with them to create sustainable solutions."

Empowering Staff: Building Careers and Cultivating Leadership

African Bush Camps is equally committed to empowering its staff, many of whom come from local communities. All ABC employees receive 100 percent paid health coverage, transport, accommodation, meals, and compensation well above statutory requirements. Additionally, ABC offers extensive in-camp training programs that focus on both hard and soft skills, enabling employees to grow within the company.

"We don't just hire people—we invest in them," Beks emphasizes. "Our team is the heart of ABC, and their growth is our growth. Many of our managers and senior staff started in entry-level positions and worked their way up through dedication and training."

One standout initiative is ABC's female guide program, designed to empower women in traditionally male-dominated roles. "In many of the communities we work in, women face significant barriers to employment," says Beks. "Our female guide program is breaking those barriers, showing young girls that they can pursue any career they dream of."

Regular consultations with staff committees ensure open communication and address any concerns, while the "ABC Way"—a guiding document shared among all employees—outlines the company's values and practices. "The ABC Way is about creating a culture of respect and excellence," Beks explains. "It's how we treat our colleagues, our guests, and the land we're privileged to work on."

Conservation in Action: Tackling Urgent Challenges

As a safari operator, ABC recognizes that its role extends far beyond hospitality. Conservation is woven into every aspect of its operations, from reducing plastic use to finding innovative ways to repurpose waste.

"We don't separate ourselves from being a conservation organization," Beks explains. "The challenges we face—habitat loss, poaching, human–wildlife conflict—require constant innovation and collaboration. There's always room to improve."

The Foundation's boma project, for instance, addresses human–wildlife conflict by building fortified livestock enclosures that protect animals from predators while reducing retaliatory killings of wildlife. Meanwhile, community gardens provide food security and alternative livelihoods, further reducing dependence on natural resources.

"Our approach to conservation is holistic," says Beks. "It's not just about protecting wildlife—it's about creating systems where communities, wildlife, and tourism thrive together."

For Beks, the guest experience at ABC camps goes beyond wildlife encounters. It's about creating "WOW moments" that leave a lasting impact, from sunrise mokoro excursions to heartfelt conversations around the campfire.

"We want our guests to feel like they're part of something bigger," he says. "Every time they stay with us, they're contributing to the communities and wildlife that make Africa so special. That's the true magic of the ABC experience."

Looking ahead, Beks remains driven by the urgency of his mission. "The need is immense," he reflects. "In some places, wilderness areas are disappearing before our eyes. But I'm inspired by the change we've already seen. Every project, every partnership, every guest—it all adds up to something extraordinary. Together, we can shape the future of travel and conservation."

With its commitment to people, place, and wildlife, the company continues to lead the way in creating a brighter, more sustainable future for Africa and its communities. "The ABC Way is not just a philosophy," Beks concludes. "It's a promise—to ourselves, to our guests, and to Africa."

Empowering Employees as the Core of Regeneration

At the heart of regenerative tourism lies a fundamental truth: The people who work in hospitality are its lifeblood. The well-being of employees influences every aspect of a tourism enterprise, from the quality of the guest experience to the operational efficiency and long-term sustainability of the business. When employees are valued, supported, and empowered, they become passionate advocates for the mission and contribute significantly to its success.

Regenerative tourism prioritizes employees by ensuring fair compensation, access to comprehensive health benefits, professional growth opportunities, and inclusive workplace policies. This holistic approach not only improves job satisfaction but also fosters loyalty, innovation, and a sense of purpose, creating a self-reinforcing cycle of prosperity that benefits employees, businesses and the broader community.

KEY PRACTICES

- Comprehensive health and wellness support: Offering fully funded health insurance, wellness programs, and financial safety nets like pensions and emergency loans.
- Opportunities for growth: Providing training and development pathways to help employees advance in their careers.
- Inclusive workplace policies: Ensuring equity, safety, and respect for all employees, fostering a supportive and welcoming work environment.

Paul Salmon, an Australian native from Melbourne, began in the bustling world of finance in New York City before becoming a pioneer of responsible hospitality and sustainable tourism thirty years ago. Today, he is the chairman of the award-winning Rockhouse Hotel and its sister property, Skylark Negril Beach Resort, two boutique hotels that have redefined hospitality on Jamaica's western coast. He also serves as Co-Founder and Chairman of the Rockhouse Foundation, the hotels' education nonprofit.

Salmon's foray into hospitality began modestly but quickly gained momentum as his vision for the kind of impact-driven business he wanted to create solidified. In the mid 1990s, he took the helm at Rockhouse Hotel, a boutique property perched on the rugged cliffs of Negril, Jamaica. Originally designed by two architects who met while working for Frank Lloyd Wright, this boutique hotel offers breathtaking views of the turquoise Caribbean Sea, framed by lush tropical foliage and dramatic rock formations. Though initially a hidden gem known for its stunning cliffside location, the hotel lacked the community connection and purposeful operations that Salmon envisioned.

"I wanted Rockhouse to be more than just a place to stay," Salmon explains. "I wanted it to be a place where the staff, the community, and the guests all felt connected—where the experience of being there extended beyond luxury to something meaningful."

Rockhouse's approach illustrates how prioritizing employee well-being strengthens the entire hospitality ecosystem. Empowered employees deliver exceptional service, inspire guests, and become advocates for the broader mission of regenerative tourism.

Guided by this ethos, Salmon transformed Rockhouse into a globally celebrated model of sustainable hospitality. The hotel now seamlessly blends thoughtful design, environmental stewardship, and community engagement, offering an experience that reflects the vibrant spirit of Jamaica while actively supporting its people and culture.

"At Rockhouse, we believe in the ripple effect of good," Salmon explains. "When we invest in our team, we're investing in their families, our community, and the future of Jamaica. It's not just about providing a great guest experience—it's about creating a lasting legacy of positive impact."

The hotel demonstrates this commitment through:

- **Exceptional benefits:** Employees receive fully funded health insurance, a matched savings pension plan, and access to emergency loans. These benefits exceed industry norms, fostering stability, loyalty, and trust.
- **Workplace well-being:** Paid meal breaks with quality meal options encourage camaraderie, while training programs ensure that employees can grow and thrive within the organization.
- **Career development:** The hotel is dedicated to promoting from within, offering pathways for advancement that transform entry-level staff into leaders.

Supporting Staff: Empowerment Through Benefits, Opportunities, and Respect

At the heart of Rockhouse's success is its commitment to the well-being of its team. Employees at Rockhouse enjoy a comprehensive suite of benefits that go beyond industry norms. Fully funded health insurance, life insurance, and access to a matched savings pension plan ensure financial and physical security for every staff member. For those facing unexpected hardships, Rockhouse provides emergency loans, creating a critical safety net that fosters trust and stability.

The hotel also prioritizes career development, offering robust training programs that equip employees with the skills and knowledge to advance. With a firm belief in promoting from within, Rockhouse consistently fills open positions by elevating its existing team. This approach not only creates opportunities for growth but also builds a deep sense of loyalty and pride.

"Our general manager started as a front desk agent," Salmon recalls. "Through hard work, dedication, and the support of our programs, they climbed the ranks to become a leader. Stories like this are what make Rockhouse special—we believe in the potential of every person who joins our team."

Everyday practices at Rockhouse also reflect its commitment to staff well-being. Team members receive a paid, one-hour meal break during their shifts, a rare offering in the hospitality industry. This time is designed not only for nourishment but also for fostering camaraderie and connection among colleagues. "It's a small gesture, but it has a big impact," says Salmon. "It's about showing our team that we value them—not just as employees but as people."

Inclusivity and Equity: Championing Diversity in a Complex Landscape

Jamaica's history of homophobia and societal intolerance for LGBTQ+ individuals presents challenges that Rockhouse is determined to address head-on. The hotel incorporates comprehensive orientation and training programs that emphasize tolerance, inclusivity, and understanding. A zero-tolerance policy for discrimination ensures that everyone, whether staff or guest, feels safe and respected.

"Jamaica has a complicated relationship with these issues," Salmon acknowledges. "But at Rockhouse, we've chosen to be a part of the solution. Through education and dialogue, we're fostering an environment where everyone can thrive."

When incidents of discrimination arise, Rockhouse handles them as opportunities for growth rather than punishment. Stories of these incidents and the lessons learned are shared in weekly management and monthly departmental meetings, creating a culture of transparency and accountability.

This commitment to equity extends to gender representation as well. Rockhouse boasts a leadership team where 70 percent of management positions are held by women. "This isn't about meeting quotas," Salmon explains. "It's about recognizing and rewarding talent. When you create an environment where everyone has an equal chance to succeed, amazing things happen."

Building a Stronger Community: Education and Local Engagement

Rockhouse's connection to the community runs deep, beginning with its hiring practices. By employing 100 percent Jamaican nationals, the hotel provides meaningful opportunities for local talent and strengthens the regional economy. Whenever possible, positions are filled from within, creating a pipeline for growth that starts at the line level.

But Rockhouse's commitment to the community extends far beyond its staff. Since 2004, the hotel has operated the Rockhouse Foundation, a charitable organization dedicated to improving education in Negril and its surrounding areas. To date, the foundation has invested over $10 million to transform and modernize seven schools and the Negril Community Library, creating better learning environments for thousands of children.

"Education is the key to unlocking potential," Salmon asserts. "When we invest in schools, we're not just helping today's children—we're paving the way for a better future for generations to come."

The Covid-19 pandemic highlighted the foundation's adaptability and commitment to the community. When schools closed and families faced unprecedented challenges, the foundation pivoted to food distribution, delivering over 250 tons of staples to sustain more than 1,000 people weekly for over a year.

"When the pandemic hit, we knew we couldn't stand by and do nothing," Salmon recalls. "Our food distribution program became a lifeline for so many families. It was one of the most humbling and rewarding initiatives we've ever undertaken."

Rockhouse ensures that its hospitality extends to the local community by offering discounted rates for Jamaican residents. During the high season, locals receive a 30 percent discount, which increases to 50 percent for last-minute bookings. Additionally, local guests benefit from reduced rates at the spa and dining outlets, making Rockhouse a welcoming space for all.

"We're not just a hotel for tourists," Salmon emphasizes. "We're a part of this community, and it's important to us that locals feel just as welcome here as anyone else."

As Rockhouse celebrates its 50th anniversary in 2024, plans are underway to deepen its impact. The Rockhouse Foundation is expanding the Savanna La Mar Inclusive Academy, the first school built from the ground up by the Foundation, where students with and without disabilities to learn in an inclusive setting. This expansion is made possible through a partnership with Jamaica's Ministry of

Education, ensuring that all children, no matter their learning needs, have access to quality education from pre-K through high school.

Strengthening Communities for Mutual Prosperity

In regenerative tourism, the health and prosperity of the surrounding community are fundamental to the success and sustainability of a destination. Businesses cannot thrive in isolation—when local communities flourish, they create the conditions for tourism to thrive as well. Regenerative tourism emphasizes building strong, reciprocal relationships with communities by creating meaningful employment, supporting local enterprises, and addressing systemic challenges such as education, healthcare, and infrastructure.

This approach fosters resilient communities that act as stewards of the land and culture, ensuring the long-term viability and authenticity of the destination. By embedding community well-being into their operations, regenerative tourism businesses become active participants in creating a shared future of mutual prosperity.

KEY PRACTICES

- **Local hiring:** Providing meaningful employment opportunities to residents, prioritizing their development and growth.
- **Supporting local economies:** Partnering with local entrepreneurs, artisans, and farmers to integrate local products and services into operations.
- **Investing in social infrastructure:** Addressing challenges in education, health, and environmental sustainability through targeted initiatives and partnerships.

Spanning over 45 acres of lush coastal forest in Hopkins, Belize, Hamanasi Adventure and Dive Resort epitomizes how regenerative tourism can uplift communities while providing exceptional guest experiences. Founded by Dana and David Krauskopf, Hamanasi is a model of sustainable luxury that deeply intertwines its success with the well-being of the local village.

Dana Krauskopf's journey to Hamanasi began far from the Caribbean, in small-town Ohio. Growing up, her wanderlust was sparked by family road trips and stories of her brother's adventures in the Peace Corps. That curiosity drove her to explore the world, diving in exotic locales, dining with Bedouins, and studying and working abroad in Europe. "Traveling helps you empathize with other people, cultures, and perceptions," Krauskopf reflects. "It keeps your mind and body active and enriches your perspective."

It was during a trip to Mexico's Yucatan Peninsula with her husband, David, that the seed of owning a boutique hotel was planted. Drawn to the idea of combining their love for diving, cultural exploration, and the natural world, the couple began dreaming of a place where guests could enjoy all three. "It started as a crazy idea," Krauskopf recalls. "But the more we thought about it, the more we realized—why not?"

The path from dream to reality wasn't straightforward. After living and working in Prague and Moscow during the turbulent 1990s, the couple gained the confidence to pursue their vision in a new corner of the world. They eventually landed in Belize, drawn by its natural beauty, commitment to environmental preservation, proximity to the U.S., and English-speaking population.

Building a Foundation in Hopkins

In 1999, the Krauskopfs began construction on Hamanasi in the village of Hopkins, a small coastal community known for its vibrant Garifuna culture. The decision to build near Hopkins was intentional: the couple wanted their guests to have authentic interactions with locals and to contribute meaningfully to the village's economy. The property's name, "Hamanasi," was inspired by the Garifuna word for the almond tree, reflecting the resort's commitment to honoring the local culture.

Opening its doors in October 2000, Hamanasi started modestly but with an ambitious vision. The early years were fraught with challenges—delayed construction, sourcing quality materials, and training a team with little hospitality experience. The Krauskopfs took a hands-on approach, teaching staff everything from setting a table to anticipating guest needs. "We were all in it together," Dana says. "It was like a shared journey of learning and growth."

Building trust within the local community was another hurdle. "It took years to earn respect," Dana reflects. "Many locals were wary, having seen outsiders come in with big ideas that didn't pan out. We had to prove ourselves through consistency, fairness, and our genuine commitment to the village."

At Hamanasi, approximately 50 percent of employees hail from the nearby village of Hopkins, ensuring that the resort's economic impact directly benefits the community. Beyond employment, the resort collaborates with local leaders on projects that address pressing issues like road improvement, youth needs and conservation. These partnerships not only enhance the resilience of Hopkins but also preserve the natural resources that attract visitors to the region.

"Our employees are the bridge between Hamanasi and the community," explains Dana. "Their insights guide us on how to best support local needs. For us, it's not just about being a successful business—it's about creating a lasting, positive impact."

Dana's passion for women's empowerment drives many of Hamanasi's policies and initiatives. Recognizing the systemic challenges women face in Belize and Central America—such as patriarchal structures, domestic abuse, and limited access to education—Hamanasi actively creates opportunities for women to grow and succeed.

Each year, the resort hosts an International Women's Day rally planned by female employees, with a focus on gender equality and leadership development. "This year's theme was 'Gender Equality Today for a Sustainable Tomorrow,'" Dana explains. "It's about recognizing the critical role women play in building sustainable businesses and communities and helping them see themselves as leaders."

Hamanasi also prioritizes hiring women, balancing representation across all levels of the resort. By providing training and support, the resort helps women break free from cycles of poverty and build fulfilling careers. "We believe in giving women the tools they need to succeed," says Dana. "When women thrive, families thrive, and communities thrive."

Hamanasi's approach exemplifies the interconnected nature of community well-being and tourism. By investing in the people and environment of Hopkins, the resort creates a foundation for mutual prosperity that benefits residents, employees, and guests alike. This model reinforces the essence of regenerative tourism: Thriving communities are essential to thriving destinations.

Protecting the Environment: Regenerative Practices and Partnerships

Hamanasi's approach to guest experiences goes beyond luxury. The resort fosters meaningful connections between visitors and the local culture, environment, and people. Staff are encouraged to engage with guests, creating a warm, welcoming atmosphere. "Guests often comment on how special it feels to be greeted by name, even in the village," says Dana. "Those personal connections are what make their stay unforgettable."

The resort's culinary offerings celebrate Belize's cultural diversity, featuring dishes inspired by Garifuna, Creole, and Mayan traditions. Locally sourced ingredients support nearby farmers and showcase the flavors of Belize. Guests can also participate in immersive activities like drumming and dance performances, cultural tours, and "Green Hour" sessions that highlight Hamanasi's sustainability initiatives.

"Our goal is to inspire guests to leave Hamanasi not just with great memories, but with a deeper understanding of Belize's culture and environment," says Dana. "We hope they'll take what they've learned and apply it in their own lives."

As a pioneer in sustainable tourism, Hamanasi integrates eco-friendly practices into every aspect of its operations, from reforestation projects to reef conservation. The resort also supports innovative initiatives like sustainable seaweed farming, which combines ecological restoration with economic opportunity.

Seaweed farming, known locally as "Belize Gold," is a project spearheaded by The Nature Conservancy (TNC) and supported by Hamanasi. This regenerative practice provides alternative livelihoods for fishers, restores marine habitats, and mitigates climate change impacts.

"Seaweed farming is a game-changer for Belize," says Dana. "It supports strong communities and healthy ecosystems—both of which are vital for sustainable tourism. We're proud to support TNC and help scale this incredible project."

Hamanasi also incorporates seaweed into its offerings, using it in smoothies and spa treatments. "It's not just about the economic and environmental benefits," Dana explains. "Seaweed has wellness properties that our guests can experience firsthand, creating a deeper connection to its importance."

As Hamanasi continues to grow, Dana and David remain focused on their vision of holistic well-being. Plans include expanding wellness offerings with a jungle yoga studio and spa, scaling sustainability efforts, and deepening partnerships with organizations like TNC. "Sustainability is a journey, not a destination," Dana reflects. "Every step we take—whether it's supporting our employees, empowering women, or protecting the environment—brings us closer to a future where tourism is truly regenerative."

Aligning with Environmental and Cultural Stewardship

Holistic well-being in regenerative tourism extends beyond individuals and communities to encompass the natural and cultural ecosystems that define a destination's identity. Regenerative tourism acknowledges the intrinsic connection between the health of the environment, the preservation of cultural heritage, and the well-being of the people who inhabit and visit these places. This approach requires businesses to adopt eco-friendly practices, actively restore degraded ecosystems, and integrate local traditions into the guest experience. By doing so, they ensure that tourism supports—not diminishes—the vitality of the land and culture.

The principles of environmental and cultural stewardship manifest through sustainable design, reforestation, wildlife conservation, and the celebration of local arts and traditions. This commitment transforms tourism destinations into living systems that thrive ecologically, economically, and socially, fostering resilience and authenticity in the process.

KEY PRACTICES

- Sustainable design and construction that minimizes environmental impact.
- Supporting biodiversity through reforestation, wildlife conservation, and sustainable agriculture.
- Preserving cultural heritage through partnerships with local communities.

Nestled on the fringes of Gujarat's Gir Forest, Woods at Sasan is a shining example of how tourism can align with environmental and cultural stewardship. Founded by Maulik Bhagat, the retreat operates on biophilic design principles that emphasize a deep connection between people and nature. Its 16-acre property is a lush sanctuary of over 900 trees, including eight varieties of mango, and provides a haven for more than 50 species of birds and 20 species of butterflies. "We are not just preserving the environment—we are enhancing it," Maulik explains.

Beyond its elegant accommodations and wellness offerings, Woods at Sasan serves as a gateway to explore the Gir National Park, where guided safaris bring visitors face-to-face with the rare and regal Asiatic lion, alongside a rich diversity of wildlife. Deeply committed to conservation and community, the resort provides eco-conscious experiences that celebrate the region's unique biodiversity and cultural heritage, making it an ideal escape for travelers seeking both adventure and tranquility.

The retreat's commitment to sustainability begins with its design. Built using locally sourced, non-toxic, and reclaimed materials, the structures blend seamlessly into the natural landscape. Lime plastering, a traditional technique, keeps interiors cool, while terracotta installations and bamboo-crafted furnishings celebrate Gujarat's rich artisan heritage. This thoughtful approach minimizes environmental impact while fostering a sense of place and connection for guests.

Built on the biophilic design principles of connecting humans with nature, Woods at Sasan creates a serene environment for guests to unwind and reflect. The retreat's architecture utilizes locally sourced, non-toxic, and reclaimed materials, with structures designed to blend seamlessly into the natural landscape. The 38-key property occupies just 12-17 percent of the land, preserving the area's ecological integrity.

The interiors feature handcrafted furniture, bamboo accessories, terracotta installations, and macrame decorations made by local artisans. Traditional techniques, such as lime plastering for cool interiors and lippan mudwork for decoration, further root the retreat in the region's heritage. "Our design choices reflect our respect for this land and its people," explains Maulik. "Every detail speaks of Gir Forest's story and its cultural richness."

Bridging Guests with Gujarat's Rich Heritage

A pillar of Woods at Sasan's mission is its commitment to preserving and celebrating the cultural heritage of the Gir region. The retreat's Community Development Program engages with 25,000 residents across 13 villages, focusing on education, healthcare, and economic empowerment. Programs like the Community Library, which brings over 2,000 books to rural schools, and skill-building workshops for women in crafts like macrame and stitching ensure that local traditions are passed down and livelihoods are supported.

This ethos extends to guest well-being through biophilic design and thoughtfully curated programs and guest experience. Yoga, meditation, and wellness workshops allow visitors to reconnect with nature and themselves, fostering peace and introspection. "Our retreat is a sanctuary for those seeking harmony," Maulik explains. "Through quiet contemplation, immersive experiences, and thoughtful design, we help our guests reconnect with their inner selves and the natural world."

Biophilic design is an approach to architecture and interior design that aims to connect people more closely with nature. It incorporates natural elements such as daylight, vegetation, natural materials, and organic shapes into built environments to enhance well-being, reduce stress, and improve cognitive performance. Examples include large windows for natural light, indoor green walls, water features, and the use of materials like wood and stone. The term is rooted in the concept of "biophilia," first popularized by biologist Edward O. Wilson, who described humans' innate affinity for nature. Studies have shown that biophilic design can create healthier, more engaging spaces, particularly in workplaces, healthcare settings, and hospitality environments.[6]

Even the culinary experience is a harmonious blend of tradition, health, and sustainability. The retreat's signature restaurant, Swadesh, pays homage to Gujarat's rich culinary heritage with its seasonal, locally sourced offerings. Dishes like *khatta dhokla* (steamed sour rice cakes), *ringan na oro* (smoked brinjal mash), and *mohanthal* (a classic sweet) connect guests with the region's flavors while celebrating its time-honored recipes. Each meal is thoughtfully curated to provide an authentic taste of Gujarat, emphasizing the importance of locally grown produce.

Elevating the dining experience is the Sattvic Meal Plan, inspired by ancient Ayurvedic principles. This innovative, plant-based, five-meal-a-day plan aligns with the body's natural circadian rhythms, offering fresh, organic ingredients sourced directly from the retreat's Edible Garden. "Our Sattvic Meal Plan is not just a dining option—it's a philosophy," explains Maulik. "It's about nourishing the body and soul while respecting the environment. This approach challenges conventional hospitality norms and redefines wellness." Through this commitment, Woods at Sasan reimagines culinary practices as a vehicle for holistic well-being and sustainable living.

"We consider ourselves destination enablers," Maulik explains. "Our goal is to give guests an authentic sense of place—its geography, culture, and cuisine. By connecting them to the essence of Gir Forest, we hope to inspire a deeper appreciation for the land and its people."

Environmental Stewardship and a Haven for Well-Being

Sustainability is woven into every facet of Woods at Sasan's operations, extending beyond cuisine and architecture to embrace the surrounding ecosystem. The retreat has planted over 4,000 trees across 21 villages, fostering reforestation and biodiversity. Biodiversity monitoring and the installation of bird feeders and baths further enhance this natural haven.

The retreat's eco-friendly practices include water treatment systems, composting initiatives, and the elimination of single-use plastics. "Sustainability is not just a practice for us—it's a promise," says Maulik. "We're working towards a net-zero future and sharing our journey to inspire others in the hospitality industry to follow suit." As a signatory of the World Animal Protection pledge, Woods at Sasan is dedicated to ethical tourism and peaceful coexistence with wildlife. The retreat employs low-impact lighting to minimize disruption to nocturnal ecosystems, ensuring harmony between its operations and the natural environment.

Looking forward, Woods at Sasan plans to deepen its impact by developing a permaculture-based food forest, expanding to other regions in India, and encouraging sustainable lifestyles among guests. "Regenerative travel is the future of hospitality," Maulik asserts. "It's about creating spaces that honor the land and its culture while inspiring guests to live more consciously. At Woods at Sasan, we're not just hosting travelers—we're shaping a movement."

Through its commitment to sustainability, cultural preservation, and guest well-being, Woods at Sasan sets a high standard for what regenerative hospitality can achieve. By seamlessly blending environmental stewardship with community empowerment, the retreat offers a compelling model for a more humane and sustainable future in travel.

As Woods at Sasan grows, its focus remains on deepening its impact on people and the planet. Plans include developing a permaculture-based food forest, expanding to other regions in India, and promoting sustainable lifestyles among guests.

Woods at Sasan's commitment extends beyond hospitality, fostering a deeper connection between guests, the land, and its people. "Regenerative travel is the future of hospitality," Maulik asserts. "It's about honoring the land and culture while shaping a movement toward conscious living."

Enhancing Guest Experience Through Meaningful Connections

At the core of regenerative tourism is the philosophy that travel should inspire and enrich both the traveler and the destination. Holistic well-being in tourism goes beyond luxurious accommodations and breathtaking landscapes—it is about fostering authentic, meaningful connections between guests, local communities, and the environment. This ethos is brought to life at Tiger Mountain Pokhara Lodge, a retreat steeped in history, where every detail reflects a commitment to regeneration, conservation, and cultural preservation.

> **KEY PRACTICES**
>
> - Introduce culturally immersive activities, such as village visits and artisan workshops, fostering authentic connections with local communities.
> - Provide unique offerings blending mindfulness and nature immersion for transformative guest experiences.
> - Collaborate with local conservation groups to protect and preserve surrounding ecosystems, ensuring biodiversity thrives alongside tourism.

The story of Tiger Mountain Pokhara Lodge began in the 1980s with the success of trekking tourism in Nepal. Colonel Jimmy Roberts in 1965, the founder of Nepal's first trekking company, Mountain Travel Nepal, envisioned creating an experience for travelers seeking tranquility and cultural immersion beyond the rigors of trekking. Initially a stopover with basic tents and facilities, on the route of the 'Royal Trek' he organized for King Charles III (then the Prince of Wales), the site evolved into a permanent lodge with a vision to blend the comforts of boutique hospitality with Nepal's natural beauty and rich cultural heritage.

In 1998, after years of planning the lodge officially opened its doors. Sir Edmund Hillary, the legendary mountaineer who first summited

Mount Everest with Tenzing Norgay, inaugurated the property. His connection to Nepal and admiration for its people made him the ideal figure to launch a lodge dedicated to celebrating the country's unique landscapes and traditions.

From the outset, Tiger Mountain was designed to reflect Nepal's architectural vernacular. Using local stone, sustainably sourced timber, and traditional mud mortar crafted by local women, the cottages were clustered, like local villages, below the ridgeline to preserve the natural skyline. Simple lime-washed walls, Nepalese artifacts, and terracotta accents created interiors that honored the region's aesthetic while offering a serene retreat for guests.

"Our aim was to create a lodge that felt as if it belonged to the land," recalls Marcus Cotton, the lodge's owner and manager. "Every material, every design choice was rooted in the traditions and environment of rural Nepal."

Immersive Guest Experiences

Today, Tiger Mountain Pokhara Lodge continues to embody its founding principles, offering guests immersive experiences that foster a deep connection to Nepal's culture and environment. Guests can explore the surrounding *Schima-castanopsis* woodlands on guided walks led by local naturalists, who share insights into the region's flora, fauna, and conservation efforts. Cultural exploration provides an intimate look at village life, allowing visitors to engage with artisans, farmers, and community members.

A unique offering is *Ban Magan*, a Nepalese adaptation of forest bathing that combines mindfulness with nature immersion. Guests are encouraged to slow down, breathe deeply, and absorb the serenity of the Himalayan landscape—a practice that Marcus believes fosters moments of profound reflection.

"Our goal is to create moments of tranquility and connection," Marcus explains. "When guests experience the peace and beauty of rural Nepal, they leave with a deeper appreciation for its people and landscapes."

Commitment to Community and Conservation

Tiger Mountain Pokhara Lodge's history is also deeply intertwined with its surrounding community. From its inception, the lodge has prioritized hiring from local villages, with over half its staff coming from the area. Many of these team members, like Jhalak, Lalu, and Shiva, have grown into leadership roles, showcasing the lodge's culture of empowerment and growth.

Through its Community Support Partnership Programme, the lodge channels resources into locally led initiatives, particularly in education and conservation. From building schools to supporting historically marginalized groups, the lodge aligns its development efforts with the aspirations of the community. "Our philosophy has always been to listen first," Marcus shares. "The community knows what it needs better than we do. Our role is to support their vision, not impose our own."

The lodge's commitment to conservation is equally profound. In partnership with the Community Forest User Group, Tiger Mountain collaborates on forest preservation initiatives, ensuring that the surrounding ecosystems remain vibrant and intact. The lodge's operations emphasize sustainability, from sourcing fresh, local ingredients to eliminating single-use plastics and adopting a zero-waste policy.

Over the years, Tiger Mountain Pokhara Lodge has weathered political instability, natural disasters, and global challenges like the Covid-19 pandemic. Each obstacle has strengthened its resolve to remain a beacon of regenerative tourism in Nepal.

"Tourism in Nepal is not for the faint-hearted," Marcus reflects. "But the rewards are immense. Every challenge we face is an opportunity to grow stronger and make a greater impact."

As the lodge looks to the future, it continues to uphold its legacy of thoughtful hospitality and stewardship. By creating transformative guest experiences, empowering local communities, and preserving Nepal's natural and cultural heritage, Tiger Mountain Pokhara Lodge exemplifies the potential of regenerative tourism to inspire a more harmonious and sustainable world.

Marcus concludes, "It's about being part of something much larger—a legacy of resilience, renewal, and respect for the land and its people."

Far from the limited scope of traditional tourism, which often prioritizes profits and superficial guest satisfaction, regenerative tourism integrates the health and vitality of employees, communities, ecosystems, and travelers into a cohesive and mutually reinforcing system. It asserts a simple yet profound truth: When one element thrives, the entire system flourishes, creating enduring prosperity that elevates destinations far beyond sustainability.

Holistic well-being challenges businesses to shift from incremental improvements to systemic transformation. It is a call to action for the tourism industry to evolve into a force that heals, uplifts, and inspires. These pioneering destinations do not just adopt this philosophy; they lead by example, proving that when care, connection, and purpose drive decision-making, the benefits extend far beyond the boundaries of a single business.

Key Takeaways

Regeneration starts within–personal well-being as a foundation:

- Regeneration begins with individuals living in alignment with natural rhythms.
- Holistic well-being encompasses physical, mental, emotional, social, and spiritual health.
- Practices like mindfulness, nature immersion, and intentional living nurture inner balance.

Interdependence of people, communities, and nature:

- Holistic well-being and regeneration are rooted in systems thinking.
- Individual health, community resilience, and ecosystem vitality are interconnected.
- Thriving people foster strong communities, which protect and regenerate natural environments.

Reconnecting with nature for healing and resilience:

- Nature provides mental, emotional, and spiritual restoration.
- Time in natural environments strengthens individual resilience and inspires environmental stewardship.

- Biophilic design connects built spaces to natural surroundings, enhancing well-being.

Redefining holistic well-being beyond traditional health:

- Holistic well-being focuses on proactive balance and purpose, not merely absence of illness.
- Encourages a whole-person approach, integrating body, mind, emotions, and spirit.
- Fosters fulfillment and a deeper sense of connection and meaning in life.

Regenerative tourism's systems-based approach:

- Moves beyond profit-focused tourism to ensure the well-being of all stakeholders.
- Aims for long-term sustainability, ecological restoration, and social equity.
- Measures success through collective flourishing, not just guest satisfaction.

Community empowerment and cultural preservation:

- Regenerative tourism preserves local cultural heritage and traditions.
- Supports community-led initiatives in education, conservation, and economic development.
- Builds strong local partnerships for mutual prosperity and resilience.

Empowering employees as stewards of regeneration:

- Employees are central to regenerative tourism's success.
- Fair wages, health benefits, and professional development foster loyalty and well-being.
- Inclusive policies and workplace cultures empower staff to become sustainability champions.

Guests as active participants, not passive consumers:

- Regenerative tourism invites guests into immersive cultural and conservation experiences.

- Travelers engage deeply with local communities and ecosystems.
- Meaningful travel transforms guests into advocates for sustainability and cultural respect.

Environmental stewardship and active ecosystem restoration:

- Regenerative tourism prioritizes restoring biodiversity and healthy ecosystems.
- Sustainable building practices, reforestation, and conservation efforts are core commitments.
- Healthy ecosystems ensure tourism's long-term viability and contribute to climate resilience.

Real-world examples of holistic regeneration:

- Hamanasi Resort, Belize: Combines community projects, women's empowerment, sustainability, and guest engagement.
- Woods at Sasan, India: Integrates biophilic design, cultural preservation, and environmental stewardship, offering safaris into the Gir Forest to see Asiatic lions.
- Tiger Mountain Pokhara Lodge, Nepal: Exemplifies community-led conservation, cultural immersion, and regenerative guest experiences.

Holistic regeneration as the core of sustainable tourism:

- Regenerative tourism creates a self-reinforcing cycle where staff, community, and guests all thrive.
- Aligns tourism with healing and uplifting people, places, and the planet.
- Demonstrates tourism's potential to become a force for widespread, lasting good.

Notes

1 Harvard T H Chan School of Public Health. The impact of lifestyle choices on health and wellbeing, 2021.
2 National Institutes of Health (NIH). Mind–body practices and resilience in health, NIH, 2020. www.nih.gov (archived at https://perma.cc/6TAK-N4F9)
3 World Economic Forum (WEF). The future of workplace wellbeing, WEF, 2022. weforum.org (archived at https://perma.cc/TVB9-CZKR)
4 United Nations Environment Programme (UNEP). Sustainable tourism and biodiversity restoration, UNEP, 2022.
5 Travel Foundation. Transformative travel and guest engagement in sustainability, Travel Foundation, 2021.
6 E O Wilson (1984) *Biophilia*, Harvard University Press, Cambridge, MA.

Economic Viability   06

Regenerative tourism offers a transformative approach to the tourism industry by prioritizing long-term economic, environmental, and social benefits for local communities, ecosystems, and stakeholders. Unlike traditional mass tourism, which often emphasizes short-term profits and can lead to resource depletion and economic leakage, regenerative tourism focuses on fostering equitable, sustainable, and resilient economic outcomes. By creating systems that support local economies and ecosystems, this model of tourism is designed to ensure that the benefits of tourism are widely distributed and that destinations can thrive without compromising their natural and cultural heritage.[1]

At its core, regenerative tourism emphasizes empowering local economies through community-owned enterprises. By promoting locally run businesses such as guesthouses, restaurants, and craft markets, it ensures that tourism revenue remains within the community, directly benefiting local families and workers rather than external corporations. This approach helps to build economic resilience by creating dignified and sustainable job opportunities in sectors like hospitality, guiding, and cultural education, empowering residents to play an active role in their local economy.[2] Regenerative tourism represents a departure from the extractive practices of mass tourism, offering a more sustainable and inclusive model that fosters long-term prosperity for both people and the environment.

Enhancing Local Economic Resilience Through Sustainable Tourism

High-impact, low-volume tourism is a growing approach within the broader concept of regenerative tourism. Unlike mass tourism, which can lead to environmental degradation and economic dependence on a few major operators, high-impact, low-volume tourism emphasizes the quality of the visitor experience over quantity, while prioritizing sustainable practices that benefit local communities. This model provides a powerful means of empowering local economies, fostering cultural preservation, and ensuring that the economic benefits of tourism remain within the community. By focusing on fewer but more engaged travelers, this tourism model ensures that both environmental and social impacts are positive, creating long-term benefits for local stakeholders.

One of the key advantages of high-impact, low-volume tourism is its ability to generate significant economic benefits while minimizing the negative impacts often associated with mass tourism. Unlike traditional tourism, which often leads to overcrowding, resource depletion, and exploitation, high-impact tourism focuses on attracting a select number of visitors who are willing to engage deeply with the local culture, environment, and community. According to the Global Sustainable Tourism Council, this model helps ensure that the money spent by tourists stays within the local economy, directly benefiting local businesses such as boutique accommodations, restaurants, and artisanal markets.[3] This localized spending also supports local employment, creating meaningful, well-paying jobs that are aligned with sustainable practices and cultural preservation.

For instance, in regions like Bhutan, the government has actively promoted high-impact, low-volume tourism by implementing a "high-value, low-impact" policy, which ensures that visitors pay a daily fee to access the country's unique cultural and natural sites. This approach limits the number of visitors while ensuring that the revenue generated is reinvested into conservation and community development initiatives. As a result, Bhutan has successfully minimized the negative effects of mass tourism while empowering its local communities through sustainable revenue streams.[4]

Supporting Community-Owned Enterprises

High-impact, low-volume tourism is also critical for developing and supporting locally owned businesses. By attracting visitors who are more interested in authentic, immersive experiences than traditional tourist activities, local entrepreneurs are encouraged to offer unique services that reflect the true character of the area. This includes locally-run accommodations, guided cultural tours, and the sale of handmade crafts, which directly contribute to the community's economy.

These businesses help reduce economic leakages, where much of the money spent by tourists ends up benefiting large corporations rather than local families. The success of these enterprises fosters a sense of ownership within the community and empowers locals to maintain control over their resources. According to a report by the World Travel and Tourism Council, community-based tourism enables residents to retain more of the economic benefits generated from tourism, ensuring that wealth stays within the local area and promoting greater economic equality.[5]

In regions like the Galápagos Islands, for example, tourism is deliberately restricted, to prevent overcrowding and protect biodiversity. Tourists pay for exclusive access to specific conservation areas, which supports the local community and encourages the development of sustainable, small-scale tourism ventures. This model has led to the creation of community-run lodges and eco-tours, ensuring that economic benefits are distributed directly to local families while preserving the delicate ecosystem of the islands.

Attracting Conscious Travelers and High-Value Experiences

One of the defining features of high-impact, low-volume tourism is its ability to attract conscious travelers who are willing to pay a premium for sustainable, authentic, and meaningful experiences. These travelers are motivated by a desire to learn about local cultures, contribute to conservation efforts, and minimize their environmental footprint. Unlike mass tourism, where the focus is on visiting as many attractions as possible in a short period of time, high-impact tourism encourages a slower pace, allowing for deeper connections between visitors and the destinations they visit.

As noted by the Global Sustainable Tourism Council, conscious travelers often spend more on local goods and services, thereby contributing more significantly to the local economy. They are more likely to engage in activities such as eco-tours, cultural workshops, and local dining experiences, which not only provide financial support to local businesses but also contribute to the preservation of local traditions and natural resources. For example, in Costa Rica's sustainable tourism sector, high-value experiences like guided rainforest tours and wildlife conservation programs offer tourists a chance to directly contribute to the protection of local ecosystems while providing economic benefits to the communities involved in these projects.[6]

Promoting Environmental Sustainability and Preservation

High-impact, low-volume tourism also ensures that the natural environment is respected and protected. By limiting the number of visitors, this model reduces the strain on local ecosystems, preventing overexploitation of resources such as water, land, and wildlife. Furthermore, the revenues generated from high-value tourists are often reinvested into conservation efforts, ensuring that the natural beauty of the area is preserved for future generations.

In many cases, these conservation efforts are linked to community development projects that help local populations adapt to climate change, preserve biodiversity, and maintain sustainable livelihoods. For instance, in Kenya, tourism revenue from wildlife safaris is reinvested into local conservation projects, such as anti-poaching initiatives and habitat restoration programs, which benefit both the local community and the broader ecosystem.[7]

Preserving Pemba: The Vision Behind The Manta Resort

Known for its infamous Underwater Room, built to attract and educate its guests about the underwater world, The Manta Resort is a beacon of regeneration located on the sister island to Zanzibar, Tanzania. Juma Bakar Mohamed, the General Manager of The Manta Resort, has dedicated his career to fostering a culture of purpose and sustainability on the island of Pemba, part of the Zanzibar Archipelago. At the heart of this mission is the concept of *Kwanini*, a Swahili word meaning "why," which underpins the resort's philosophy. Through *Kwanini*, The Manta Resort seeks to balance tourism, conservation, and community well-being, ensuring a brighter future for Pemba and its people.

The Manta Resort is located on Pemba, an island distinct from its neighbor, Unguja, the main island of Zanzibar. Juma emphasizes the unique attributes of Pemba that set it apart. "Pemba is greener, more hilly, and closer to nature compared to Unguja," he explains. "While Unguja has over 660 hotels, Pemba has only eight. This lower density of tourism has allowed Pemba to remain more natural and less impacted by human activity."

Kwanini serves as the guiding principle for The Manta Resort, shaping its operations and its role within the local community. Juma describes *Kwanini* as more than a philosophy—it is a bond that unites the resort's team. "It's like a tribe, with its own customs, culture, and traditions," he explains. "It represents our way of relating as a family at The Manta Resort and keeps us focused on our goals."

This sense of purpose extends beyond the resort itself. According to Juma, *Kwanini* prompts reflection on deeper questions: "Why work at The Manta Resort and not at another hotel? Why stay in Pemba and not elsewhere in Zanzibar or Tanzania?" For Juma, the answer is clear: "I am here because I love Pemba. I believe in its future. That's what *Kwanini* represents—it keeps us focused on the bigger picture."

The scarcity of large-scale tourism on Pemba highlights the importance of sustainable practices. "Having a small number of hotels means less impact on the environment and the culture and traditions of the local community," Juma notes. "This is why we believe in high-end, low-volume tourism. Instead of building massive hotels with low nightly rates and high environmental costs, we focus on creating meaningful, sustainable experiences."

Tourism as a Tool for Conservation

The Manta Resort champions the idea that tourism can serve as a powerful tool for conservation. "For conservation projects to be effective, they need funding," Juma explains. "Instead of relying on external donations, tourism provides a self-sustaining solution. Revenue from guests allows us to allocate funds directly to conservation initiatives."

Central to this effort is the resort's partnership with the Kwanini Foundation. Juma highlights the foundation's impact, saying, "Our guests contribute a certain amount each night they stay, which goes directly to the foundation. This allows us to fund conservation efforts, while also involving guests in the process. It's a way to showcase the positive impact of their stay and attract further support."

The Kwanini Foundation is a cornerstone of The Manta Resort's efforts to protect Pemba's natural and cultural heritage. Juma stresses the importance of transparency in its operations. "Guests often ask, 'Where does the money go, and what does it do?' A big part of staying at The Manta Resort is seeing the tangible results of their contributions, whether it's marine conservation, community development, or protecting Pemba's unique biodiversity."

Through the foundation, the resort has been able to demonstrate the potential of tourism to drive meaningful change. "The foundation allows us to integrate tourism, conservation, and community development," Juma says. "It ensures that tourism benefits not just the visitors, but also the people and the environment of Pemba."

Empowering Pemba: The Role of the Kwanini Foundation and The Manta Resort

The Kwanini Foundation and The Manta Resort are spearheading efforts to uplift the communities around Pemba through sustainable initiatives and the creation of sustainable fishing methods that address both environmental conservation and socio-economic development. At the heart of their mission is a focus on preserving the marine ecosystem while creating alternative livelihoods for the local population. Through innovative programs and partnerships, these organizations are fostering growth, education, and economic stability in the region.

The Kwanini Foundation was established to support communities around Pemba, with a strong emphasis on marine conservation. The foundation's efforts are particularly evident in the creation of a no-take zone in front of The Manta Resort. This protected area is fully supported by contributions from the resort's guests, who pay a percentage of their fees to the foundation. According to Sele, a representative of the foundation, the initiative demonstrates the collaboration between the resort and the local fishing committees, which represent villages such as Makangale.

"The idea is to reduce pressure on the marine resources by providing locals with alternatives to fishing," Sele explains. By focusing on sustainable livelihoods, the Kwanini Foundation is helping to balance the need for conservation with the economic needs of the community.

One of the foundation's key strategies is the establishment of cooperative groups that empower local residents to diversify their sources of income. For instance, women in the Makangale area have formed a cooperative to produce and sell soaps made from seaweed and plants like lemongrass. Sele highlights the impact of this initiative: "They received full training from government-supported NGOs, and now they sell their soaps at better prices, increasing their daily income."

The foundation is also exploring mariculture opportunities, including sea cucumber farming, lobster farming, and prawn cultivation. Sele notes, "We've conducted small assessments, and these projects have great potential in this area." These efforts not only improve living standards but also align with the foundation's conservation goals by reducing the community's reliance on overfished marine resources.

Sele has taken personal steps to contribute to the community's development by establishing an English school in his village. "I started my school after graduating because I wanted to do something for my community," he explains. The school provides English lessons to children from surrounding villages, equipping them with skills essential for future opportunities.

"For me, English is a key subject," Sele emphasizes. "It's not only important for education but also for economic opportunities in Pemba. With more hotels being built, speaking English is a critical skill for locals to access training and employment, even without attending a formal tourism college." Sele's school underscores the importance of education in preparing Pemba's youth for a rapidly evolving economy driven by tourism.

Tourism's Role in Pemba's Development

Tourism is a relatively new industry in Pemba but holds significant potential for transforming the island's economy. Historically, Pemba has struggled with high levels of poverty and low economic activity. The government has identified North Pemba as a tourism investment zone, encouraging investors to support local development. The Manta Resort is a prime example of this approach in action.

Sele points out that "99 percent of the people working for The Manta Resort come from the surrounding villages and Pemba." This commitment to hiring locally has created numerous opportunities for residents, improving their living standards and fostering a sense of empowerment.

The Kwanini Foundation and The Manta Resort demonstrate how tourism can serve as a force for good when coupled with community-focused initiatives. Their work highlights the importance of balancing conservation efforts with socio-economic development. By preserving marine ecosystems, providing alternative livelihoods, and investing in education, they are creating a sustainable model for growth that benefits both people and the environment.

As Sele reflects on the broader impact of these efforts, he notes the importance of collaboration: "Tourism is a chance for Pemba to improve its living standards. The Manta Resort and the Kwanini Foundation are examples of how investors can support locals and raise daily incomes." Through their innovative and inclusive approach, these organizations are paving the way for a brighter future for Pemba and its people.

High-impact, low-volume tourism offers a transformative model for empowering local economies, fostering cultural preservation, and ensuring environmental sustainability. By focusing on fewer, more conscious travelers who prioritize authentic, meaningful experiences, this model creates a more equitable distribution of tourism revenues and minimizes the negative impacts associated with mass tourism. Through supporting locally owned businesses, generating sustainable employment, and promoting the preservation of natural and cultural resources, high-impact tourism offers a sustainable pathway forward for communities worldwide. As the demand for more responsible travel options grows, this approach will play a key role in shaping the future of tourism and ensuring that local economies can thrive while preserving the unique characteristics of their environments and cultures.

Economic Benefits of Regenerative Tourism: Cayuga Collection as a Case Study

Regenerative tourism minimizes economic leakages by reducing reliance on external suppliers and labor. By prioritizing local sourcing of materials, products, and services, tourism revenue remains within the community, strengthening the local economy. Furthermore, investing in capacity-building through training and education enhances local skills, reducing the need for outside expertise and fostering long-term economic benefits. As communities create unique and authentic cultural experiences, they can charge a premium for these services, attracting conscious travelers who value meaningful engagements.

At the same time, regenerative tourism supports cultural preservation by providing a platform for communities to monetize their heritage sustainably. Whether through the sale of handmade crafts, cultural performances, or cooking classes, these activities generate income while incentivizing the safeguarding of cultural traditions. This approach ensures that both the local economy and cultural heritage thrive in harmony.

Unlike traditional mass tourism, which often prioritizes short-term profits, regenerative tourism fosters equitable, sustainable, and resilient economic outcomes. The Cayuga Collection, under the leadership of Hans Pfister, serves as a powerful example of how these principles can be implemented effectively.

The Cayuga Collection's commitment to locally-owned and operated businesses ensures that economic benefits remain within the community rather than being extracted by external corporations. Hans Pfister emphasizes, "Our approach is local and people focused. When we center everything on these principles, we make the right decisions." This philosophy underpins initiatives like hiring local staff even in challenging environments. For instance, in Guatemala, where Cayuga took over a property in a nascent tourism market, Hans recalls, "It would be easy to hire a Cornell grad to come in and fix everything, but that's not our way. We invest in training locals to not just meet our standards but exceed them." Once these staff members thrive, Hans notes, "It creates that upward mobility where people look at their managers and think, 'If they can do it, so can I.'"

The integration of tourism with other sectors like agriculture and artisanal crafts further diversifies local economies. Hans provides a vivid example of a women-led oyster cooperative in Costa Rica, explaining, "These oysters aren't typically consumed by locals, but they've found a market in our hotels. Guests ask, 'Where are these from?' and we proudly tell them they're harvested right here, supporting a women's cooperative." Seasonal stability is another hallmark of Cayuga's approach. By offering year-round activities such as eco-tours, wellness retreats, and cultural festivals, the properties mitigate the economic volatility associated with seasonal tourism. Luxury rewilding projects, where previously degraded lands are restored and repurposed, also play a role. Hans describes Isla Palenque as "a place that was once heavily impacted by agriculture but now has more wildlife than the nearby reserves. That's what rewilding can do."

The Cayuga Collection ensures that profits from tourism initiatives are equitably distributed across stakeholders by prioritizing local sourcing and partnerships. Hans notes their success in "keeping 90–95 percent of revenue within the local economy," adding that they aim to eliminate imported goods wherever possible. "We go through our storage rooms and try to replace imported items with local alternatives. It's not always easy—olive oil and wheat flour are hard to substitute—but where we can, we do." Revenue generated by Cayuga properties is reinvested in community infrastructure projects such as schools, healthcare facilities, and clean water systems. Hans points out, "This isn't just about running hotels; it's about creating a formal economy where suppliers get legal invoices and employees have social security."

The connection between economic benefits and conservation is another hallmark of Cayuga's approach. Hans is particularly proud of the Social Progress Index (SPI) in Costa Rica, which measures the socio-economic impact of tourism. "This isn't just theoretical. We now have data showing how tourism improves lives in our communities," he explains. Properties like Isla Palenque, which was rehabilitated from agricultural use, now serve as havens for biodiversity. Hans explains, "These areas now support more wildlife than nearby reserves, demonstrating how tourism can regenerate ecosystems." Rewilding gardens at Senda offer similar outcomes, where guests encounter more wildlife within the hotel grounds than in the surrounding nature reserves.

Cultural preservation is a key component of regenerative tourism at Cayuga properties. Guests are offered opportunities to purchase handmade crafts, participate in cooking classes, or enjoy cultural performances, all of which celebrate the unique heritage of the region. Hans underscores the importance of authenticity, stating, "I see hotels with decor brought in from halfway around the world—Buddha statues from Bali, doors from Morocco—and I think, 'Does this make sense for Costa Rica?' It's about creating a sense of place that's authentic to the region." This commitment to cultural integrity not only enriches the guest experience but also provides local artisans and performers with a sustainable source of income.

Regenerative tourism also appeals to travelers who prioritize quality over quantity. Guests at Cayuga properties tend to spend more on local goods and experiences, directly boosting the local economy. Hans reflects, "These are conscious travelers who care about where their money goes. They form deep connections with the destinations, and that brings them back again and again." This loyalty strengthens the financial resilience of the communities where Cayuga operates.

Minimizing economic leakages is another significant achievement of the Cayuga Collection. Hans explains how the company reduces reliance on external suppliers by sourcing materials and services locally. "Even though it might cost more, supporting local suppliers is integral to our mission," he states. Additionally, Cayuga invests heavily in training and education for local communities. Collaborations with organizations like Luciernagas provide underprivileged individuals with pathways to employment through internships and job training. Hans explains, "We don't just give people handouts. We give them opportunities to work, to learn, and to grow. That's how you create lasting change."

Finally, Cayuga's commitment to sustainability attracts values-aligned investors and funding institutions. Hans ensures that all developments align with the company's mission, stating, "We say no to developments that are too invasive or don't align with our mission." This careful selection process has solidified Cayuga's reputation as a responsible operator, making them a preferred partner for local banks and international funding organizations. Furthermore, government programs like Costa Rica's Certification for Sustainable Tourism (CST), which Hans praises as "rigorous and accessible," offer additional support and recognition for regenerative tourism initiatives.

The Cayuga Collection illustrates how regenerative tourism can harmonize economic viability with social and environmental stewardship. By empowering local economies, promoting diversification, enhancing resilience, incentivizing conservation, and fostering cultural preservation, Cayuga proves that financial success and sustainability can go hand-in-hand. As Hans Pfister states, "When tourism is done right, it truly becomes a force for good."

Driving Conservation and Economic Resilience

Regenerative tourism is a transformative approach that aims to restore and enhance the natural, cultural, and social environments of a destination while minimizing the negative impacts typically associated with traditional tourism. This model emphasizes a symbiotic relationship between environmental conservation and economic development, drawing sustainable investments and fostering long-term partnerships that benefit both ecosystems and local communities.

A core strength of regenerative tourism is its ability to attract investors and organizations dedicated to sustainability. These stakeholders play a crucial role in funding infrastructure projects, conservation efforts, and community development initiatives. By focusing on long-term partnerships, regenerative tourism ensures that investments are directed toward lasting positive change. This, in turn, strengthens local economies and ecosystems, fostering resilience and sustainability. Through these collaborations, regenerative tourism provides a model for economic growth that supports both the environment and the people living within it.

Governments and international organizations are increasingly recognizing the value of regenerative tourism and providing various forms of financial support to encourage its development. For example, the U.S. Economic Development Administration's Travel, Tourism, and Outdoor Recreation program invested $750 million from the American Rescue Plan to support communities impacted by the Covid-19 pandemic. This funding is aimed at rebuilding and strengthening the tourism sector while fostering a more equitable and resilient industry.[8]

Additionally, initiatives such as The Ocean Foundation's Regenerative Tourism Catalyst Grant Program, in partnership with the U.S. National Oceanic and Atmospheric Administration (NOAA) and the Local2030 Islands Network, have provided approximately $118,266 in funding to regenerative tourism projects in island nations. This funding aims to help these regions build climate resilience while advancing sustainable development goals.[9]

By embracing regenerative tourism, communities can transform their tourism sectors into engines for positive change. The integration of sustainable investment, government support, and community-driven initiatives creates a model for growth that enhances both environmental and economic well-being. As more regions adopt regenerative tourism principles, we can create a future where tourism contributes to the preservation of our planet's beauty and the empowerment of local communities, ensuring that these areas remain vibrant for generations to come.

Regenerative tourism creates a sustainable link between economic benefits and the preservation of natural resources. By integrating eco-tourism activities like wildlife safaris and guided hikes, local communities receive direct financial incentives for maintaining ecosystems and biodiversity. Additionally, regenerative models incorporate payments for ecosystem services, such as reforestation or carbon sequestration, ensuring communities are compensated for their role in safeguarding the environment.

This model also fosters economic diversification, reducing communities' dependence on tourism alone by supporting sectors like agriculture and artisanal crafts. Agritourism, for example, combines farming with tourism, offering farmers supplementary income while promoting local agricultural practices. By focusing on year-round activities such as eco-tours, wellness retreats, and cultural festivals, regenerative tourism stabilizes local economies and reduces the volatility associated with seasonal tourism.

By attracting conscious travelers who prioritize sustainability and authentic experiences, regenerative tourism drives higher spending on local goods and services. These travelers not only contribute more directly to the economy but are also likely to return, fostering repeat visits and spreading positive word-of-mouth, further bolstering local businesses and promoting long-term economic growth.

Furthermore, regenerative tourism promotes financial resilience through equitable revenue-sharing models, ensuring that the economic gains from tourism are fairly distributed, particularly benefiting marginalized groups. Revenue generated from tourism can also be reinvested into local infrastructure, enhancing roads, schools, and healthcare facilities and creating lasting benefits for communities.

Balancing Profit, People, and Planet: Sarah Dusek's Vision for a Regenerative Economy

Sarah Dusek, co-founder of Under Canvas and Few and Far, is an entrepreneurial pioneer committed to creating a regenerative economy. Through her work in eco-lodging, carbon sequestration, and land restoration, Sarah has developed a business model that harmonizes profitability with social and environmental impact. Sarah's entrepreneurial journey began with a bold vision but limited resources.

"It's exceptionally difficult to get these kinds of projects funded just as a baseline," she admitted, describing the uphill battle she faced in attracting investment for Under Canvas which eventually sold for $100 million. Despite the growing awareness of sustainable tourism, alternative lodging remains "an alternative asset class," she explains. "It's not seen as a very dependable, reliable asset class. It'll get there... but we're still not there yet."

In the early days, Under Canvas relied heavily on debt to fund its growth. "We understood debt, and we just understood how debt worked," she recalled. "Thankfully, we had a cash-flowing business, so we could service a little bit, borrow a little bit of money for equipment, and know we'd probably be able to pay it back." This pragmatic approach enabled Sarah to scale the business gradually until it reached a tipping point. "When you generate huge amounts of earnings before interest, taxes, depreciation and amortization (EBITDA)—1 million, 2 million, 3 million and up—that's when professional, large-scale investors start to take notice," she explains. But the path from startup to profitability was fraught with challenges, requiring careful financial management and determination.

Natural Capital: A New Economic Paradigm

Sarah is a passionate advocate for natural capital, an emerging economic model that values biodiversity and land restoration. "We are on the cusp of natural capital becoming a thing," she said, though she acknowledged that the mechanisms for quantifying and trading natural assets are still in their infancy. "When people get their brains around the idea of having nature on their balance sheets, it will get easier. But we're still not there yet."

At Few and Far, Sarah is pioneering projects as a tour and hotel operator that aim to restore ecosystems while generating economic returns. "Our goal is to sequester a million additional tons of carbon a year through all the projects we do," she shared. The company's first project alone aims to sequester 100,000 tons annually by planting grasslands, reforesting areas, and removing invasive species. "This work is scientifically measured, rigorously documented, and tied to generating carbon credits that we can sell directly or through a market," she explains. These efforts exemplify how natural capital can be monetized to benefit both the planet and investors.

For Sarah, the success of regenerative projects hinges on their ability to uplift local communities. "One of the things discovered in the last five years was that it was possible for people to develop carbon projects without having any impact on local people whatsoever," she said. In response, new standards now require carbon projects to include robust community development plans. "You have to demonstrate how the project impacts the local community, whether it's building a school, creating jobs, or providing carbon credit revenue to community members."

Few and Far is committed to ensuring that local stakeholders benefit directly from its initiatives. "We're partnering with communal lands for an expansion area of land, where partners will receive some of the carbon credits themselves," Sarah explains. She highlighted a landmark project in Namibia involving one million hectares of community-managed land. "Carbon developers are working with local communities, teaching them how to manage their land so they get paid for it. I think that alone has the potential to completely upend rural poverty," she said.

The benefits of these projects extend beyond carbon revenue. By restoring ecosystems, they create opportunities for biodiversity, tourism, and economic diversification. "Some land isn't prime for tourism—like flat grasslands in the middle of nowhere," Sarah noted. "But if you restore those grasslands, you can sequester carbon, increase wildlife, and create new opportunities for tourism, making the whole thing extraordinarily regenerative."

The Three-Legged Stool: People, Planet, and Profit

Sarah's philosophy for regenerative business is rooted in the metaphor of a three-legged stool, representing people, planet, and profit. "If one of those legs is out of balance, the stool falls over," she explains. "To be regenerative, all three legs must be equal and in harmony." This balance, she believes, is the key to ensuring long-term sustainability in any business.

In Few and Far, Sarah has structured her team to reflect this philosophy. "I have a general manager for hospitality and an ecology manager for land management, and they are peers. One isn't the boss of the other," she shared. "They each have a specific responsibility to drive their area forward, and together they ensure we're making progress across all three pillars."

Sarah also stressed the importance of profitability in driving impact. "When something functions as a business and has to pay its way, it forces us to get very creative," she said. She contrasted this approach with philanthropic conservation models, which she criticized for their reliance on "billionaire philanthropy" that often lacks sustainability. "As soon as the funding dries up, the system collapses. We need solutions that pay for themselves and can stand the test of time."

While Sarah acknowledges the role of government in creating incentives and regulatory frameworks, she believes the private sector must lead the charge. "If we wait for the government to do it, it just takes too long," she argued. "Government's responsibility is to govern, create rules, and protect its people—not to innovate. That's the role of the private sector."

She envisions a complementary relationship between the private sector and government, where businesses pioneer new systems and governments provide governance. "Look at AI or social media," she said. "Without strong governance, you see the pitfalls clearly. But the innovation always comes from the private sector first."

For Sarah, a regenerative economy is one where all outputs—economic, environmental, and social—are overwhelmingly positive. "It's about creating more benefit in every arena," she said. This vision requires rethinking traditional capitalism to prioritize long-term sustainability over short-term gains. "It's like running a three-legged race," she reflected. "We might move slower, but we ensure that no one is left behind and no resources are depleted beyond repair."

Sarah emphasized that achieving this balance requires intentionality and accountability. "The more impactful your project is—whether it's restoring biodiversity, supporting communities, or increasing wildlife—the higher the value of the carbon credits you can generate," she explains. "People are looking for high-quality projects with significant impact."

By aligning business objectives with environmental and social impact, Sarah is redefining what it means to succeed in the 21st century. As she succinctly put it, "If we want to have a planet that exists for thousands more years, we have to go together."

Blended Finance: A New Model for Sustainable Funding

Blended finance is emerging as an innovative approach to financing sustainable development. It combines public or philanthropic funds with private investment to address global challenges, particularly in sectors that require long-term funding and have high risks but also high potential returns, such as climate change mitigation, poverty reduction, and social development. This model offers a pathway to scale up investments in sustainable development by leveraging the strengths of both sectors. By blending different types of financial resources, blended finance aims to create a self-sustaining funding model that not only attracts private investment but also supports the achievement of social, environmental, and financial goals.

Blended finance is the strategic use of development finance and philanthropic funding to mobilize private capital for investments in sustainable development. The World Economic Forum defines it as a mechanism where donor or concessional funds are used to de-risk or provide incentives for private investors to engage in projects that they might otherwise consider too risky.[10] By reducing risks, these public and philanthropic funds act as a catalyst for private investments in areas such as renewable energy, infrastructure development, and sustainable agriculture, where the returns may take longer to materialize but are critical for achieving the United Nations' Sustainable Development Goals (SDGs).[11]

The blending of public and private finance is crucial for filling the financing gap needed to achieve the SDGs. According to the United Nations, the estimated financing gap for sustainable development is trillions of dollars annually.[12] While public funds alone are insufficient to meet this gap, blended finance can catalyze private investment and create a multiplier effect by increasing the volume of capital directed towards sustainable projects.

Advantages of Blended Finance

One of the primary benefits of blended finance is its ability to attract private capital to development projects that would otherwise be considered too risky or unattractive to investors. By using public or philanthropic funding to cover a portion of the risk, private investors are more willing to participate in projects that align with their financial objectives while contributing to social and environmental outcomes. This is particularly important in sectors like renewable energy and sustainable agriculture, where the long-term nature of investments and uncertain returns may discourage private investors.

Additionally, blended finance has the potential to scale up sustainable investments. According to the Global Impact Investing Network (GIIN), blended finance has the ability to mobilize large amounts of private capital, thereby increasing the amount of financing available for SDGs.[13] The blending of funds from different sources creates a more diversified financial base, reducing the overall risk for all parties involved. Moreover, blending finance allows for the structuring of deals that cater to a wider range of investors, from those looking for low-risk, low-return investments to those willing to take on higher risks for potentially higher returns.

Despite its potential, blended finance also faces several challenges. One of the key concerns is the complexity of structuring deals that meet the interests of both public and private investors. Often, these projects involve long-term commitments and require the coordination of multiple stakeholders, which can lead to delays and inefficiencies. Additionally, there is the issue of measuring the impact of blended finance projects. While financial returns are relatively easy to measure, social and environmental outcomes are more difficult to quantify. Without robust impact measurement frameworks, it becomes challenging to assess the effectiveness of blended finance in achieving sustainable development objectives.[14]

Another challenge is the need for appropriate governance structures to ensure that blended finance projects are managed effectively. This involves establishing clear guidelines for the use of public funds, ensuring transparency, and maintaining accountability to ensure that funds are allocated efficiently and that the intended outcomes are achieved.[15]

Examples of Blended Finance in Action

One of the most notable examples of blended finance is the Green Climate Fund (GCF), which is designed to support the transition to a low-carbon, climate-resilient world. The GCF uses a blend of concessional and non-concessional funds to provide financing for projects in developing countries that address climate change. By blending donor contributions with private sector investments, the GCF has been able to finance large-scale renewable energy projects and climate adaptation initiatives in countries such as India and South Africa.[16]

Similarly, the International Finance Corporation (IFC), a member of the World Bank Group, has been active in using blended finance to support private sector investments in sustainable development. For example, the IFC has used blended finance mechanisms to support renewable energy projects in emerging markets, where access to financing for clean energy is limited. By offering concessional financing and guarantees, the IFC has been able to attract private investors to projects in countries such as Kenya and Vietnam, contributing to the global transition to renewable energy.[17]

Blended finance represents a powerful tool for financing sustainable development by mobilizing both public and private capital to address the world's most pressing challenges. Through its ability to reduce investment risks, scale up funding, and attract private capital, blended finance is playing an essential role in achieving the SDGs. However, challenges related to deal structuring, impact measurement, and governance remain. To unlock the full potential of blended finance, it is crucial to create efficient frameworks, improve transparency, and ensure effective management of these funds. As more examples of successful blended finance initiatives emerge, this model has the potential to revolutionize the way sustainable development is funded, driving positive social, environmental, and financial outcomes globally.

The Role of Blue Alliance and Blended Finance in Conservation

Blue Alliance (BA), a non profit NGO, is reshaping the way marine protected areas (MPAs) are financed by creating sustainable financing models. BA co-manages almost two million hectares of MPAs with local/national governments in Indonesia, the Philippines, and Zanzibar. MPA management centers around community development, compliance, science, and the blue economy. In each country, work is administered by local teams who are guided by workplans developed with the governments.

Most MPAs are underfunded, and while public expenditure on biodiversity averages $6.1 billion per annum globally, only 4 percent of this is directed towards marine biodiversity. Traditional sources, such as governments and philanthropy, are required for conservation but are inadequate and unreliable. "With grants, you get funding for two years, then scramble to get another grant, and so on," Angelique Brathwaite, Director of Conservation and Science and Co-Founder, explains. "That doesn't work for sustainable management. If you don't know whether you'll be able to pay your staff in two years, it's impossible to plan effectively." The same is true for government subventions and philanthropy.

Angelique is a marine ecologist responsible for coordinating conservation and science programs for MPAs. She is an expert in both coral reef science and integrated coastal management, with over 25 years' global experience. She headed the marine research section for government in Barbados for over a decade, developing coral reef related research projects in addition to reef system management protocols compatible with integrated coastal zone management (ICZM) frameworks. She holds a PhD in marine biology from the Paris Sciences et Lettres Research University and is a professional scuba diving educator.

New financing means must be found quickly given the small window of opportunity, reported to be less than 50 years, for both mitigation against stressors and adaptation to a changing climate. With this timeframe, it is imperative that effective action is taken now.

Blue Alliance believes in business as a force for good and private investment is a key component of its sustainable financing program. In addition to sourcing traditional means of funding for MPAs, the NGO owns and runs bankable, reef-positive businesses in and around the MPAs that it co-manages. These businesses are community-based aquaculture, nature-based tourism and sustainable sea food. They all aim at generating long-term income for MPA management and alleviating poverty in the surrounding communities. Ultimately, after eight years, profits from these businesses will finance the MPAs, with less reliance on traditional financing means.

Impact investing, a cornerstone of Blue Alliance's work, represents a significant shift in how conservation projects are funded. "Impact investors are very different from the regular investors who only care about profit," Angelique says. "They still need a return on investment—they're not giving their money away—but they also require social and environmental returns. Three pillars—profit, social impact, and environmental impact—are central to their model."

Investors track the impact of their investments via a series of predetermined metrics. Blue Alliance's metrics reflect its holistic approach. "While we collect data on over 25 indicators that encompass biodiversity, fisheries, livelihoods, and revenues, we selected seven metrics for impact investors. These specific metrics, such as fish biomass, are expected to improve during the life cycle of the loan. Other metrics, such as coral cover, for example, might not improve, in spite of our best efforts, due to circumstances out side of our control. For the first time in my career, I've had to project what our management interventions will achieve over one to ten years," Angelique says. In some cases, "If we overachieve, our interest rate is lower. If we underachieve, it's higher. This brings a level of discipline to conservation that we're not really accustomed to." This results-based approach ensures accountability and transparency, essential for building trust with investors. "We have to be very clear about what we're going to do, how we're going to do it, and what outcomes we expect," Angelique explains. Angelique emphasizes the importance of trust and collaboration with communities. Beyond biodiversity, Blue Alliance also tracks social and economic metrics to evaluate the broader impact of MPAs. "A key livelihood metric is the number of jobs generated by the MPA," Angelique explains. "We also measure how many people are supported by the MPA—whether through training, workshops, or alternative revenue-generating activities."

Community engagement is critical to the success of any MPA. "An MPA is not just about enforcement; it's about communication and education that goes both ways," Angelique says. "A hungry fisher will not be a good conservationist, and at the same time people need to understand why the MPA exists and how it benefits them. Without that, any MPA is likely to fail."

One of Blue Alliance's core strategies is blended finance, and the NGO has developed a blended finance vehicle with anchor investor—BNP Paribas, with the Global Fund for Coral Reef (GFCR), Swiss Re Foundation and other donors, providing a catalytic grant to de-risk the investment. To date, the NGO has partnered with a variety of organizations which aid either in financing or de-risking the business ventures. The facility combines grants, refundable grants, and impact loans to finance the reef-positive businesses. Such a facility is attractive to impact investors as the due diligence has already been done and the investments de-risked by catalytic grants and diversification across revenue models, sectors, and geographies.

Blue Alliance's work addresses a significant gap in the conservation world: The ability to structure deals with impact investors. "There aren't many scientists who can go to an impact investor and structure a deal," Angelique says. "Most conservationists aren't trained in that." The expertise of BA's CEO—Nicolas Pascal, whose skills include marine biology and investment banking—allows Blue Alliance to connect their MPAs with the funding they need, creating a bridge between conservation goals and financial sustainability.

The ultimate goal of Blue Alliance's work is to create MPAs that are financially sustainable and environmentally robust, while supporting communities. "Regarding the reef-positive businesses, nature-based tourism is aimed at improving the visitor experience. In community-based aquaculture, the communities play major roles in all aspects of farming and in sustainable sea food, again communities are involved in sustainable fishing and effective processing of fish. "In all, conservation is at the forefront."

Blue Alliance is also exploring opportunities in blue carbon, a field focused on the carbon stored in marine ecosystems such as mangroves and seagrass beds. "We're primarily working with mangroves at this stage," Angelique says. "Mangroves are incredibly effective at storing carbon, and protecting or restoring them is essential for climate change mitigation." Despite its potential, the blue carbon market is still in its infancy. "The markets for trading carbon credits are relatively new and extremely complicated," Angelique explains. "Our work here is at a very nascent stage, aimed at managing, mapping, and measuring suitable forests, and identifying owners."

Blue Alliance's approach is transforming attitudes toward private investment in conservation. "In the past I've viewed investors as the 'baddies,'" Angelique admits. "But impact investing shows that private capital can be a force for good, provided it's tied to clear social and environmental metrics."

Through initiatives like blue carbon, aquaculture, and ecotourism development, Blue Alliance is proving that conservation and the private sector can work together to protect the planet's most precious ecosystems. This innovative approach not only ensures the long-term success of marine protected areas but also redefines the role of private investment in building a sustainable future.

Angelique's work with Blue Alliance highlights the importance of balancing ecological goals with the needs of local communities. By integrating scientific, social, and economic metrics, the organization creates management plans that benefit both ecosystems and the people who depend on them.

"We need to look at science as well as social metrics," Angelique emphasizes. "The success of an MPA depends on its ability to improve ecosystem health while also supporting local livelihoods." Through rigorous monitoring and collaboration, Blue Alliance is setting a new standard for marine conservation, proving that well-managed MPAs can deliver tangible benefits for both people and the planet.

Ensuring Long-Term Sustainability

The economic viability of regenerative tourism presents a promising pathway for creating long-term, sustainable benefits for local communities, ecosystems, and stakeholders. By focusing on community-owned enterprises, job creation, and the equitable distribution of tourism revenues, regenerative tourism fosters resilient economies that are less reliant on external entities and short-term profits. This approach not only empowers local residents but also ensures that tourism development aligns with environmental preservation and cultural respect. As more destinations adopt regenerative tourism principles, this model can play a crucial role in reshaping the global tourism industry into one that prioritizes sustainability, inclusivity, and long-term economic health for all involved. By fostering a conservation-led economy, we can generate revenue through blue economy social enterprises while also providing socio-economic and employment benefits. This approach shows how people and nature can thrive together in a shared seascape.

Key Takeaways

Regenerative tourism as an economic model:

- Prioritizes long-term benefits for local communities, ecosystems, and stakeholders rather than short-term profits.
- Aims to distribute tourism revenues equitably, avoiding economic leakage to external corporations.
- Empowers communities through community-owned enterprises like locally run lodges, restaurants, and craft markets.

High-impact, low-volume tourism:

- Focuses on quality over quantity—attracting fewer visitors who engage deeply with local culture and nature.
- Helps prevent overcrowding, resource depletion, and cultural erosion typical of mass tourism.
- Examples like Bhutan's high-value, low-impact model show how tourism fees can fund conservation and development.

Supporting community-owned enterprises:

- Encourages local entrepreneurship in authentic, place-based experiences, from crafts to cultural tours.
- Reduces economic leakage, ensuring money stays in local economies and benefits families directly.
- Regions like the Galápagos Islands use restricted tourism to protect biodiversity while fostering community-led eco-tourism businesses.

Attracting conscious travelers:

- Appeals to visitors seeking meaningful, sustainable experiences who are willing to pay a premium.
- Conscious travelers spend more on local goods and services, directly benefiting the community.
- Example: In Costa Rica, eco-tours and conservation programs connect travelers with local biodiversity and culture.

Tourism as a tool for conservation:

- Tourism revenue funds critical environmental conservation and community development projects.
- Models like The Manta Resort in Pemba use guest contributions to support marine conservation via foundations like Kwanini.
- Combines tourism with ecological stewardship for mutual benefit.

Economic resilience through diversification:

- Regenerative tourism integrates with other sectors like agriculture, crafts, and conservation.
- Initiatives like the Cayuga Collection invest in local sourcing, reducing reliance on imports.
- Year-round tourism activities mitigate risks from seasonal downturns.

Blended finance for sustainable tourism:

- Combines public, philanthropic, and private funds to finance sustainable projects.
- Attracts private capital by de-risking investments through grants or guarantees.
- Examples include the Green Climate Fund and IFC projects in renewable energy.

Blue Alliance and conservation finance:

- Pioneers sustainable financing for Marine Protected Areas.
- Funds conservation via reef-positive businesses like aquaculture and eco-tourism.

- Measures impacts through social, economic, and biodiversity indicators to ensure accountability.

Natural capital and regenerative investment:

- Entrepreneurs like Sarah Dusek integrate carbon sequestration and land restoration into tourism models.
- Natural capital initiatives monetize ecosystem services, creating new revenue streams while protecting biodiversity.
- Emphasizes a "three-legged stool" approach—balancing people, planet, and profit for sustainable business.

Long-term sustainability:

- Regenerative tourism offers a resilient path forward, creating economic stability and protecting cultural and natural heritage.
- Helps communities build a conservation-led economy that supports livelihoods and ecosystem health.
- Positions tourism as a driver of equitable, inclusive economic growth worldwide.

Notes

1 McKinsey & Company. The future of sustainable tourism: A comprehensive outlook, McKinsey & Company, 2020.
2 World Travel and Tourism Council. Travel and tourism: Economic impact 2020, World Travel and Tourism Council, 2020. www.wttc.org (archived at https://perma.cc/5D8Y-J3L8)
3 Global Sustainable Tourism Council. The role of community-based tourism in sustainable development, Global Sustainable Tourism Council, 2019. www.gstcouncil.org (archived at https://perma.cc/R2F6-QAAG)
4 S Pankaj. High value, low impact tourism: Lessons from Bhutan and Costa Rica, *Tourism and Sustainable Development Journal*, 2020, 14 (2), 118–35.
5 World Travel and Tourism Council. Travel and tourism: Economic impact 2020, World Travel and Tourism Council, 2020. www.wttc.org (archived at https://perma.cc/5D8Y-J3L8)

6 L Vera. Empowering local communities through high-impact tourism, *Tourism and Development Review*, 2020, 15 (2), 49–58.
7 McKinsey & Company. The future of sustainable tourism: A comprehensive outlook, McKinsey & Company, 2020.
8 Economic Development Administration. Travel, tourism, and outdoor recreation, US Economic Development Administration, nd. www.eda.gov/funding/programs/american-rescue-plan/travel-tourism (archived at https://perma.cc/5GKH-E6C2)
9 The Ocean Foundation. The Ocean Foundation awards funding to eight island-led regenerative tourism initiatives around the world, The Ocean Foundation, 2022. oceanfdn.org/the-ocean-foundation-awards-funding-to-eight-island-led-regenerative-tourism-initiatives-around-the-world (archived at https://perma.cc/XR2H-2SN3)
10 World Economic Forum. Blended finance: The future of sustainable funding, World Economic Forum, 2020. weforum.org (archived at https://perma.cc/TVB9-CZKR)
11 Organisation for Economic Co-operation and Development (OECD). Blended finance: A review of the current landscape, OECD, 2018. www.oecd.org (archived at https://perma.cc/AV2T-YA26)
12 United Nations (2015) *Transforming Our World: The 2030 Agenda for Sustainable Development*, United Nations, New York.
13 Global Impact Investing Network (GIIN). Blended finance: A new model for sustainable investment, GIIN, 2019. thegiin.org (archived at https://perma.cc/NY82-QEUU)
14 World Economic Forum. Blended finance: The future of sustainable funding, World Economic Forum, 2020. weforum.org (archived at https://perma.cc/TVB9-CZKR)
15 Organisation for Economic Co-operation and Development (OECD). Blended finance: A review of the current landscape, OECD, 2018. www.oecd.org (archived at https://perma.cc/AV2T-YA26)
16 World Economic Forum. Blended finance: The future of sustainable funding, World Economic Forum, 2020. weforum.org (archived at https://perma.cc/TVB9-CZKR)
17 International Finance Corporation (IFC). Blended finance for sustainable development, IFC, 2020. ifc.org (archived at https://perma.cc/4D8F-C65G)

Community Empowerment   07

Tourism, when thoughtfully designed, can play a pivotal role in empowering local communities by fostering meaningful interactions between travelers and hosts. Guest engagement serves as a bridge between visitors and local populations, enabling cultural exchange, economic growth, and environmental stewardship. When tourism prioritizes authentic connections and community-driven initiatives, it creates a sustainable model that uplifts both the hosts and the guests.

One of the most significant ways guest engagement empowers communities is by creating economic opportunities and capacity-building. Direct involvement of local artisans, farmers, and service providers ensures that tourism revenue benefits the community rather than external intermediaries. For example, G Adventures' Ripple Score highlights how much of a trip's expenditure stays within local economies, encouraging travelers to choose experiences that directly support local businesses.[1] The United Nations World Tourism Organization (UNWTO) further emphasizes that community-led tourism initiatives help marginalized groups access markets, reducing inequality and fostering financial independence.[2]

Cultural preservation is another critical benefit of community-focused tourism. Through activities such as storytelling, traditional crafts, and culinary workshops, communities can showcase their heritage while preserving it. Cultural tourism not only educates travelers but also ensures the survival of intangible cultural practices that might otherwise be lost. According to the UNWTO, programs that celebrate and monetize cultural heritage have successfully sustained traditions in regions such as Southeast Asia and Africa.[3]

Guest engagement also promotes environmental stewardship, aligning tourism with conservation goals. Many destinations involve visitors in activities such as reforestation, wildlife monitoring, and marine conservation, encouraging travelers to take an active role in protecting the environment. At Fogo Island Inn in Canada, for example, guests are invited to learn about local ecosystems and participate in sustainability initiatives. This approach not only enriches the guest experience but also strengthens community resources for managing and protecting natural assets.

Key strategies are essential for ensuring the success of guest engagement programs. First, communities must actively co-create tourism experiences to ensure authenticity and alignment with local values. The Indigenous Tourism Association of Canada (ITAC) highlights the importance of community leadership in shaping tourism offerings, which ensures that initiatives reflect local priorities.[4] Second, education and interpretation play a critical role in fostering meaningful guest interactions. Providing travelers with context about the cultural and ecological significance of their experiences enhances appreciation and respect. Finally, partnerships between local governments, NGOs, and tourism operators amplify the impact of these programs. The Maasai Mara Conservancies in Kenya, for example, demonstrate how collaborative efforts can balance wildlife conservation with the socioeconomic needs of local communities, creating a sustainable tourism model.[5]

Despite its potential, community-focused tourism faces challenges such as overtourism, cultural commodification, and unequal power dynamics. To address these issues, ethical guidelines and sustainable practices are necessary to protect communities from exploitation. Organizations like the Global Sustainable Tourism Council (GSTC) provide frameworks to ensure that tourism initiatives prioritize community well-being and environmental sustainability.[6]

Empowering communities through guest engagement transforms tourism into a force for positive change. By creating economic opportunities, preserving cultural heritage, and promoting environmental stewardship, tourism uplifts local populations while offering travelers deeper, more meaningful experiences. When communities actively shape their tourism futures, the benefits extend far beyond economic gains, fostering resilience, cultural preservation, and environmental sustainability.

Regenerative hospitality goes beyond environmental stewardship; it requires a deep commitment to the communities that surround and support it. Engaging with local communities as equal partners ensures that the benefits of tourism are shared equitably and that the cultural integrity of the area is preserved. This principle recognizes that without the involvement and support of the community, a hospitality operation cannot truly be regenerative.

Strategies for Engaging Communities

The travel industry has immense potential to influence local communities, economies, and environments positively. By adopting regenerative tourism principles, businesses can shift from simply minimizing harm to actively contributing to the resilience and vitality of the places they operate. Below are actionable strategies for fostering community engagement and advancing regenerative practices in tourism.

Engage Local Communities from the Outset

Involving local communities from the earliest stages of tourism projects is critical to ensuring that their voices are heard and their needs are addressed. Community engagement can be achieved through a combination of consultations, advisory boards, and the integration of local knowledge. Workshops, town hall meetings, and focus groups allow businesses to gather valuable insights into cultural sensitivities and community priorities. For example, the Indigenous Tourism Association of Canada highlights the importance of collaborative planning that respects indigenous knowledge and traditions. Forming community advisory committees ensures ongoing communication, while incorporating traditional practices into tourism offerings honors cultural heritage in an authentic and respectful way.

At the heart of Song Saa's operations is the principle of engaging the local community in every aspect of its activities. The resort hires 35 percent of its workforce from Prek Svay, a nearby underserved community with significant barriers to employment. These employees are integrated into roles across the resort, from guest-facing services to operational support. Local hires receive competitive salaries, benefits exceeding Cambodia's living wage, and extensive training programs in hospitality and life skills. This commitment ensures that community members develop long-term career prospects while contributing to the resort's operations.

Song Saa also involves the local community in decision-making. With dedicated community liaison officers and ongoing consultations with village chiefs and community leaders, the resort aligns its initiatives with the needs and aspirations of the local population. This collaborative approach not only builds trust but also enables the resort to design programs that reflect the local culture and environment, enriching the guest experience with authentic and immersive activities.

The resort's policy of sourcing goods and services locally further reinforces its commitment to community engagement. Approximately 96 percent of Song Saa's supplies come from within 50 miles, with much of the produce sourced directly from Prek Svay. Items like seafood, coconut oil, and bamboo straws are not only environmentally sustainable but also support local livelihoods. This approach strengthens the local economy and allows guests to enjoy fresh, authentic, and environmentally conscious products.

To ensure transparency, Song Saa communicates the economic impact of its practices to guests. By adopting a model similar to Fogo Island Inn's Economic Nutrition labels, the resort demonstrates how guest spending directly supports local communities. This transparency fosters a deeper connection between visitors and their host community, encouraging more mindful and impactful travel behavior.

Song Saa's engagement extends beyond employment and sourcing. The resort, through its foundation, actively contributes to the development of local infrastructure and education. Initiatives include the creation of water catchment systems, the establishment of Cambodia's first waste management center in the archipelago, and support for community-led projects like bamboo straw and coconut oil production. The foundation also supports educational workshops and skill-building programs, addressing systemic barriers to opportunity and fostering long-term development in the region.

One of the most ambitious initiatives involves transforming an old wooden house near the local primary school into a community center. This facility will provide extracurricular activities, a library, a computer room, and sports fields. By addressing gaps in creative education and sports programming, the project aims to empower local youth and create new opportunities for personal growth.

Song Saa's commitment to the environment is integral to its relationship with the local community. The resort established Cambodia's first marine protected area in 2006, safeguarding coral reefs and marine ecosystems. Guests can actively participate in conservation initiatives such as coral planting, mangrove restoration, and beach cleanups. These activities allow visitors to connect with the natural environment while supporting the resort's efforts to balance tourism and ecosystem health.

The deep integration of community engagement into Song Saa's operations translates directly into an unparalleled guest experience. Guests are welcomed "home" upon arrival and encouraged to form personal connections with staff. These interactions are enhanced by the resort's training programs, which emphasize authenticity, professionalism, and cultural sensitivity. Many guests leave with a sense of having formed genuine friendships with the staff, enriching their memories of the resort.

Song Saa also provides structured feedback mechanisms, including daily monitoring of guest satisfaction and real-time responses to inquiries or complaints. These systems ensure that the resort continuously improves its offerings, while its philosophy of "service from the heart" inspires staff to deliver exceptional hospitality.

Song Saa Private Island demonstrates how prioritizing community engagement can elevate both the local population and the guest experience. By creating a holistic model that integrates employment, education, conservation, and cultural exchange, the resort has set a benchmark for regenerative tourism. Guests not only enjoy a luxurious stay but also contribute to the well-being of the surrounding community, fostering a sense of purpose and connection.

This approach positions Song Saa as a leader in sustainable tourism, proving that businesses can succeed while benefiting the people and ecosystems they depend on. As the hospitality industry continues to evolve, Song Saa's example serves as a reminder that community engagement is not just an ethical imperative but also a pathway to creating transformative guest experiences.

Invest in Local Education and Capacity-Building

Education and capacity-building are essential pillars of community empowerment, particularly in remote and underserved regions. By equipping local populations with knowledge, skills, and opportunities, businesses can create pathways for long-term socio-economic growth while enhancing the tourism experience. Kasbah du Toubkal, located in Morocco's High Atlas Mountains, demonstrates how integrating educational initiatives into a tourism model can transform lives and communities while supporting cultural preservation and environmental sustainability.

Supporting Education Through "Education for All"

One of Kasbah du Toubkal's most impactful contributions is its support for Education for All (EFA), a non-profit organization founded by Mike McHugo, the co-owner of Kasbah du Toubkal. EFA addresses a critical gap in access to secondary education for girls from remote Berber villages. In the rural High Atlas Mountains, education for girls is often inaccessible due to cultural barriers, the lack of local schools, and the prohibitive distance to secondary institutions. Recognizing these challenges, EFA established six culturally appropriate boarding houses near schools, enabling over 250 girls to pursue secondary education in a safe and supportive environment.

The initiative is funded in part by a 5 percent levy on all invoices from the Kasbah, ensuring that tourism revenue directly supports this transformative program. As Mike explains, "Providing girls with an education does not just change their lives—it changes the future of their families and communities." Educated girls are more likely to secure stable employment, advocate for their rights, and support their families, creating a virtuous cycle of empowerment and resilience. The success of EFA is not just reflected in the number of girls who graduate but in the long-term socio-economic impact on their communities. The program has become a model for how tourism businesses can address systemic barriers to education while fostering gender equality.

Education and skill development are critical for empowering local communities to benefit fully from tourism. By equipping individuals with expertise in areas such as hospitality, eco-tourism management, and conservation, businesses can create a skilled workforce that supports sustainable tourism while enhancing local livelihoods. Kasbah du Toubkal exemplifies this approach through its innovative and community-driven initiatives.

Developing Skills and Careers Locally

Kasbah du Toubkal also focuses on developing the skills and careers of its employees, most of whom are from the local community. Approximately 80 percent of the staff were born within two kilometers of the Kasbah, and many have risen through the ranks to leadership roles or gone on to start their own hospitality businesses. This localized hiring approach not only creates jobs but also ensures that the region retains its talent and benefits from tourism.

Training is a key element of the Kasbah's operations. Employees receive comprehensive instruction in hospitality, customer service, and cultural interpretation. Mike emphasizes the importance of empowering staff to share their heritage with guests authentically, saying, "From the beginning, we described the Kasbah as a 'Berber hospitality center' rather than a hotel. Our goal was to make sure guests experience the real culture of this region, and our team is central to that."

Integrating Education into the Guest Experience

Kasbah du Toubkal integrates its educational initiatives into the guest experience, offering travelers a deeper understanding of the region's culture and challenges. Complimentary introductory walks are designed to highlight the work of the Association des Bassins d'Imlil, a village association supported by the resort's levy. These walks allow guests to see firsthand the community projects funded by tourism, including waste management services, public amenities, and EFA's boarding houses.

Additionally, Kasbah du Toubkal offers personalized trekking experiences led by local guides. These treks not only showcase the stunning landscapes of the High Atlas Mountains but also facilitate cultural exchange, as guides share their knowledge of Berber traditions and way of life. Through these initiatives, the resort fosters a connection between visitors and the local community, enriching the guest experience while supporting cultural preservation.

Since its establishment in 1995, Kasbah du Toubkal has acted as a catalyst for the development of the Imlil Valley. The village, once reliant on subsistence farming, has grown into a thriving hub for sustainable tourism, with over 100 hospitality properties now operating in the area. By sourcing food and services locally, the Kasbah further strengthens the community's economic fabric while reducing its environmental footprint.

As Mike reflects, "Tourism can be a force for good when it's done thoughtfully and with respect for the people and environment it touches. Our goal has always been to create opportunities for the community and show that sustainable tourism is not just possible but transformative."

Kasbah du Toubkal's investment in education and capacity-building demonstrates the profound impact tourism can have when aligned with community needs. By supporting initiatives like EFA, prioritizing local employment, and integrating cultural education into the guest experience, the Kasbah has created a model of regenerative tourism that benefits both residents and visitors.

This approach not only empowers the local community but also enhances the authenticity and richness of the guest experience. Visitors leave with a deeper understanding of the region's culture and the knowledge that their stay has contributed to meaningful change. As the tourism industry evolves, Kasbah du Toubkal serves as a powerful example of how businesses can leverage education to foster sustainable development and cultural preservation.

Training and Capacity-Building Through Local Employment

Beyond its support for formal education, Kasbah du Toubkal emphasizes on-the-job training and skill development for its staff. Approximately 80 percent of the resort's workforce comes from within two kilometers of the property, ensuring that economic benefits stay within the community. Staff are provided with comprehensive training in hospitality, customer service, and cultural interpretation, enabling them to thrive in their roles and advance their careers.

Many former employees have gone on to establish their own hospitality ventures, further contributing to the region's economic diversification. This capacity-building model demonstrates how tourism can serve as a catalyst for entrepreneurship and long-term community development. Additionally, the resort fosters an environment where employees are encouraged to embrace and share their cultural heritage with guests, creating an authentic and enriching experience for visitors.

Kasbah du Toubkal exemplifies how investing in education and capacity-building can create a regenerative tourism model that benefits both communities and visitors. By supporting EFA, providing local employment and training, and integrating educational initiatives into the guest experience, the resort has become a beacon of sustainable development in the High Atlas Mountains.

Travelers leave with a deeper appreciation of the region's culture and the knowledge that their stay has contributed to meaningful change. As tourism continues to evolve, Kasbah du Toubkal's model serves as a powerful example of how businesses can create lasting social and economic impact through education and community engagement.

Prioritize Local Sourcing and Economic Integration

Economic integration is a regenerative model that seeks to restore and enhance the social, cultural, and environmental systems upon which the industry depends. By prioritizing local sourcing and embedding the local economy into tourism operations, businesses can directly contribute to the economic resilience of host communities. This approach not only reduces environmental impacts but also enriches the guest experience by offering an authentic connection to the destination.

Local sourcing, where goods and services are procured from nearby producers, plays a critical role in regenerative tourism. Hotels and restaurants that feature locally made furniture, decorations, or menu items crafted from ingredients grown by nearby farmers contribute to both community prosperity and environmental sustainability. For example, sourcing furniture from local artisans reduces the carbon footprint associated with long-distance transportation while supporting traditional craftsmanship. Similarly, restaurants that use local produce provide guests with an authentic culinary experience that reflects the region's agricultural heritage. According to the United Nations World Tourism Organization (UNWTO), embedding the local economy into the tourism value chain ensures that the benefits of tourism are widely distributed within the community, fostering equitable development.

In addition to sourcing, creating localized supply chains strengthens the economic fabric of communities. This can include direct partnerships with local farmers, fishers, and craftsmen to meet the operational needs of tourism businesses. For instance, a resort that collaborates with local farmers to supply fresh produce not only ensures high-quality ingredients for its guests but also provides consistent income for agricultural workers. The establishment of these supply chains creates a symbiotic relationship where tourism operations and community livelihoods are interconnected and mutually supportive.

Tourism businesses can further enhance economic integration by hosting local markets or providing platforms for local vendors to showcase their products. This approach allows entrepreneurs to connect directly with travelers, broadening their customer base and increasing visibility for their goods. For example, a resort that invites local artisans to display their crafts on-site offers guests an immersive cultural experience while enabling the artisans to generate income.

These initiatives exemplify how tourism can move beyond transactional models to build sustainable community-driven economies.

The impact of economic integration extends beyond direct financial benefits. It fosters pride within the community by showcasing local talents, traditions, and innovations. Moreover, when tourists witness the positive effects of their spending on local livelihoods, they are more likely to engage in responsible travel behaviors, creating a virtuous cycle of support for sustainable practices.

As UNWTO highlights, embedding local economies into tourism operations is not merely a strategy for fostering economic growth but a means of achieving inclusivity and resilience in host communities.[7] This integration aligns with broader global objectives, such as the United Nations Sustainable Development Goals, which emphasize the importance of partnerships and local engagement in advancing sustainable development.

Transparency fosters trust between tourism operators and local communities. Businesses can adopt practices that clearly communicate how tourism revenues are shared and reinvested. Initiatives like the Economic Nutrition^{CM} labels, created by the Canadian charity Shorefast and used by Fogo Island Inn as well as other social businesses under the parent charity, which show how much of each dollar spent by the business goes back into the local economy. These help guests and consumers make informed, mindful spending decisions. Equitable revenue-sharing models are another effective tool, ensuring that a portion of profits supports community infrastructure, healthcare, or education. Additionally, fair compensation for local contributors, such as artists and guides, ensures that they are appropriately rewarded for their work, avoiding exploitative practices.

In conclusion, economic integration is a vital component of regenerative tourism. By sourcing goods and services locally, creating supply chains that support community livelihoods, and offering platforms for local entrepreneurs, tourism businesses can contribute to the economic well-being of host communities. These practices not only strengthen local economies but also enhance the authenticity and sustainability of guest experiences, making economic integration a cornerstone of a thriving and regenerative tourism model.

The Genesis of a Regenerative Vision with Fogo Island Inn

Situated on a remote island off the coast of Newfoundland and Labrador, Canada, Fogo Island Inn is more than an architectural marvel; it's a story of regenerative design, community empowerment, and sustainable tourism. Dreamed into reality by Zita Cobb, an eighth-generation Fogo Islander, the Inn exemplifies how thoughtful design and deep-rooted respect for local culture can harmonize with the environment while uplifting a close-knit community.

Zita's perspective on community at Fogo Island Inn highlights this approach: "The word community here means a physical, tangible place where people live together in some kind of tangle with each other, where, by virtue of their shared geography, they have a shared fate." This shared fate drives the Inn's business model, which prioritizes economic agency and dignity for the local people, ensuring they can continue to care for the natural environment. By focusing on creating economic opportunities that respect the island's culture and traditions, while connecting it to the world beyond, Fogo Island Inn has helped to revitalize the local economy while evolving the island's unique way of life.

Born and raised on Fogo Island, in the very town of Joe Batt's Arm where the Inn now stands, Zita left the island to pursue education and a successful career in the fiber optics industry. After finding financial success, she returned to Fogo Island with a vision—to help her home community thrive sustainably while preserving its cultural richness. This vision led to the founding of the Shorefast Foundation, a charity dedicated to building cultural and economic resilience on Fogo Island. Through Shorefast, Zita established the Fogo Island Inn, which has since become a global symbol of sustainable and community-based tourism.

During my visit to Fogo Island in 2018 as a journalist, the connection between the Inn and the local community was evident in every aspect of the experience. The Executive Chef took me on a foraging tour, where we gathered mushrooms and local berries to be incorporated into the evening's meal. Later, I dined on a feast of local snow crab, prepared with care and reverence for the island's culinary traditions. In between touring the island with my host, I spent an afternoon baking a berry pie and later soaked in a wood-fire sauna, gazing out at the icy North Atlantic waves crashing on the shore.

Zita's story is a testament to the power of place-based, regenerative design. The creation of the Fogo Island Inn was not just an architectural endeavor but a deeply collaborative process involving the entire town. Zita describes this approach as prioritizing community and nature, saying, "Place holds people and holds nature. Whatever we do has to optimize for the community." This philosophy became the bedrock of the Inn's design and operations, ensuring that every decision was made with careful consideration of its impact on the local ecosystem and residents.

A Community-Centric Approach to Design

The design of the Fogo Island Inn was guided by a series of conversations and charrettes—formal and informal gatherings that included architects, designers, and community members. These discussions ensured that the Inn's development would be deeply intertwined with the island's history, culture, and environment. Zita recalls, "We had to weave as many elements of our community—its past, its practices, its dreams, its stories—into the fabric of this Inn and how it's built and operates."

One example of this community-centric design is the inclusion of fragments of old sailing poems in each room's shower. These poems, used by Zita's father's generation for navigation, are a tangible link to the island's maritime heritage. Guests who stay in any of the 29 rooms will discover the full poem, guiding them metaphorically from St. John's to Fogo Island—a journey steeped in history and local tradition.

This attention to detail extends to the Inn's culinary offerings, which are built around ingredients sourced from the island. Gardens that had been abandoned after the daily ferry service began were reactivated, leading to a resurgence in local growers. Forgotten ingredients, like oyster leaves, have been rediscovered and are now featured in the Inn's cuisine. Zita explains, "We take every action, everything we have to do in the way we operate at the Inn, and ask, how do we build community into it?"

The environmental impact of the Inn was carefully considered from the start. It was the first hotel in the province to install a primary sewage treatment plant, ahead of any legal requirement to do so. The Inn sets a strong example of environmental stewardship, using solar panels to heat water and implementing a greywater system to minimize waste. "Our approach has been to be as absolutely gentle as we can with the natural world," says Zita. "If we can create economic dignity for the people of Fogo Island, they're going to continue to be able to take care of the natural world."

Economic Nutrition: Redefining Financial Transparency and Community Impact in Regenerative Tourism

Zita's commitment to economic sustainability is evident in her introduction of Economic Nutrition labeling, a concept that transparently shows where every dollar spent by the Inn is allocated. This tool, also practiced at Fogo Island Workshops, a furniture and textile retailer and maker, and at Growlers, an ice cream shop, helps educate guests about the importance of sustaining local economies. "When you spend a dollar, you should know where that dollar goes at the moment of purchase," Zita explains. "It's a way of reattaching money to place."

Economic Nutrition represents a paradigm shift in understanding financial flows within communities, particularly in the context of tourism. Developed by Shorefast on Fogo Island, this concept integrates the strengths of for-profit, nonprofit, and entrepreneurial sectors to create a holistic economic model that prioritizes community well-being and resilience. Economic Nutrition challenges the traditional profit-driven mindset by emphasizing financial transparency, right pricing, local investment, and sustainable community impact.

Integrating Economic and Community Values

Shorefast's Economic Nutrition model emerged from the need to blend the innovative drive of entrepreneurship with the financial rigor of the private sector and the community-oriented focus of the nonprofit world. Operating through a dual structure, Shorefast's nonprofit arm manages community and cultural initiatives, while its for-profit ventures, including the renowned Fogo Island Inn, generate revenue that is directly reinvested into local projects.

This structure exemplifies a radical departure from conventional business practices by ensuring that economic activities are not only profitable but also deeply aligned with the needs and aspirations of the community. Shorefast's model leverages its unique position to reinforce the local economy, channeling business surpluses into preserving cultural heritage, enhancing educational opportunities, and creating sustainable employment.

Shorefast's vision is for prosperous economies that serve people, nature and culture, in local places. The central question driving Shorefast's approach is how communities, big and small, can effectively participate in a globalized economy. The answer lies in redefining the relationship between business and community, ensuring that economic activities contribute to local prosperity rather than merely extracting value. This integrated model sets a new standard for how tourism can be leveraged as a tool for community development, rather than just a commercial enterprise.

Economic Nutrition: A Philosophy of Financial Impact

At its core, Economic Nutrition reimagines how we perceive spending and investment. Unlike traditional economic models that treat financial transactions as isolated events, Economic Nutrition positions every dollar spent as an opportunity to support and strengthen communities. This philosophy demands a comprehensive understanding of where money goes, who benefits, and how these flows impact local economies.

Economic Nutrition prioritizes transparency in financial transactions, making economic flows visible and actionable. Inspired by nutritional labels on food, which provide consumers with critical information about their health choices, Economic Nutrition offers a similar level of transparency regarding financial decisions. This approach enables consumers, businesses, and community stakeholders to make informed choices that align with broader social and economic goals.

For Shorefast, this philosophy is not merely theoretical; it is a practical tool for driving change. Economic Nutrition compels businesses and consumers to rethink their financial decisions, pushing beyond the narrow focus of price and profit to consider the broader impact on community resilience, local culture, and environmental sustainability. By making economic flows transparent, Economic Nutrition transforms routine financial decisions into deliberate acts of community support.

The Economic Nutrition Label: A Tool for Financial Transparency

The Economic Nutrition label developed by Shorefast represents a groundbreaking innovation in financial transparency. Modeled after food nutrition labels, it provides a detailed breakdown of the costs associated with a product or service and how these expenditures are distributed geographically. This tool reveals the true economic footprint of spending, showing how much money remains within the local community versus how much flows to regional, national, or global entities.

The label consists of two key components: an analysis of input costs, such as labor and supplies, and a detailed geographic distribution of spending. For instance, the Economic Nutrition label at Fogo Island Inn highlights the significant portion of expenditures that support local wages and suppliers, demonstrating a commitment to reinforcing the local economy. Furthermore, the geographic distribution demonstrates that 70 percent of the money paid for a stay at the Inn stays on Fogo Island and the province. This level of transparency sets a new benchmark in the tourism industry, where the economic impact of visitor spending is often obscured by complex supply chains and opaque financial practices.

The label empowers consumers by providing critical insights at the point of purchase, allowing them to make choices that directly benefit local communities. This tool not only enhances consumer awareness

Figure 7.1   Economic Nutrition label

Economic Nutrition^{CM}

Fogo Island Inn
Community Enterprise

Where does the money go?

Fogo Island	54%	**Rest of Canada**	26%
Newfoundland	16%	**International**	4%

What does the money pay for?

Salaries, Wages	53%
Food, Room Supplies	12%
Business Operations	15%
Building Costs	10%
Insurance	3%
Sales, Marketing	4%
COVID-19 Debt Service	3%

* Values are calculated retrospectively and updated when changes are material. Figures shown are for illustrative purposes.

Economic Nutrition[CM] is a certification trademark of Shorefast, used under license by Fogo Island Inn.

SOURCE Shorefast (nd). Economic Nutrition

but also serves as a powerful differentiator for businesses committed to sustainable and responsible economic practices. By adopting the Economic Nutrition label, businesses can demonstrate their commitment to community impact, setting themselves apart in an increasingly conscientious marketplace.

Cultivating a Culture of Economic Accountability

Economic Nutrition is a call to action for businesses, consumers, and communities to embrace a culture of economic accountability. Shorefast's model disrupts conventional financial communication by prioritizing transparency and challenging stakeholders to engage with their economic impact on a deeper level. This approach fosters a broader understanding of value, extending beyond the traditional metrics of profit and cost to include social and environmental considerations.

Shorefast's journey in developing the Economic Nutrition label revealed the limitations of conventional financial reporting, which often fails to capture the real impact of economic activities on communities. Traditional accounting methods lack the granularity needed to reveal how financial flows affect local economies and overlook the broader implications of economic decisions. To address this gap, Shorefast reengineered its financial communications, creating a tool that distills complex data into a format that is both accessible and actionable.

This approach redefines how we assess value in economic transactions. In a market dominated by price-driven decisions, Economic Nutrition provides a critical counterbalance, highlighting the unseen dimensions of value—how spending supports local employment, preserves cultural heritage, and sustains community services. This deeper insight challenges consumers and businesses alike to move beyond superficial price comparisons and consider the broader implications of their financial choices.

Scaling Economic Nutrition for Global Impact

While rooted in Fogo Island, the principles of Economic Nutrition are universally applicable and scalable. Shorefast envisions a future where this approach becomes a standard feature of economic transactions worldwide, empowering consumers and businesses to make informed, responsible decisions. As part of this vision, Shorefast is expanding the Economic Nutrition label into a practice that can be adopted by other organizations, catalyzing a global movement toward greater economic transparency and place-based accountability.

The potential applications of Economic Nutrition extend far beyond the tourism sector. Any industry can benefit from this approach, particularly those that seek to understand and enhance their impact on local communities. By embedding Economic Nutrition into broader economic frameworks, we can foster a network of interconnected, resilient local economies that collectively contribute to a more sustainable and equitable global system.

The Power of Community-Led Tourism

Reflecting on the journey of creating the Fogo Island Inn, Zita admits that there were challenges along the way. One of the biggest lessons she learned was the importance of pacing. "I had to slow down because the community wasn't going as fast as I wanted it to go," she says. "If I had to do it again, I would be even more holistic in the design process."

Looking to the future, Zita aspires to expand the Inn's Economic Nutrition label to capture its carbon footprint and achieve carbon neutrality in its operations. She envisions projects like vertical seaweed farming, which could serve as a carbon offset and a guest attraction. "Why can't Fogo Island be carbon neutral?" she asks. "Small places can be little petri dishes for bigger places, where we can be a proving ground for things."

One of the most significant social impacts of the foundation of Shorefast and the Inn has been the revitalization of the local cod fishery. After the collapse of the stocks, a stewardship fishery was established, focusing on handline cod fishing—a method that is less destructive and more sustainable than gillnets. The Inn helped create a market for this high-quality cod in Toronto and Ottawa, allowing fishers to earn a premium price for their catch. "If you're selling something too cheaply, how do you expect the fisher to go out and spend hours with one line and a hook?" asks Zita. "Our human quest for cheap pushes people toward behaviors that are really quite destructive."

The Inn's success in promoting sustainable fishing practices is just one example of how it has empowered the Fogo Island community. Zita emphasizes that tourism should never be the sole industry for any community, noting that the fishery remains the most important industry on Fogo Island. "What we do at the Inn is continue to showcase that, support it, and try to deepen it," she says. "I don't think you can really separate social and ecological considerations. It's an 'and,' not an 'or.'"

Fogo Island Inn stands as a model for how tourism can be a force for good, fostering economic, social, and environmental resilience in remote, and often vulnerable, communities. For Zita, the ultimate hope is that guests leave the Inn with a renewed understanding of the importance of relationships—with each other, with nature, and with the communities they are part of. "The quality of your life is the quality of your relationships," says Zita. "That's where meaning comes from."

Zita's work at Fogo Island Inn highlights the vital role that community-led tourism can play in regenerative travel. By empowering local communities and respecting the environment, tourism can become a catalyst for positive change, ensuring that both people and places thrive together. As Zita aptly puts it, "If you're coming into a place as an outsider, it doesn't mean you can't do good work, but you have to empower the local community. You have to give power."

Through her efforts, Zita has shown that it's possible to create a tourism model that not only sustains but also regenerates—a model where the community leads the way, and the world follows.

Fogo Island Inn's commitment to community-led tourism highlights how deeply engaging local voices can transform tourism into a regenerative force. Their community-centered approach not only revitalized Fogo Island's economy but also preserved its unique way of life.

Foster Long-Term Relationships, Not Transactions

Tourism should prioritize building enduring relationships with local communities over short-term gains. Establishing long-term partnerships with local organizations and suppliers helps create sustainable and mutually beneficial collaborations. Supporting community-led initiatives ensures that local residents have agency in shaping their futures. For example, funding or providing resources for community-driven conservation projects can lead to long-lasting environmental and social benefits. Furthermore, respecting and preserving cultural heritage by avoiding commodification or misrepresentation fosters trust and meaningful engagement between travelers and hosts.

Basata, on the Red Sea coast of Egypt, embodies this ethos of community empowerment. The co-lodge was built in partnership with the local Bedouin tribes, whose knowledge and traditions form the backbone of Basata's operations. Just as Fogo Island Inn weaves the narratives of its community into the guest experience, Basata thrives on its deep connections with the Bedouins, honoring their customs, supporting local livelihoods, and fostering sustainable tourism practices. Both Fogo Island Inn and Basata stand as testaments to the power of community-led tourism—where the voices of local people not only shape the visitor experience but also drive meaningful, lasting change.

Basata as a Model of Community Empowerment in Egypt

Following the 2022 United Nations Climate Change Conference or Conference of the Parties of the UNFCCC (more commonly referred to as COP27) taking place in Sharm El Sheikh, Egypt, I brought a group of 13 climate change makers and professionals to our member hotel Basata Eco-Lodge for a retreat. Basata stands as a pioneering example of community empowerment and community-led tourism—a vital pillar of regenerative tourism.

Founded in the 1980s by Sherif El-Ghamrawy, Basata was conceived as an eco-friendly retreat that honors the natural environment and the local Bedouin culture. Through innovative practices, collaboration with local communities, and an unwavering commitment to sustainability, Basata has become a leading example of how tourism can empower communities while preserving cultural heritage.

Building Trust and Relationships with Local Communities

One of Basata's most significant achievements has been its ability to build strong, trust-based relationships with the local Bedouin communities. Sherif El-Ghamrawy, born in Giza, Egypt, attended the German School of Cairo before earning a degree in civil engineering from Cairo University. However, it was his deep passion for the environment and a commitment to conserving Egypt's natural resources that ultimately inspired him to establish Basata Ecolodge. When Sherif first arrived in the area, the Bedouins were skeptical of his intentions, as they had seen other investors come and exploit the land without regard for the local people or environment. Over time, however, Sherif demonstrated that Basata was different. "I made it clear that I wasn't here for business; I was here to live, to learn from the Bedouins, and to share what little knowledge I had that could help them," he says.

This commitment to mutual respect and collaboration laid the foundation for Basata's community empowerment initiatives. Basata has worked closely with the Bedouins to support sustainable livelihoods, such as educating local fishermen about the impact of overfishing on marine ecosystems and introducing sustainable fishing practices. Abdullah, a local fisherman, explains, "Basata taught us about the effects of overfishing on our tribe. They helped us see that sustainable fishing is not just about preserving fish—it's about preserving our way of life."

The relationships forged between Basata and the Bedouin communities have been instrumental in fostering a sense of shared responsibility for environmental stewardship. As Sherif puts it, "Trust is the most important thing. You have to trust people, and they have to trust you. Once you build that trust, you can achieve anything together."

Education has been an integral aspect of Basata's approach to community empowerment. Recognizing the limitations of local government schools, which were often underfunded and lacked quality resources, Basata established a private school on its property to provide better educational opportunities for local children. The school teaches multiple languages, environmental conservation, and practical skills that help students engage with the modern world while preserving their cultural heritage.

A Bedouin woman who lived on Basata's property with her children shares her experience: "Sherif's school taught us more than just reading and writing. We learned English, how to eat healthy, and how to respect our environment. The government school was not good, but here, my kids learned things that will help them for life." This focus on education is not just about academics—it's about equipping the next generation with the tools they need to thrive while maintaining a strong connection to their cultural roots.

Basata's educational initiatives extend beyond the classroom. The eco-lodge regularly hosts workshops and training sessions for community members on topics such as sustainable agriculture, natural building techniques, and eco-friendly business practices. These programs empower locals to take ownership of their own economic futures, aligning with Basata's philosophy of providing "a hand up, not a handout." As Sherif notes, "Education is key. It's not just about teaching children; it's about empowering the whole community to be self-sufficient and resilient."

In addition to its work directly through the eco-lodge, Basata has established the Hemaya Foundation, a non-profit organization dedicated to conservation and community development. The foundation's projects are designed to be community-led, ensuring that local voices guide the direction of conservation efforts. Hemaya works with local Bedouins to protect marine and terrestrial ecosystems, addressing issues such as illegal fishing, waste management, and habitat restoration.

One of Hemaya's key initiatives involves working with Bedouin fishermen to promote sustainable fishing practices. This project not only aims to protect the marine environment but also to preserve the cultural practices of the Tarabine Bedouin tribe, whose way of life has been intimately connected to the sea for generations. Abdullah, a Bedouin fisherman, describes the impact: "Before Hemaya, many of us didn't realize how our fishing practices were affecting the coral reefs and fish populations. Now, we're learning to fish in ways that keep the sea healthy for our children."

The Hemaya Foundation also collaborates with international partners to conduct environmental audits, develop conservation guidelines, and engage in cross-sector partnerships that enhance the effectiveness of their programs. By involving the community at every stage of the process, Hemaya ensures that conservation efforts are not imposed from the outside but are rooted in local knowledge and priorities.

While Basata's model of community-led tourism has brought numerous benefits, it also faces ongoing challenges, particularly in balancing the need for preservation with the pressures of development. As Maria, Sherif's wife and a key member of Basata's team, observes, "We live in a very pristine area, and we've always wanted to keep it that way. But with more development in the region, it's becoming harder to preserve the environment as it was."

Basata's commitment to minimal environmental impact means that every aspect of the lodge's operations is carefully considered, from waste management to energy use. Without access to municipal infrastructure, Basata has had to develop its own systems for water, electricity, and waste, often at great expense. "We are far from any big city, so bringing in the tools and materials we need is difficult and costly. But we do it because we believe it's the right thing to do," Maria explains.

Sherif echoes these sentiments, highlighting the importance of maintaining Basata's environmental integrity: "We are here for a very short time, and everything around us is much older than we are. Most of the trees are older than us, and the corals have been here for millions of years. How can we justify damaging these ancient ecosystems for our short-term gain? We have to think long-term, for the generations that will come after us."

One of Basata's most innovative contributions to the field of ecotourism has been its work in establishing new standards and guidelines for eco-friendly accommodations in Egypt. Faced with the challenge of operating within a regulatory system that did not recognize the unique needs of eco-lodges, Basata partnered with the Ministry of Environment to develop a set of criteria tailored to ecotourism. This collaboration has helped to pave the way for other eco-lodges in Egypt, providing a framework for sustainable tourism development that respects both the environment and local communities.

Sherif emphasizes the importance of public–private partnerships in achieving these goals: "One hand cannot clap by itself. We need the private sector, the government, and the local communities to work together if we want to create a truly sustainable tourism model. It's not just about building eco-lodges—it's about changing the entire system."

The impact of these partnerships extends beyond Basata's immediate surroundings, influencing national policies and setting a precedent for other tourism operators in Egypt and beyond. By working collaboratively with government authorities, Basata has helped to demonstrate that ecotourism is not just a niche market but a viable, sustainable alternative to conventional tourism.

Basata's journey exemplifies the transformative potential of community-led tourism as a pillar of regenerative tourism. By honoring place, building trust with local communities, and creating opportunities for education and empowerment, Basata has shown that tourism can be a force for positive change. The eco-lodge's commitment to sustainability, community collaboration, and cultural preservation offers a powerful model for other tourism operators seeking to integrate regenerative principles into their practices.

As Sherif reflects, "We didn't come here to impose our way of doing things. We came to learn, to live humbly, and to share what we could. Basata is not just a place—it's a philosophy, a way of life that respects the land, the people, and the traditions that make this corner of the world so special. And if we can inspire others to do the same, then we have achieved something truly worthwhile."

The travel industry has a unique opportunity to redefine its impact on communities and the environment by adopting regenerative practices. By prioritizing community engagement, education, economic transparency, environmental stewardship, and long-term relationships, tourism businesses can transform their operations into powerful forces for positive change. The examples of Fogo Island Inn and Basata illustrate that when communities lead, tourism can become a tool for cultural preservation, economic empowerment, and environmental regeneration. For the travel industry, embracing these principles is not just an ethical choice—it is the path to a more sustainable and resilient future.

Key Takeaways

Guest engagement empowers communities:

- Thoughtfully designed tourism fosters cultural exchange, economic growth, and environmental stewardship.
- Authentic, community-driven interactions enhance traveler experiences while uplifting host communities.

Economic opportunities through local involvement:

- Direct engagement of local artisans, farmers, and service providers ensures tourism revenue stays within communities.
- Tools like G Adventures' Ripple Score and Shorefast's Economic Nutrition labels promote financial transparency and local benefits.

Cultural preservation as a pillar of tourism:

- Community-focused tourism safeguards intangible cultural heritage through storytelling, crafts, and traditional practices.
- Cultural experiences enrich tourism while sustaining local identity and traditions.

Environmental stewardship through active participation:

- Guests contribute to conservation efforts such as reforestation, wildlife monitoring, and marine protection.
- Examples like Fogo Island Inn integrate guests into sustainability initiatives, deepening connections to place.

Co-creation ensures authentic tourism experiences:

- Successful guest engagement requires communities to co-create tourism offerings, ensuring alignment with local values and priorities.
- Education and context enhance travelers' respect and appreciation for cultural and ecological significance.

Partnerships amplify impact:

- Collaborations among governments, NGOs, and tourism operators foster sustainable models balancing conservation and community needs.

Investing in education and capacity-building:

- Initiatives like Kasbah du Toubkal's support of Education for All empower marginalized groups, particularly women and girls.
- Training in hospitality and entrepreneurship equips locals for long-term socio-economic growth.

Local sourcing strengthens economies:

- Sourcing goods and services locally reduces environmental impact and enriches guest experiences.
- Economic integration fosters pride, preserves traditions, and builds resilient local economies.

Financial transparency drives responsible tourism:

- Shorefast's Economic Nutrition label offers clarity on where tourism dollars go, promoting mindful consumer choices.
- Transparency fosters trust between businesses and local communities.

Community-led tourism as a regenerative model:

- Examples like Fogo Island Inn and Basata Eco-Lodge demonstrate how tourism can regenerate communities rather than extract from them.
- True regenerative tourism requires respect for local leadership, cultural preservation, and long-term relationship-building.

Sustainability requires holistic vision:

- Tourism businesses must balance social, cultural, environmental, and economic goals.
- Regenerative tourism is not only ethical but essential for the industry's sustainable future.

Notes

1 G Adventures. Ripple score: How tourism benefits local economies, G Adventures, 2024. gadventures.com (archived at https://perma.cc/BYA4-QAKD)

2. United Nations World Tourism Organization (UNWTO). Tourism for inclusive growth, UNWTO, 2021.
3. United Nations World Tourism Organization (UNWTO). Tourism for inclusive growth, UNWTO, 2021.
4. Indigenous Tourism Association of Canada (ITAC). Indigenous tourism and reconciliation, ITAC, 2022.
5. Maasai Mara Conservancies. Community-driven conservation efforts, Maasai Mara Conservancies, 2024.
6. Global Sustainable Tourism Council (GSTC). Sustainable tourism frameworks, GSTC, 2023.
7. United Nations World Tourism Organization (UNWTO). Tourism for inclusive growth, UNWTO, 2021.

The Role of Destination Management Companies in Regenerative Tourism

08

Tourism is undergoing a fundamental transformation, shifting from traditional sustainability efforts toward regenerative models that restore, revitalize, and enhance both environmental and social systems within destinations.[1] While sustainability focuses on minimizing harm, regenerative tourism takes a proactive approach by actively improving ecosystems, strengthening local economies, and fostering deeper cultural connections. This shift requires more than operational change—it demands a rethinking of how regenerative travel is marketed, structured, and experienced. For regenerative tourism to gain widespread adoption, marketing strategies must communicate not only its ethical benefits but also its potential to provide richer, more immersive, and community-centered travel experiences.[2]

Destination management companies (DMCs) are at the core of this transformation, serving as architects of immersive travel experiences that align with local knowledge, sustainability principles, and community-driven tourism. Unlike traditional tourism models that prioritize efficiency and mass appeal, regenerative tourism prioritizes direct engagement with local businesses, cultural stakeholders, and ecological initiatives. This ensures that tourism revenue remains within the destination, directly benefiting local economies while reinforcing long-term resilience.[3]

Beyond logistics, well-integrated DMCs play a crucial role in facilitating genuine cultural exchange. By collaborating closely with indigenous leaders, local artisans, and conservation groups, DMCs help design travel experiences that respect local traditions, promote small businesses, and encourage responsible tourism behaviors.[4] Their ability to create ethical, community-centered experiences positions them as key players in reshaping tourism into a force that uplifts rather than exploits.

Travel Agencies and Tour Operators: Educators and Advocates for Regenerative Travel

Travel agencies and tour operators serve as gatekeepers of regenerative tourism, influencing traveler awareness, guiding responsible booking decisions, and partnering with ethical service providers. Their influence extends beyond simple itinerary planning—they shape the industry by promoting travel that prioritizes long-term environmental and social well-being over short-term economic gains. By encouraging travelers to seek out regenerative experiences, these agencies redirect tourism dollars toward initiatives that actively restore ecosystems, empower communities, and preserve cultural heritage.

The growing consumer interest in sustainable and ethical travel presents both opportunities and challenges. Research shows that while many travelers express a desire to support responsible tourism, cost and convenience often drive final purchasing decisions.[5] To bridge this gap, regenerative travel must be positioned not just as an ethical alternative but as a superior travel experience—one that offers deeper engagement, cultural authenticity, and personal transformation.[6]

Authentic Storytelling as a Tool for Regenerative Tourism

A key strategy for marketing regenerative tourism lies in authentic storytelling—creating narratives that illustrate the tangible benefits of regenerative travel for communities, cultures, and the environment. Studies indicate that emotionally compelling stories encourage traveler engagement and foster a deeper connection between tourists and destinations.[7] By sharing firsthand accounts of how tourism dollars support reforestation projects, empower indigenous guides, or revitalize local economies, stakeholders can reshape consumer perceptions and make responsible tourism more relatable and aspirational.[8]

Community-Driven Marketing: Giving Local Voices a Platform

Beyond storytelling, community engagement is essential in effectively marketing regenerative tourism. Instead of relying solely on external narratives, the most impactful marketing efforts center local perspectives in shaping destination branding and tourism messaging. Studies suggest that destinations that authentically integrate community voices into their marketing strategies are perceived as more credible, ethical, and culturally enriching.[9] By allowing local artisans, conservationists, and business owners to share their stories, tourism businesses can foster a sense of place that resonates deeply with travelers seeking meaningful experiences.

The Future of Regenerative Tourism: A Shift in Industry Mindset

Embracing regenerative tourism across the supply chain is essential for creating enduring ecological and social prosperity. Shifting away from extractive tourism models toward restorative and community-driven approaches allows destinations to actively regenerate, thrive, and offer travelers profoundly meaningful experiences. Regenerative tourism is not just an industry trend—it is a necessary evolution that ensures travel remains a force for good.

The success of regenerative tourism depends on rethinking industry priorities, reframing traveler expectations, and demonstrating the long-term benefits of responsible tourism models. It requires a collective shift—from industry leaders, destination management companies, travel agencies, and travelers alike—to recognize that tourism should leave destinations better than it found them. By integrating authentic storytelling, community engagement, and meaningful partnerships, regenerative tourism can transition from a niche concept to the mainstream standard—ensuring that travel is not just sustainable, but truly transformative.

Unequal Expectations in Ethical Tourism

Wazha Dube, Director of the Africa Collection at Index Select, highlights how the traditional structure of travel agencies relying on tour operators as intermediaries is breaking down. Increasingly, travel agents are forming direct partnerships with local DMCs and suppliers, cutting out the middleman and ensuring that a greater share of tourism revenue remains within the destination.

"That system is being dismantled," Wazha explains, emphasizing that direct collaborations allow for more personalized experiences and greater financial benefits for local businesses. The old model, where tour operators acted as middlemen between travel agencies and local providers, is being replaced by a more direct, transparent, and community-driven approach to selling travel.

As a result of this shift, tour operators are under growing pressure to redefine their value propositions. No longer just facilitators of travel logistics, they must now demonstrate their expertise, network strength, and service quality to remain relevant. "Tour operators now must be better," Wazha asserts, highlighting the need for specialization and deeper engagement with local communities to justify their role in the industry.

Wazha also addresses the double standard in tourism ethics, where African tourism businesses are held to higher ethical expectations than their Western counterparts. While companies in Africa and other emerging destinations are consistently expected to demonstrate social responsibility, European and American tourism operators face no such pressure to prove their positive impact.

"Why must we always be doing good and prove it, whereas the European or American company has no impetus or backlash as a result of them just wanting to make a profit?" Wazha questions, pointing out that this bias creates an unfair burden on African businesses to justify their ethical commitments while allowing Western operators to prioritize profitability without scrutiny.

This disparity highlights the need for a more balanced global approach to ethical tourism. If regenerative tourism is to be truly effective, the same ethical expectations must be applied across the industry, ensuring that all businesses, regardless of location, contribute meaningfully to environmental and social well-being.

The Covid-19 pandemic initially accelerated interest in regenerative travel, as the pause in global tourism allowed businesses to reflect on more sustainable models. However, as the industry recovers, Wazha notes a troubling regression.

"People started making money again and put feelings to the side," he observes, explaining that financial pressures have led many businesses to deprioritize regenerative principles in favor of short-term economic gains. The urgency of rebuilding after the pandemic has, in some cases, overshadowed the momentum toward sustainability.

Despite this regression, Wazha commends businesses that have remained committed to their regenerative missions. The most successful regenerative tourism efforts, he argues, come from long-term dedication rather than short-lived trends. This underscores the importance of embedding sustainability into core business strategies rather than treating it as a temporary response to crises.

The Role of Travel Agents in Promoting Regenerative Tourism

Travel agents play a pivotal role in shifting consumer behavior toward more sustainable choices. With their ability to educate and influence traveler preferences, they act as gatekeepers of responsible tourism. Traditionally, high-end travel agents catered to markets where convenience and luxury were prioritized over sustainability. However, Wazha observes a growing shift as more agents now actively present regenerative options to their clients.

By introducing immersive, ethically driven experiences, travel agents are reshaping consumer expectations. The key to selling regenerative travel lies in framing it as an elevated experience, rather than merely an ethical choice. Travelers are more likely to engage with regenerative tourism when it is marketed as offering deeper cultural connections, richer experiences, and a greater sense of purpose.

Diversity and inclusion are crucial for the success of regenerative tourism. Wazha argues that having a broader range of voices in leadership positions leads to more impactful and equitable outcomes.

"With more diversity, you'll naturally see broader impacts," he asserts, reinforcing the connection between inclusive leadership and innovative, community-centered tourism models. A diverse tourism industry ensures that a wide range of cultural perspectives and sustainability solutions are integrated into travel experiences.

Wazha's insights highlight the need for a comprehensive, collaborative approach to marketing and selling regenerative tourism. The industry must move beyond surface-level sustainability claims and actively promote travel models that prioritize direct community engagement, fair economic distribution, and genuine cultural exchange.

The success of regenerative tourism depends on authentic storytelling, consumer education, and the elimination of traditional profit-driven tourism structures that marginalize local communities. For regenerative tourism to thrive, it must be positioned as not just a responsible choice, but the most compelling and enriching way to explore the world.

As more tourism stakeholders redefine their business models, build stronger partnerships, and actively educate travelers, the industry can transition toward a truly regenerative approach—one that ensures tourism actively benefits both the traveler and the destination. By embedding these principles into marketing and sales strategies, the industry can shift from simply promoting sustainable tourism to actively creating a future where travel is a force for regeneration, connection, and long-term prosperity.

Disrupting Traditional Tourism Channels

One of the most significant shifts in regenerative tourism is the disruption of traditional tourism distribution channels. "When the world stopped traveling, we had a chance to rethink everything," Craig explains. "For decades, travel was dictated by foreign operators who painted a picture of destinations through their own lens. We wanted to flip that—giving full control back to the local communities, ensuring they tell their own stories and benefit directly from tourism dollars."

Craig Zapatka is the co-founder of Elsewhere by Lonely Planet, a groundbreaking travel company established in 2020 alongside Alexis Bowen during the peak of the Covid-19 pandemic. Recognizing the rare opportunity presented by the global pause in tourism, Craig envisioned a travel model that disrupted traditional practices, focusing instead on deeply authentic local experiences directly curated by in-destination travel experts.

Under Craig's leadership, Elsewhere champions regenerative travel, intentionally addressing economic leakage by partnering exclusively with locally owned businesses rather than multinational hotel chains or large, international tourism operators. "Most people don't realize that when they book through a traditional agency, a huge percentage of their money never reaches the destination. It stays with the middlemen—agencies, big brands, and international conglomerates. With Elsewhere, we eliminate that. Your money stays in the place you're visiting, supporting small businesses, independent guides, and the people who know their destination best."

Elsewhere's meticulously developed vetting process guarantees that partner DMCs operate with transparency, uphold fair labor standards, and prioritize eco-friendly practices. "We don't just work with anyone," Craig says. "We vet every single DMC we partner with. We look at their commitment to sustainability, their economic practices, how they treat their staff, and their engagement with local communities. We want to work with companies that care—those that don't just see travelers as transactions, but as opportunities to foster meaningful cultural exchange."

Craig has passionately advocated for responsible tourism by implementing stringent guidelines that ensure ethical interactions, particularly regarding wildlife tourism, human interactions, and culturally sensitive experiences. "One of the hardest things we had to do was say no—to lucrative partnerships, to high-end properties that don't align with our values, and to popular but unethical experiences. But we stand firm. We refuse to support wildlife interactions that exploit animals. We don't do poverty tourism. We don't put people in a position where they feel like they're on display for visitors. Travel should be about genuine connection, not about ticking off a list of Instagrammable moments."

Additionally, Craig champions the reduction of travel's carbon footprint. He advocates for the use of trains over cars and prioritizes accommodations that demonstrate commitment to sustainability. Elsewhere proactively addresses unavoidable emissions through initiatives such as ocean plastic cleanup, reforestation programs, and purchasing verified carbon offsets. "I've always said that offsetting should be treated like a donation—because in reality, that's what it is. It's not a get-out-of-jail-free card for emissions. What we should be focusing on is changing our habits—using trains, booking eco-friendly stays, and choosing experiences that don't harm the planet."

With extensive firsthand experience traveling globally—from the vibrant streets of India and Nepal to remote regions of Iceland and the culturally rich landscapes of Morocco and Panama—Craig deeply understands the nuances of impactful travel. His experiences inform Elsewhere's policy to decline engagements involving unethical wildlife interactions, poverty tourism, or exploitative cultural practices. "I've seen firsthand how tourism can either build communities up or tear them down. That's why we're so deliberate with our approach. We don't just want to be another travel company—we want to set the standard for what responsible tourism should look like."

Under Craig's leadership, Elsewhere continues to pioneer meaningful travel that not only enriches travelers' experiences but also positively impacts the destinations visited, firmly establishing itself at the forefront of regenerative tourism. "Travel should be transformative—not just for the traveler, but for the places they visit. If we do it right, tourism can be a powerful force for good. That's the future I believe in."

Building a Travel Model That Gives Back

The tourism industry is at a crossroads. For decades, mass tourism has driven economic growth but often at a cost—disrupting local cultures, depleting natural resources, and funneling profits away from the very communities that make destinations unique. As the demand for more ethical and sustainable travel rises, a new approach is emerging—one that ensures tourism is not just an extractive industry, but a regenerative force that directly benefits local economies, protects cultural heritage, and restores ecosystems.

Building a travel model that gives back requires a fundamental shift in the way trips are designed, marketed, and experienced. It prioritizes locally owned businesses over multinational corporations, ensuring that tourism dollars stay within the destination. It fosters genuine cultural exchange by working with community-led initiatives rather than offering superficial, transactional experiences. It integrates conservation and sustainability at every level, from carbon-conscious transportation choices to regenerative accommodations and waste-free operations.

Beyond sustainability, this model actively seeks to restore and uplift—whether by empowering indigenous communities through responsible tourism partnerships, supporting artisans and small business owners, or investing in conservation projects that safeguard the landscapes travelers come to see. The shift toward regenerative travel is not just an ethical imperative; it is a smarter, more resilient approach to tourism that ensures destinations thrive long after visitors have gone.

As travelers become more conscious of their impact, the industry must evolve. A travel model that gives back does not just minimize harm—it creates lasting benefits for the people and places that make travel meaningful. The future of tourism belongs to those who are willing to rethink the status quo, reimagine their business practices, and rebuild an industry that truly serves both travelers and the world they explore.

Empowering Communities and Preserving Culture

Rebecca Brack's life took an unexpected turn in 2014, one that would ultimately reshape not just her own future, but also the way countless travelers experience Latin America. Born and raised in the Netherlands, she had followed a conventional path—earning an MBA, securing a coveted position at KLM Royal Dutch Airlines, and excelling in the structured corporate world. On paper, she had everything she had worked for: financial security, career growth, and a well-defined trajectory. "I had everything I had studied for—a great job, financial stability, a structured life—but something was missing. I couldn't shake the feeling that I was meant to do something different, something more connected to people and the world around me," she recalls. Seeking clarity, she made the bold decision to step away from her corporate career and travel to Ecuador, where she volunteered at a horse ranch in the Andes.

It was there, amidst the sweeping mountain landscapes and close-knit communities, that her perspective on life and travel began to shift. The people she met—farmers, artisans, and indigenous families—had a deep-rooted connection to their land and traditions. They lived simply but fully, prioritizing community over competition, a stark contrast to the fast-paced, individualistic world she had left behind. "I arrived in Ecuador with my own European way of seeing the world, but very quickly I realized that the people here had something we had lost—this incredible connection to family, to land, to traditions," she says.

This realization planted the seeds of a new idea. Could tourism be more than just a business? Could it become a force for good, one that not only showcased the beauty of a destination but also uplifted the people who called it home? She stayed in Ecuador, determined to build something different. In 2015, she founded Rebecca Adventure Travel, a boutique travel company committed to immersive, sustainable, and culturally enriching experiences. But this wasn't just another tour company. It was a platform for regenerative travel, ensuring that tourism actively improved the places it touched rather than merely sustaining them.

From the very beginning, Rebecca Adventure Travel was designed to function differently. Most traditional tourism models funnel profits away from the destination, with large multinational companies reaping the financial benefits while local communities see little return. Rebecca was determined to change that. "For me, the question has always been: how do we make sure that travel isn't just extractive? How do we ensure that visitors don't just take memories, but also leave something positive behind?"

Creating Meaningful Travel Experiences

Beyond simply redirecting financial benefits, Rebecca also wanted to reshape how travelers interact with destinations. Too often, tourism reduces places to a checklist of attractions—monuments to see, landscapes to photograph, activities to tick off a list. But for her, true travel was about human connection and cultural immersion.

"I believe that travel should be about more than just seeing a place. You should feel it, touch it, interact with it," she explains.

To foster this deeper engagement, Rebecca Adventure Travel curates experiences that bring travelers into direct contact with local traditions and ways of life. Visitors don't just stay in a hotel; they might join a family for a home-cooked meal in the Andes, learning about traditional recipes and sharing stories over steaming bowls of locro de papa. Instead of visiting a souvenir shop, they might spend an afternoon in a local artisan's workshop, shaping clay into pottery using techniques passed down through generations. For those drawn to conservation efforts, the company offers experiences like volunteering at an animal rescue center in Costa Rica, where travelers can assist with the rehabilitation of injured wildlife.

"When you sit in someone's home and listen to their stories, when you share a meal, when you work side by side in a community project—you don't just learn about a place, you feel a sense of responsibility toward it," Rebecca says.

This hands-on approach transforms travel from a passive experience into an active exchange. Visitors leave not just with photographs, but with a deeper understanding of the people and cultures they encountered—and in turn, communities feel valued and respected, rather than treated as mere backdrops for tourism.

Rebecca's approach to travel is a direct challenge to the traditional tourism industry, which too often prioritizes growth over ethics and efficiency over authenticity. While regenerative tourism is still a relatively new concept, she believes it represents the future of responsible travel.

"It's not just about sustainability anymore," she says. "Sustainability is about maintaining the status quo. But regenerative tourism? That's about actively making things better—restoring ecosystems, empowering communities, and creating deeper, more meaningful connections between travelers and the places they visit."

As Rebecca Adventure Travel continues to expand, its mission remains the same: to prove that travel can be a force for good. By ensuring that every journey supports local economies, preserves cultural traditions, and fosters meaningful connections, the company is setting a new standard for what tourism can—and should—be.

For Rebecca, what started as a journey of self-discovery in the Ecuadorian Andes has evolved into a mission to transform the travel industry. And in doing so, she has created more than just a business—she has built a movement, one where travelers, communities, and the planet all thrive together.

Overcoming the Challenges of Promoting Regenerative and Sustainable Travel

Building a successful business rooted in regenerative tourism is no small feat. While travelers increasingly express interest in sustainability, their booking decisions often tell a different story. Convenience and cost remain dominant factors, making it difficult to persuade travelers to prioritize ethical and regenerative experiences. "A lot of travelers say they care about sustainability, but when it comes to booking, most people still prioritize convenience and cost," says Brack. "It's frustrating because we know that people would get so much more out of an immersive experience, but they don't always actively seek it out."

To bridge this gap, Rebecca Adventure Travel integrates sustainability seamlessly into its trips—without labeling them as "eco-tours" or "voluntourism." Rather than positioning sustainability as an obligation, the company ensures that regenerative elements are embedded naturally into the experience. "When a traveler stays at a solar-powered lodge or participates in a reforestation project, they're contributing to sustainability—whether they actively sought that out or not,"

Brack explains. "The key is to make it feel effortless, something they want to do rather than something they feel they should do." By making sustainability an inherent part of every trip rather than a separate selling point, the company attracts a broader audience while still upholding its commitment to responsible tourism.

Another significant challenge is countering negative media perceptions of certain destinations. Political instability, crime, and economic struggles can deter potential visitors, even when on-the-ground realities tell a different story. Brack has seen this firsthand with Ecuador. "Ecuador, for example, has been in the news for political unrest and crime, and that scares people away. But what they don't see is the day-to-day reality. I've lived here for years, I raise my children here, and I've never felt unsafe," she says. "The media focuses on the extremes, but our job as tour operators is to show the reality—that Ecuador is full of warm, welcoming people and incredible places that deserve to be explored."

Despite these challenges, Rebecca Adventure Travel has successfully expanded beyond Ecuador, bringing its regenerative tourism model to destinations such as Costa Rica, Colombia, Chile, Argentina, and Peru. Among these, Costa Rica stands out as an inspiring example of a country where sustainability is deeply embedded in the national identity. "Costa Rica has done such an incredible job. They've made sustainability part of their national identity—everyone understands it, from the government to the taxi drivers. I think it's a model for the rest of Latin America," Brack notes.

The company's dedication to responsible tourism is reflected in its B Corp certification, a distinction held by only a handful of travel agencies in the region. This accreditation underscores its commitment to social and environmental responsibility, yet Brack acknowledges that certifications alone don't necessarily drive bookings. "Travelers don't necessarily look for certifications—they look for experiences. So we focus on creating something unforgettable, and sustainability comes as part of the package," she explains. While partnerships and industry recognition benefit the business, the true key to promoting regenerative travel lies in crafting compelling, transformative experiences that speak to travelers on a personal level.

Looking ahead, Brack remains steadfast in her mission to reshape the tourism industry. Her focus is on educating travelers, expanding partnerships with ethical businesses, and advocating for policies that place local communities at the center of tourism economies. "I want people to think about travel differently—not just as a getaway, but as an opportunity to connect, to learn, to contribute," she says. "If we can shift that mindset, we can change the entire industry."

At its core, regenerative travel is about fostering deeper connections, creating lasting impact, and encouraging meaningful cultural exchange. "At the end of the day, travel should leave a place better than we found it. Not just in terms of the environment, but in the people we meet, the stories we tell, and the way we choose to experience the world," Brack reflects. Through Rebecca Adventure Travel, she continues to challenge the traditional tourism model, proving that travel can be both ethical and extraordinary.

Marketing Regenerative Tourism: A Shift in Strategy

To successfully promote regenerative tourism, the industry must adopt marketing approaches that resonate with conscious travelers while appealing to mainstream audiences. Authentic storytelling plays a crucial role in this shift. By crafting compelling narratives that illustrate the tangible impacts of regenerative travel—on both communities and the environment—stakeholders can foster deeper emotional connections with travelers. Stories that highlight transformative travel experiences are particularly effective in encouraging engagement and shifting consumer behavior toward more responsible choices.

Community involvement is another essential component of effective marketing. By incorporating local voices and perspectives into tourism promotion, destinations ensure that cultural narratives remain authentic, inclusive, and representative of the people who live there. This approach not only enhances credibility but also reinforces the social and economic benefits of regenerative tourism. Additionally, educational initiatives provide travelers with insightful resources on regenerative practices, helping them understand how their choices contribute to long-term sustainability and cultural preservation.

Different players in the tourism industry each have a unique role in advancing regenerative travel. DMCs can design itineraries that highlight local regeneration efforts, including ecosystem restoration projects and community empowerment initiatives, ensuring that tourism directly contributes to the resilience of destinations.[10] Travel agencies play a crucial role in raising awareness, guiding travelers toward responsible choices, and recommending experiences that align with regenerative values. Tour operators work directly with local communities and conservation organizations to design immersive experiences that protect cultural heritage, restore ecosystems, and support sustainable livelihoods.

Transitioning to a regenerative tourism model requires more than just operational changes—it demands a complete reimagining of marketing strategies. By leveraging authentic storytelling, engaging communities meaningfully, and emphasizing traveler education, tourism businesses can effectively communicate the value of regenerative tourism in a way that resonates with both socially conscious travelers and mainstream consumers. These approaches not only enhance consumer engagement but also drive tangible positive impacts, transforming regenerative tourism from an ethical concept into a widely marketable reality.

A New Era of Travel

The shift toward regenerative tourism is not just a trend—it is an essential evolution in the way people experience the world. The industry must move beyond merely minimizing harm and embrace travel as a force for positive change. By prioritizing community-driven models, fostering deeper traveler engagement, and shifting industry-wide narratives, regenerative tourism has the potential to reshape global travel into something more meaningful, sustainable, and transformative.

The challenge lies not just in implementing these practices, but in effectively communicating their value. By embedding sustainability into seamless, enriching experiences, countering misconceptions about destinations, and educating travelers on the true impact of their choices, the industry can pave the way for a new kind of travel—one that not only benefits those who explore but also enriches and revitalizes the places they visit.

Key Takeaways

Regenerative tourism—a new paradigm:

- Moves beyond sustainability's "do no harm" mindset to actively restore ecosystems, cultures, and communities.
- Seeks to revitalize local economies and foster deeper cultural connections through tourism.
- Requires both operational changes and innovative marketing to communicate its value as a superior travel experience.

The pivotal role of DMCs:

- Act as architects of immersive experiences, integrating local knowledge, sustainability, and community engagement.
- Prioritize partnerships with local businesses and cultural stakeholders to keep tourism revenue within destinations.
- Collaborate with indigenous leaders, artisans, and conservationists to design experiences that promote cultural respect and environmental stewardship.

Travel agencies and tour operators as educators:

- Influence traveler choices by educating clients about the benefits of regenerative tourism.
- Help shift tourism spending toward experiences that restore ecosystems and empower communities.
- Face challenges convincing travelers to prioritize ethical choices over cost and convenience, requiring innovative marketing and storytelling.

Authentic storytelling—the power of narrative:

- Emotionally engaging stories illustrate the tangible benefits of regenerative tourism, making ethical travel relatable.
- Highlight how tourism dollars support conservation, local businesses, and cultural preservation.
- Transform perceptions of regenerative travel from niche to desirable mainstream experiences.

Community-driven marketing—centering local voices:

- Successful regenerative tourism marketing elevates local narratives and perspectives.
- Destinations that feature community voices in branding are perceived as more credible, ethical, and authentic.
- Encourages travelers seeking deeper cultural connections and meaningful experiences.

Disrupting traditional tourism channels:

- Entrepreneurs like Elsewhere by Lonely Planet eliminate middlemen, ensuring money stays local.
- DMCs are vetted for sustainability, ethical practices, and fair labor standards, ensuring transparent and responsible tourism.
- Moves away from mass-market tourism to locally curated, authentic experiences.

Confronting ethical double standards:

- Highlights the need for a universal standard of ethical tourism worldwide, regardless of geography.
- Points to systemic biases that burden certain regions with proving their regenerative impact while others face less scrutiny.

Post-Covid 19 realities and industry regression:

- The Covid-19 pandemic created momentum for regenerative thinking, but economic recovery pressures have led many businesses to revert to old practices.

- Sustainable practices must be embedded into core business strategies to withstand short-term economic challenges.
- Businesses that remain committed to regenerative principles demonstrate long-term resilience and leadership.

The role of travel agents in shaping consumer behavior:

- Act as gatekeepers, steering clients toward regenerative options by reframing them as elevated travel experiences.
- Diversity and inclusion in tourism leadership produce more impactful and community-centered tourism models.
- Effective marketing frames regenerative travel as offering deeper connections, richer experiences, and a sense of purpose.

Building a travel model that gives back:

- Regenerative tourism is about leaving destinations better than found—ecologically, socially, and culturally.
- Focuses on locally owned businesses, genuine cultural exchange, and integrated conservation.
- Seen as a smarter, more resilient tourism model that ensures long-term benefits for communities and ecosystems.

Overcoming challenges in promoting regenerative travel:

- Travelers express interest in sustainability but often prioritize convenience and cost.
- Effective regenerative tourism weaves sustainability into the experience without overt labels or guilt messaging.
- Authentic, immersive experiences convert travelers into advocates for responsible tourism.

A new era of travel:

- Regenerative tourism is evolving from niche to mainstream necessity, transforming travel into a force for good.
- Requires collective action across the industry to rethink business practices and marketing strategies.
- Ultimately aims for tourism that creates lasting benefits for both travelers and the destinations they visit.

Notes

1 J Mize (2025) *Regenerative Tourism: Beyond sustainability towards restoration and revitalization*, Green Travel Publications, Bradford on Avon.
2 A Pollock (2019) *Regenerative Travel: How tourism can strengthen local economies and support communities*, Earthwise Press, Bristol.
3 A Pollock (2019) *Regenerative Travel: How tourism can strengthen local economies and support communities*, Earthwise Press, Bristol.
4 P Sheldon, A Pollock and R Daniele. Sustainable and regenerative tourism: Cultural exchange and community-driven experiences, *Journal of Sustainable Tourism*, 2017, 25 (4), 512–30.
5 S Gössling and C M Hall. Sustainable tourism and consumer behavior: Bridging the intention-action gap, *Tourism Management*, 2019, 72, 251–64.
6 VisitBritain (2023) *Marketing Regenerative Tourism: Positioning sustainability as a superior experience*, VisitBritain, London.
7 MDPI (2023) The power of storytelling in regenerative tourism: Engaging travelers through impact-driven narratives, *Journal of Tourism and Society*, 15 (3), 302–18.
8 Global Sustainable Tourism Council (GSTC). Community-driven tourism marketing: The role of local perspectives in destination branding, GSTC, 2024. www.gstc.org (archived at https://perma.cc/FC4C-L62G)
9 Global Sustainable Tourism Council (GSTC). Community-driven tourism marketing: The role of local perspectives in destination branding, GSTC, 2024. www.gstc.org (archived at https://perma.cc/FC4C-L62G)
10 Global Sustainable Tourism Council (GSTC). Community-driven tourism marketing: The role of local perspectives in destination branding, GSTC, 2024. www.gstc.org (archived at https://perma.cc/FC4C-L62G).

Shifting From Fragmentation to Collective Action

09

While tourism has the potential to drive conservation, economic inclusion, and cultural preservation, it can also exacerbate environmental degradation, overtourism, and resource depletion. Achieving regenerative models in travel requires systemic change by moving beyond fragmented sustainability efforts to a coordinated, industry-wide approach. Travalyst, a global coalition dedicated to sustainable travel, is leading this transformation by aligning key industry stakeholders, promoting data transparency, and engaging policymakers. Founded by Prince Harry, The Duke of Sussex, Travalyst emerged from his conservation work and recognition that while some tourism models positively impacted ecosystems and communities, others caused significant harm. He questioned why travel companies were working in isolation rather than collectively addressing sustainability challenges.

"The first step was just getting people around the same table and proving that we could do that," explains Sally Davey, CEO of Travalyst. "This had never been done before—big travel companies working together in a non-commercial, non-competitive way." Over its first five years, Travalyst established governance frameworks that enabled collaboration and neutrality among major industry players. Now, the coalition is expanding its reach beyond its founding members to drive widespread adoption of sustainable practices across the entire travel sector.

Aligning Industry Players for Systems Change

Achieving regenerative travel requires collaboration across multiple sectors. Travalyst's coalition includes major players from various segments of the travel ecosystem, including online travel agencies, meta-search and technology companies, global payment systems, travel data aggregators, and distribution networks. It also works with policymakers, sustainability organizations, and industry bodies such as UN Tourism, the Global Business Travel Association, GSTC, and the European Commission. Recently, the coalition expanded to include on-the-ground operators such as The Travel Corporation, which integrates sustainability across its portfolio. By bringing together these diverse stakeholders, Travalyst is creating a blueprint for industry-wide systems change and demonstrating that collaboration, not competition, is key to building a regenerative future for travel.

Travalyst was born out of a collective realization that travel has a dual impact—both profoundly positive and potentially harmful. The industry had been struggling with fragmentation, with many companies taking independent sustainability initiatives but lacking a coordinated approach. Through Prince Harry's conservation work, he witnessed firsthand how tourism, when managed well, could drive conservation, economic inclusion, and protect ecosystems. However, in cases where tourism was mismanaged, it could deplete local resources and harm communities.

Prince Harry recognized that, despite widespread awareness of tourism's impact, there was no unified industry response to addressing sustainability at scale. He initiated discussions with major players in the travel sector, questioning why so many companies were working independently rather than collectively. "It became really interesting to him that tourism was coming up more and more in his conversations with local communities," Sally explains. "He saw examples where tourism was being done really well and was an incredibly powerful tool for conservation. But equally, in other cases, it was removing money from local communities and having a significant negative impact."

The goal was to create an independent, non-competitive coalition where industry leaders could collaborate for the first time and align on key sustainability efforts. "The first step was just getting people around the same table and proving that we could do that," says Sally. "This had never been done before—big travel companies working together in a non-commercial, non-competitive way."

In its first five years, Travalyst focused on demonstrating that major brands could work together in a non-commercial way to create industry-wide alignment. The coalition started with rigorous governance and operational structuring to ensure that all members could collaborate effectively while maintaining neutrality. Now, as the coalition moves into its second phase, the focus is shifting towards expanding collaboration beyond the founding members and ensuring widespread adoption of sustainable practices across the broader travel industry.

> **KEY INDUSTRY PLAYERS IN THE TRAVALYST COALITION**
>
> Travalyst's coalition consists of some of the largest travel and financial technology brands, including:
>
> - online travel agencies (OTAs): Booking.com, Expedia, Trip.com, Group
> - metasearch and technology: Skyscanner, Google
> - global payment systems: Visa, Mastercard
> - review and travel data aggregators: TripAdvisor
> - global distribution systems (GDSs): Sabre, Amadeus

Additionally, Travalyst collaborates with key industry bodies and policymakers, including UN Tourism, GBTA, GSTC, the World Sustainable Hospitality Alliance, and the European Commission. The coalition recently expanded to include on-the-ground operators, such as The Travel Corporation, which is known for integrating sustainability across its portfolio.

Beyond the core coalition, Travalyst also maintains strategic partnerships with regulators, policymakers, and sustainability certification bodies. This structure ensures that sustainability efforts are aligned not just across the private sector but also within policy frameworks that influence global travel regulations.

The Role of Data in Systems Change

Sally emphasizes that the biggest missing piece in sustainability efforts is data—specifically, aligned and scalable sustainability data that can drive real impact. "We quickly realized that if we really want to scale what 'good' looks like, we have to define it at scale first," she explains. "That meant we had to look at data—align it, scale it, and make it accessible."

Travalyst initially focused on aligning industry players to commit to collecting and displaying standardized sustainability data. Early efforts resulted in the first Accommodation Framework, which integrated millions of data points from properties worldwide into a single harmonized system. This was a major breakthrough in consolidating fragmented sustainability efforts within the accommodation sector.

On the aviation front, Travalyst facilitated the adoption of a single emissions model, spearheaded by Google, to unify aviation emissions calculations across travel platforms. This allowed 130 billion consumer searches to display standardized carbon emissions data, marking an unprecedented step in mainstreaming sustainability data at scale. "Google worked unbelievably hard and invested heavily to bring a completely free, open-source aviation emissions model to market," Sally says. "Through Travalyst, we ensured that all partners adopted the same approach, making this the first time aviation emissions data was standardized across major travel platforms."

Travalyst has also worked on expanding data collection standards across corporate travel, destination impact measurement, and transportation emissions. The coalition is now moving towards integrating cross-sector data sharing, allowing different parts of the industry—hotels, airlines, tour operators, and financial institutions—to use shared sustainability data to improve decision-making and policy compliance.

Consumer Behavior and the Impact of Sustainability Data

One of Travalyst's main objectives is to empower travelers with transparent information. "Consumers care deeply and want to make better choices," says Sally, "but they're often confused by conflicting information."

Since integrating carbon emissions data into flight searches, Travalyst has begun collecting detailed consumer interaction data to understand how sustainability information influences travel decisions. "For the first time ever, platforms that have never shared data are now providing confidential insights back to Travalyst," she explains. "That is game-changing."

As regulations around sustainability reporting continue to evolve, Travalyst has taken a proactive role in policy engagement, particularly within the European Union. "We have to make sure that all these different policies and departments are talking to each other," Sally explains. "The worst thing that can happen in systems change is fragmentation."

For small hotels and independent properties practicing regenerative travel but hesitant to engage with OTAs, Sally encourages them to explore alternative distribution models. "There are so many incredible distribution opportunities beyond OTAs," she says. "Some of the most exciting sustainability initiatives are coming from grassroots operators."

Additionally, Travalyst's recent acquisition of Weeva's assets signals a growing commitment to supporting independent properties in data collection and reporting. Sally highlights that education and capacity-building programs will be a key focus, mentioning potential collaborations with existing training initiatives to help properties navigate sustainability data collection more effectively. "Weeva was all about providing access to technology for independent businesses, and that's something we're excited to continue."

Travalyst remains committed to leveraging data as a tool for global systems change, ensuring that sustainability is not just an industry talking point, but a mainstream operational standard. "The next five years will be about making sure this data drives real behavior change," Sally concludes. "We've built the foundation—now it's about execution."

The Next Step for Hospitality Giants

While boutique hotels and eco-lodges have pioneered sustainable initiatives, the hospitality industry's comprehensive transformation hinges on large hotel corporations adopting regenerative practices. These corporations possess the influence and resources necessary to drive systemic change. The shift toward regeneration is crucial not only for mitigating environmental damage but also for strengthening social responsibility, securing market leadership, and ensuring long-term business viability.

Large hotel chains are significant consumers of natural resources, with operations that often contribute to environmental degradation. The construction of expansive resorts can disrupt ecosystems, and their daily activities generate vast amounts of waste, pollution, and carbon emissions. For instance, the proposed development of luxury hotels near the Aldabra Atoll in Seychelles poses a direct threat to fragile habitats, including those of giant tortoises and other endemic species.[1] The environmental consequences of such developments highlight the urgent need for the hospitality industry to shift toward regenerative models.

Moving beyond minimizing harm, regenerative hospitality actively restores and enhances ecosystems. This can involve rewilding degraded landscapes, investing in carbon sequestration projects, and adopting circular economy principles to eliminate waste. The Populus Hotel in Denver serves as a pioneering example, positioning itself as a carbon-positive hotel by utilizing low-carbon materials, operating on renewable energy, and engaging in reforestation efforts to offset its emissions.[2] Such initiatives demonstrate that large-scale regenerative practices are feasible and can be integrated into mainstream hospitality models.

In addition to environmental considerations, the hospitality industry heavily relies on the well-being of local communities. However, many large hotel corporations extract more value than they contribute, often sourcing supplies globally rather than locally, limiting economic benefits to surrounding communities, and, in some cases, displacing indigenous populations. A shift toward regenerative hospitality means embedding economic and social benefits directly into local economies.

This includes fair wages, prioritizing local hiring, and forming partnerships with farmers, artisans, and small businesses. The Lopesan Hotel Group has been recognized for its sustainable development efforts, emphasizing renewable energy use, energy-efficient systems, and the promotion of local products, thereby reducing its carbon footprint while fostering local economies.[3]

Beyond direct environmental and social impacts, large hotel corporations play a critical role in shaping industry standards. Their commitments influence supply chains, consumer expectations, and governmental policies. When major brands lead the way in regenerative practices, they encourage suppliers, travel agencies, and smaller operators to follow suit. The Soneva Foundation exemplifies this leadership, implementing large-scale reforestation projects in Thailand and global initiatives to improve access to safe drinking water.[4] Such efforts not only contribute to sustainability goals but also set industry-wide precedents that other hospitality businesses are pressured to adopt.

Moreover, large hotel corporations possess lobbying power that can shape tourism regulations and policies. Their advocacy for environmental protections, incentives for sustainable businesses, and stricter ecological regulations can accelerate the transition toward regenerative hospitality at a systemic level. By leveraging their influence to push for sustainability-driven policies, these corporations can foster industry-wide transformation.

Market trends further reinforce the need for regenerative hospitality. Modern travelers are increasingly conscious of their environmental and social footprint, seeking ethical and responsible travel options. Research indicates that younger generations prioritize brands that align with their values, and hotels that fail to adapt to these shifting consumer preferences risk losing relevance. Regenerative hospitality not only helps brands differentiate themselves in a competitive market but also deepens guest engagement. Offering experiences such as guest participation in conservation efforts, locally sourced cuisine, and transparent sustainability reporting builds long-term customer loyalty. Travelers are increasingly drawn to companies they trust, reinforcing the importance of authenticity and accountability in sustainability efforts.

Some hotel corporations hesitate to transition toward regeneration due to concerns over financial risks. However, integrating regenerative practices is not merely a moral obligation—it is also a sound financial strategy. Investments in energy efficiency, waste reduction, and local supply chains can lead to significant long-term cost savings. Furthermore, properties that commit to sustainability often experience increased demand and can command premium pricing. Investors and financial institutions are also prioritizing environmental, social, and governance (ESG) factors in their decision-making, making sustainable businesses more attractive to investment and favorable financing terms.[5] As financial markets shift toward sustainability-focused investments, companies that fail to adapt may face economic disadvantages.

One of the most notable examples of a hospitality brand leading the way in regenerative tourism is Six Senses. Since its founding in 1995 with the opening of Soneva Fushi in the Maldives, Six Senses has consistently demonstrated a commitment to environmental stewardship and wellness-focused hospitality. Expanding across Southeast Asia and Europe, the brand built its reputation on sustainable luxury. By 2011, Six Senses had grown into an international spa and resort chain with 26 resorts and 41 spas. However, in 2012, Six Senses underwent a major transition, selling its management contracts and intellectual property rights to Pegasus Capital Advisors. This allowed the original founders to focus exclusively on the Soneva brand while Six Senses continued to operate under new ownership.

In 2019, Six Senses was acquired by InterContinental Hotels Group (IHG), a move that integrated the brand into one of the world's largest hospitality portfolios while preserving its commitment to sustainability.[6] Post-acquisition, Six Senses has expanded globally, opening properties in new markets while continuing to push the boundaries of regenerative hospitality. The brand's approach illustrates how sustainability can be seamlessly integrated into luxury travel, proving that environmental and social responsibility need not be at odds with high-end experiences.

The transformation of the hospitality industry depends on whether large hotel corporations seize the opportunity to lead the shift toward regeneration. Boutique hotels and eco-lodges have laid the foundation, but systemic change requires the participation of major players. By embedding regenerative principles into their operations, these corporations can drive significant positive impacts on the environment, local communities, and the broader travel industry. The case of Six Senses, alongside initiatives from Soneva and Lopesan, demonstrates that sustainability and profitability are not mutually exclusive. Instead, regeneration offers a pathway for the hospitality industry to redefine luxury, secure long-term economic viability, and create meaningful, lasting change.

Jeff Smith, Vice President of Sustainability at Six Senses, has played a crucial role in shaping the company's sustainability initiatives. His journey from environmental engineering to sustainable tourism provides a unique perspective on integrating environmental responsibility with luxury hospitality.

Jeff began his career in environmental engineering in Canada but soon transitioned into sustainable tourism. His early work in elephant conservation and community-based tourism in Thailand set the foundation for his sustainability career. He spent nearly a decade working with remote communities, balancing conservation efforts with tourism initiatives to improve conditions for both wildlife and local populations. Jeff later pursued a master's degree in sustainability and worked briefly in solar energy sales in Canada before joining Six Senses in 2016 as Director of Sustainability. His promotion to Vice President allowed him to expand and refine the company's sustainability strategies.

The Evolution of Sustainability at Six Senses

Founded in 1995, Six Senses was established with a vision of delivering high-end luxury hospitality while prioritizing environmental conservation and community engagement. At a time when the concept of sustainability was not widely recognized in the hospitality sector, Six Senses integrated it as a foundational principle, redefining the traditional notions of luxury. By eliminating unnecessary formality, promoting barefoot luxury, and embedding sustainability into the guest experience, the brand sought to create a hospitality model that balanced indulgence with responsibility. Over the years, Six Senses has developed standardized sustainability performance metrics, improved impact reporting, and achieved GSTC certification for all its properties, with only newly opened locations still undergoing the certification process.

> ### GUIDING PRINCIPLES AND BRAND PILLARS
>
> Six Senses operates under a clear and holistic vision: "Helping people reconnect with themselves, others, and the world around them." This philosophy serves as the foundation for its three core brand pillars:
>
> - sustainability: a deep commitment to environmental stewardship and local community engagement
> - wellness: a focus on holistic well-being for both guests and staff
> - out of the ordinary experiences: unique and immersive guest experiences that seamlessly blend luxury with sustainability

The sustainability pillar is particularly integral to the brand's identity. Six Senses properties are expected to go beyond basic environmental practices and embrace regenerative strategies that leave a net-positive impact on their surroundings. This includes comprehensive efforts in energy conservation, water management, and waste reduction. Each property is also encouraged to implement localized initiatives that support ecosystem restoration, carbon sequestration, and social empowerment.

Rather than merely minimizing harm, Six Senses actively seeks to create long-term benefits for the environment and local communities. Through regenerative impact strategies, the brand ensures that tourism contributes positively rather than passively sustaining the status quo. These efforts include organic farming programs, marine conservation initiatives, and community-based tourism projects that integrate local culture and traditions into the guest experience.

Additionally, Six Senses has taken steps to standardize impact measurement and reporting, ensuring that sustainability efforts are not just well-intentioned but also trackable and scalable. By achieving GSTC certification across all properties, the brand provides a model for other luxury hospitality groups looking to integrate regeneration into their business practices.

Six Senses represents a pioneering approach in the hospitality industry, demonstrating that luxury and sustainability can coexist. By embedding sustainability into its operations, wellness into its guest experience, and regeneration into its impact strategy, the brand has successfully redefined the meaning of high-end hospitality. Its commitment to environmental stewardship, community engagement, and holistic well-being serves as a benchmark for the industry, illustrating that responsible tourism can be both luxurious and transformative.

Implementing Sustainability Across Properties

As an operator rather than an owner of hotels, Six Senses embeds sustainability standards into management agreements and brand guidelines. All new Six Senses properties must be constructed to at least LEED Silver certification, and many achieve LEED Gold or even Platinum. Sustainability efforts are driven by a combination of corporate policies and localized initiatives. During operations, general managers are responsible for ensuring compliance with sustainability standards, supported by on-site sustainability directors, who ideally have extensive hospitality experience.

To ensure localized impact, sustainability initiatives are guided by environmental impact assessments and close engagement with local stakeholders. Properties undergo an evaluation process before opening to identify key environmental and community needs, and this data informs the selection of sustainability projects. "We start by looking at the environmental impact assessment, talking to development partners, and listening to the communities we're working with," Jeff explains.

Financial Commitment to Sustainability

A defining aspect of Six Senses' sustainability model is its mandatory 0.5 percent revenue allocation to sustainability initiatives. Unlike many corporate sustainability funds, this money remains within the local community where the hotel operates. It funds projects such as clean water filtration, wildlife conservation, and education programs. As Jeff explains, "I like that... it seems equitable in that sense, but from an administration point of view, it's a complete nightmare."

Despite the logistical challenges, the commitment ensures that tourism revenue directly benefits the destinations. Some properties use the funds for hands-on community projects, such as installing water filtration systems, while others operate as grant-giving entities, providing financial support to local NGOs and conservation programs.

Measuring Impact and Progress

Six Senses employs rigorous measurement frameworks to track both sustainability initiatives and operational efficiencies. Impact reports are submitted quarterly, detailing how funds are spent and what outcomes they generate, such as the number of students educated or habitats protected. In addition, the company tracks energy, water, and waste metrics monthly, with most properties monitoring these on a daily basis to identify inefficiencies.

Internal audits and third-party GSTC certification ensure that sustainability standards are maintained. Properties receive performance scores based on compliance with brand standards, and the company encourages voluntary sustainability targets. "We don't impose top-down mandates," Jeff explains. "Instead, each hotel sets their own targets, which keeps them engaged and ensures progress."

Rather than relying heavily on carbon offsets, Six Senses prioritizes reducing emissions at the source. The company has adopted science-based targets through IHG and focuses on energy efficiency and renewable energy integration before considering offsets. "I'm very happy that we didn't jump into the offset world earlier on because now it's just gone off the rails," Jeff notes. A few properties offer guest-paid carbon offsets as an optional add-on, ensuring transparency in climate commitments.

Training and Knowledge Sharing

To foster sustainability knowledge across its properties, Six Senses has developed a peer-to-peer learning model. Monthly cluster calls provide a forum for sustainability directors at different locations to share challenges and best practices. A buddy system pairs sustainability leaders with regional directors for mentorship and coaching. However, Jeff acknowledges the talent gap in sustainability leadership, emphasizing the need to train hospitality professionals in sustainability practices.

"Sustainability directors should ideally have five years of hotel management experience, but the reality is, 10 years ago, no hotel schools were offering sustainability programs," he explains. "So we're working with a limited talent pool and trying to build expertise from within."

Challenges and Opportunities in Urban Sustainability

While Six Senses is primarily known for its remote and nature-focused resorts, the company has expanded into urban environments, such as Kyoto. Jeff explains that urban properties face unique challenges but also present opportunities for community networking and local partnerships. Unlike resorts, which often must operate as self-sufficient ecosystems, urban properties can leverage municipal sustainability initiatives.

"Sustainability happens in between departments," Jeff says. "The kitchen sorts the waste, the landscaping team composts it. It only works when all departments collaborate." In urban settings, this collaboration extends to external partnerships, as properties work with city governments, local waste management providers, and community organizations.

Looking ahead, Six Senses is poised to deepen its commitment to sustainability and regeneration through several key initiatives. A major focus will be on reducing plastic waste, an effort that builds on the company's Plastic Freedom Playbook. Beyond eliminating single-use plastics from its properties, Six Senses aims to extend its plastic avoidance efforts to the surrounding communities, fostering a larger movement toward waste reduction and environmental stewardship.

Another cornerstone of its sustainability strategy is the preservation of biodiversity, particularly through seed saving initiatives. By establishing seed banks, Six Senses seeks to protect both genetic and cultural biodiversity, ensuring that traditional plants and heirloom crops remain integral to local agricultural systems. This approach not only safeguards indigenous plant species but also helps maintain culinary traditions rooted in regional heritage.

In addition to these initiatives, Six Senses is committed to strengthening its adherence to the GSTC certification. Rather than simply maintaining certification, the company aims for continuous improvement, using the GSTC framework as a benchmark to enhance its environmental and social impact across all properties.

As Jeff explains, "We want each Six Senses property to become a reserve for biodiversity and a center for cultural preservation. Seed saving, working with local farmers, and maintaining heirloom crops are all part of that." By intertwining conservation with hospitality, Six Senses continues to set new standards for regenerative tourism, ensuring that its properties not only offer luxury experiences but also contribute meaningfully to the well-being of the planet and the communities they serve.

Jeff's leadership at Six Senses exemplifies how luxury and sustainability can coexist. By embedding sustainability deeply into operations, rather than treating it as an isolated initiative, the company has positioned itself as a pioneer in regenerative hospitality. "We've always been sustainable, but now we have the third-party audits to prove it," Jeff says.

As Six Senses continues to refine its sustainability strategies, it serves as an inspiration for other hospitality brands seeking to balance luxury with environmental and social responsibility. The company's model proves that with clear frameworks, local engagement, and rigorous measurement, sustainability can be both impactful and commercially viable.

The future of travel depends on a fundamental shift toward regeneration, and large hotel corporations must lead the way. Their environmental impact, social responsibility, industry influence, and financial power position them as key drivers of change. By embedding regenerative principles into their operations, these corporations can move beyond mere sustainability and actively contribute to the restoration of ecosystems, the empowerment of local communities, and the creation of a more resilient travel industry. In doing so, they not only secure their own long-term success but also help ensure that future generations can experience the world in a way that is enriching, equitable, and enduring.

UNWTO Integrates Industry into National Climate Plans

Following the COP28 UN Climate Change Conference, the United Nations World Tourism Organization (UNWTO) has expanded its climate action efforts to ensure the tourism sector contributes to global climate goals. A key initiative driving this transformation is the Glasgow Declaration on Climate Action in Tourism, introduced at COP26, which calls for urgent measures to halve emissions by 2030 and achieve net zero by 2050.[7] The declaration encourages tourism businesses, destinations, and supporting organizations to create actionable climate plans, measure and disclose emissions, and work collaboratively to mitigate environmental impacts. It serves as a framework for destinations, tourism businesses, and organizations to implement climate strategies that contribute to broader global efforts in mitigating climate change.

A central focus of the Glasgow Declaration is the need for systematic measurement and accountability. Tourism has long been recognized as a significant contributor to global carbon emissions, with air travel, energy-intensive hotels, and large-scale tourism infrastructure exerting a substantial environmental impact. By requiring signatories to track and disclose emissions, the declaration seeks to ensure that climate commitments translate into measurable progress. Beyond reducing emissions, the initiative also emphasizes the importance of ecosystem restoration and climate resilience, encouraging the industry to go beyond sustainability and adopt regenerative approaches.

One of the defining aspects of the Glasgow Declaration is its emphasis on collaboration. Recognizing that no single business or government can tackle climate change alone, the declaration calls for shared responsibility among governments, businesses, financial institutions, and local communities. It encourages knowledge exchange and partnerships that facilitate the transition toward low-carbon, resilient tourism models. This collaborative approach is crucial, as tourism supply chains are vast and interdependent, involving everything from transport providers and accommodation operators to food suppliers and waste management systems.

In addition to collaboration, the declaration stresses the importance of securing financial resources to support climate action. Tourism businesses and destinations often struggle to secure adequate funding for sustainable initiatives, and the declaration advocates for increased investment in climate-friendly tourism infrastructure. Governments and international organizations are encouraged to develop financial mechanisms that incentivize emissions reductions, support conservation efforts, and enable small and medium-sized tourism enterprises to transition toward sustainable practices.

Since its launch, the United Nations World Tourism Organization (UNWTO) has been actively driving the implementation of the Glasgow Declaration. Building on the momentum from COP28, efforts have been made to integrate tourism into national climate policies. At COP29, over 50 governments committed to incorporating tourism-related sustainability goals into their Nationally Determined Contributions (NDCs), reinforcing the industry's role in achieving national and international climate targets. The declaration has also influenced industry-wide reporting standards, with the World Sustainable Hospitality Alliance introducing frameworks to measure carbon emissions, energy consumption, water use, and waste management. These new guidelines help standardize sustainability reporting across the sector and improve transparency and accountability.[8]

The Glasgow Declaration on Climate Action in Tourism represents a turning point in how tourism is integrated into the global climate agenda. By pushing the industry beyond basic sustainability measures and toward regenerative models, it acknowledges tourism's responsibility not just to minimize harm, but to actively contribute to climate solutions. The success of the declaration will depend on continued collaboration, financing, and enforcement, ensuring that climate commitments are upheld and translated into meaningful action. As climate change intensifies, the ability of the tourism sector to adapt and lead in climate action will be a defining factor in its long-term sustainability.

Building on these efforts, COP29, held in Baku, Azerbaijan, marked a pivotal moment in the industry's climate agenda. Over 50 governments signed the Declaration for Enhanced Climate Action in Tourism, pledging to incorporate tourism into their NDCs.[9] This move signifies an increased acknowledgment of the tourism industry's role in climate change mitigation, urging nations to integrate sustainable tourism development strategies into their national climate commitments. By embedding tourism-related sustainability targets in NDCs, governments are positioning the industry as a significant player in achieving the Paris Agreement's climate goals.

To operationalize these commitments, the World Sustainable Hospitality Alliance has introduced a comprehensive framework for measuring and reporting greenhouse gas emissions, water consumption, waste generation, and energy use within the hospitality sector.[10] This initiative is designed to enhance transparency and accountability, providing standardized metrics that allow hotels and tourism operators to track their progress toward sustainability goals. The framework also seeks to promote industry-wide best practices, ensuring that businesses remain committed to tangible environmental improvements rather than engaging in greenwashing.

Beyond environmental concerns, UNWTO is also working to advance resilience-focused tourism policies, recognizing the sector's vulnerability to climate-related disruptions, such as extreme weather events and biodiversity loss. As part of this approach, nature-based solutions and carbon offset programs are being encouraged within the tourism industry, with many organizations investing in regenerative tourism models that prioritize ecosystem restoration and community benefits.[11]

Furthermore, financing mechanisms for climate action in tourism are gaining momentum. UNWTO and its partners have been advocating for increased financial support for sustainable tourism projects, including green investment funds and public–private partnerships that enable large-scale climate adaptation and mitigation initiatives. Some governments are now implementing carbon pricing models for tourism-related activities, directing funds toward conservation efforts and renewable energy projects in high-impact travel destinations.

By integrating tourism into national climate policies and encouraging industry-wide accountability, UNWTO and its partners are reshaping the sector's role in the global climate agenda. The transition from sustainability to regenerative tourism signals a shift in priorities, where the focus is no longer solely on minimizing harm but on actively contributing to environmental and social well-being. The success of these initiatives will depend on continued collaboration between governments, businesses, and civil society, ensuring that tourism evolves as a climate-positive industry capable of driving systemic change.

Key Takeaways

Systemic change over fragmentation:

- Regenerative tourism requires shifting from isolated sustainability efforts to coordinated, industry-wide action.
- Fragmentation has limited scalability; collective initiatives like Travalyst demonstrate how unified coalitions can drive broader change.

Travalyst as a catalyst for industry alignment:

- Founded by Prince Harry, Travalyst unites major industry players, from OTAs to financial institutions, in a non-competitive coalition.
- It aims to create standardized frameworks for sustainability across the travel ecosystem, enabling systemic transformation.

Data as a foundation for regenerative travel:

- Lack of harmonized sustainability data has hindered progress. Travalyst has pioneered standardized data frameworks, such as for accommodation sustainability and aviation emissions.
- Shared sustainability data enables better decision-making, regulatory compliance, and transparency across the industry.

Empowering consumers through transparency:

- Travalyst prioritizes giving travelers clear sustainability data to inform responsible choices.

- Early evidence suggests sustainability data influences consumer behavior, promoting market demand for responsible travel options.

Supporting small operators and independent hotels:

- Travalyst is extending tools and support to independent properties and smaller operators, including through the acquisition of Weeva's assets.
- Education and capacity-building are crucial to enable participation by grassroots businesses in regenerative tourism.

Hospitality industry's pivotal role in regeneration:

- Large hotel corporations are critical to systemic change due to their scale, resources, and influence over supply chains and industry standards.
- Moving beyond minimizing harm, regenerative hospitality actively restores ecosystems and benefits local communities.

Examples of regenerative hospitality leadership:

- Six Senses exemplifies how luxury and sustainability can coexist, integrating regenerative practices like carbon-positive operations, biodiversity preservation, and local community engagement.
- Other leaders, such as Soneva and Six Senses, demonstrate that sustainability initiatives can drive both positive impacts and financial viability.

Economic viability of regeneration:

- Integrating regenerative practices is not just ethical but financially strategic, offering long-term cost savings and market differentiation.
- Investors and financial institutions increasingly prioritize ESG factors, making sustainable businesses more attractive for funding.

Policy integration and global frameworks:

- The Glasgow Declaration on Climate Action in Tourism is pushing the industry toward measurable climate action and regenerative practices.
- Integration of tourism into NDCs signals governments' recognition of tourism's role in climate solutions.

Collaboration and financing are key:

- Effective climate action in tourism requires collaboration across private and public sectors, financial support, and standardized measurement frameworks.
- Partnerships between governments, industry, and civil society are essential to achieving regenerative tourism goals.

From sustainability to regeneration:

- The industry's future lies in moving beyond minimizing harm toward actively restoring ecosystems, supporting local communities, and ensuring tourism's positive legacy.
- Regenerative tourism offers a pathway for the industry to secure its long-term viability while contributing to global climate and sustainability goals.

Notes

1 D Carrington. Luxury hotel development threatens Seychelles' Aldabra Atoll, *Guardian*, 2024.
2 O Milman. Populus Hotel aims to be America's first carbon-positive hotel, Architectural Digest, 2024. architecturaldigest.com (archived at https://perma.cc/VF5J-KW5L)
3 Cadena SER. Lopesan Hotel Group and sustainable tourism, Cadena SER, 2025. cadenaser.com (archived at https://perma.cc/T22P-S6MZ)
4 Soneva. Soneva Foundation and regenerative initiatives, Wikipedia, 2023. wikipedia.com (archived at https://perma.cc/BZM2-KQHZ)
5 Cadena SER. Lopesan Hotel Group and sustainable tourism, Cadena SER, 2025. cadenaser.com (archived at https://perma.cc/T22P-S6MZ)
6 Travel Weekly. Six Senses CEO Neil Jacobs on expansion and sustainability, Travel Weekly, 2023. travelweekly.com (archived at https://perma.cc/E8A3-S9GF)
7 One Planet Network. Glasgow Declaration on Climate Action in Tourism, One Planet Network, nd. www.oneplanetnetwork.org/programmes/sustainable-tourism/glasgow-declaration (archived at https://perma.cc/E663-M6H3)

8 Reuters. More than 50 countries sign UN sustainable tourism declaration, Reuters, 2024. www.reuters.com/sustainability/more-than-50-countries-sign-un-sustainable-tourism-declaration-2024-11-20 (archived at https://perma.cc/6ZP5-SMLM)

9 Reuters. More than 50 countries sign UN sustainable tourism declaration, Reuters, 2024. www.reuters.com/sustainability/more-than-50-countries-sign-un-sustainable-tourism-declaration-2024-11-20 (archived at https://perma.cc/6ZP5-SMLM)

10 Reuters. More than 50 countries sign UN sustainable tourism declaration, Reuters, 2024. www.reuters.com/sustainability/more-than-50-countries-sign-un-sustainable-tourism-declaration-2024-11-20 (archived at https://perma.cc/6ZP5-SMLM)

11 One Planet Network. Glasgow Declaration on Climate Action in Tourism, One Planet Network, nd. www.oneplanetnetwork.org/programmes/sustainable-tourism/glasgow-declaration (archived at https://perma.cc/E663-M6H3)

Regenerative Leadership for the Future

10

Honoring Indigenous Wisdom in Regenerative Travel: Restoring Right Relationship with Place

As the global travel industry grapples with its role in ecological and social harm, a profound insight is emerging: The future of regenerative tourism cannot be designed solely through Western frameworks. Indigenous peoples—who steward over 80 percent of the world's remaining biodiversity despite representing just 5 percent of the population[1]—offer knowledge systems, worldviews, and practices that are essential to building a truly regenerative industry. Yet too often, Indigenous contributions are tokenized, their voices marginalized, and their lands commodified for the benefit of outsiders.

To shift the travel industry toward genuine regeneration, we must go beyond inclusion and toward power-sharing, reciprocity, and the restoration of right relationship with place. For regenerative leadership to foster, there must be a return to Indigenous wisdom, how it can transform tourism, and what principles can guide businesses, governments, and travelers in honoring it.

Why Indigenous Knowledge Matters

Indigenous worldviews are fundamentally relational. They do not separate humans from nature but position people as part of a web of life, governed by reciprocity, stewardship, and long-term responsibility.[2] These traditions, passed down through generations, hold sophisticated ecological knowledge—ranging from landscape management and fire regimes to sustainable hunting, farming, and water governance.[3]

For centuries, tourism development has displaced or erased Indigenous peoples, often exploiting their cultures as attractions while denying them access to decision-making or economic benefits. Yet research shows that when Indigenous communities lead conservation and development efforts, ecological outcomes are often superior to those in government-controlled or private-protected areas.[4] As Paul Hawken, an influential American environmentalist, entrepreneur, author, and activist known for his pioneering work on sustainability, climate solutions, and regenerative economics, writes, regeneration requires not only restoring ecosystems, but also restoring cultural and historical relationships to place: "It is about healing the future by addressing the wounds of the past."[5]

Integrating Indigenous wisdom into tourism is not simply about adding cultural programming or crafts into a resort experience. It requires transforming governance, ownership, and value systems.

PRINCIPLES FOR HONORING INDIGENOUS WISDOM IN TOURISM

For businesses and destinations seeking to engage Indigenous wisdom ethically, several guiding principles emerge:

1 **Power-sharing, not tokenism.**

   Indigenous communities must hold leadership roles in governance, ownership, and benefit-sharing—not simply serve as consultants or performers.

2 **Place-based design.**

   Regenerative tourism should be deeply attuned to local ecologies, histories, and cultural meanings. This requires slowing down, listening deeply, and co-creating offerings that reflect Indigenous values and priorities.

> 3 **Reciprocity and consent.**
>
> Tourism activities should be built on free, prior, and informed consent, with benefits flowing back to Indigenous communities in ways they define as meaningful[6].
>
> 4 **Cultural continuity.**
>
> Support not only the preservation of Indigenous heritage but the flourishing of living cultures—language revitalization and intergenerational knowledge transfer.
>
> 5 **Educating travelers.**
>
> Guests should be offered opportunities to understand the local context—not through extractive or romanticized storytelling, but through respectful learning, guided by Indigenous hosts.

The integration of Indigenous wisdom into regenerative tourism is not a symbolic act; it is a structural transformation. It requires the industry to grapple with histories of dispossession, to relinquish control, and to reorient itself toward the flourishing of people and place.

As Vandana Shiva, a world-renowned Indian scholar, environmental activist, ecofeminist, author, and advocate for biodiversity, food sovereignty, and social justice, explains, "Regeneration is the renewal of life and the celebration of diversity, not the uniformity imposed by monocultures of the mind and market."[7] For travel to become a force of healing rather than harm, we must elevate the voices, governance, and knowledge systems of the world's first stewards.

The path forward is clear: regeneration begins with honoring those who have long known how to live in right relationship with the land.

How Companies Are Innovating by Giving Nature a Seat at the Table

As the global tourism industry moves beyond sustainability and toward regeneration, a radical new idea is emerging at the forefront of innovation: Treating nature not merely as a resource or backdrop but as a living stakeholder with agency, voice, and rights. Across sectors and continents, a small but growing number of companies are reshaping their governance, operations, and values to honor the land—and, in some cases, they are even giving nature a formal place in decision-making.

One of the most profound innovations in this space is the movement to grant legal rights or personhood to ecosystems. This concept, rooted in Indigenous worldviews, recognizes that landscapes, rivers, and forests are not passive objects, but active members of the ecological community. In New Zealand, the Whanganui River was granted legal personhood in 2017 as part of a landmark settlement between the government and Māori iwi (tribes), reflecting the Māori belief that the river is an ancestor and kin.[8] The settlement established a co-governance model where Māori and government representatives act as guardians, not owners, of the river's well-being. Similarly, Te Urewera, formerly a national park in New Zealand, now holds legal personhood status, with stewardship led by the Tūhoe people. These legal frameworks have rippled into tourism, where eco-lodges, tour companies, and regional operators increasingly align their practices with Indigenous-led governance, ensuring their operations reflect the rights and dignity of local ecosystems.

Another striking example comes from the United Kingdom, where the ethical beauty brand Faith in Nature made headlines in 2022 by becoming the first company in the world to appoint nature to its board of directors. This innovative governance model gives nature a formal vote in board decisions, represented by an independent environmental law firm and nature advocates.[9] While Faith in Nature operates outside the travel sector, its experiment has sparked conversations worldwide about how tourism companies could similarly elevate nature's interests in business governance.

In the United States, Patagonia—long regarded as a pioneer in environmental and social responsibility—took an unprecedented step in 2022 when it restructured its ownership so that all profits, approximately $100 million per year, are now directed toward protecting the planet through the Holdfast Collective. While Patagonia has not gone so far as to appoint nature to its board, its governance framework effectively positions the Earth as its top shareholder, embedding planetary interests into its deepest corporate structures.[10]

Indigenous-led governance offers some of the most inspiring examples of regeneration in action. In Canada, the Haida Nation's co-management of Gwaii Haanas National Park Reserve has become a global model for conservation tourism, balancing ecological protection with cultural revitalization and local employment.[11] In Australia, 100 percent Indigenous-owned enterprises like Nitmiluk Tours provide tourism experiences that are grounded in Jawoyn stewardship, blending cultural education with land protection.[12] These examples demonstrate that honoring the land requires not only listening to Indigenous wisdom but structurally embedding it into decision-making, ownership, and benefit-sharing.

Beyond governance, companies are innovating by embedding ecosystem services into their business accounting. In Costa Rica, a country renowned for its ecotourism leadership, businesses increasingly invest in reforestation and agroforestry projects that deliver measurable ecosystem benefits, including carbon sequestration, biodiversity conservation, and water retention. Some companies are experimenting with tracking these benefits alongside financial performance, signaling a move toward internalizing nature's value in corporate balance sheets.

In some cases, companies are forming informal nature advisory councils, bringing together environmental scientists, Indigenous leaders, and conservationists to guide business practices. Blue Apple Beach, a boutique beachfront hotel in Colombia, for example, works closely with marine biologists and local community members to ensure that reef health, coastal protection, and community resilience shape the hotel's sustainability initiatives.

This movement, which spans from legal innovation to operational practice, signals a broader paradigm shift. It invites the travel industry to move from an extractive model—where land and water are seen as assets to be exploited—to a relational model, where ecosystems are recognized as living partners and stakeholders. As Paul Hawken writes, "Regeneration is not about sacrifice or moralizing; it is about falling in love with life and seeing all systems as living, dynamic, and worthy of respect."[13]

By honoring the land as a stakeholder, embedding Indigenous governance, measuring ecosystem services, and designing operations around the health of place, companies across the world are showing that regeneration is not a fringe experiment—it is the next frontier of business leadership. For the travel industry, which depends so deeply on the beauty, health, and resilience of the natural world, this is not just an ethical shift. It is a business imperative.

The global travel industry is at a turning point. For decades, tourism has been hailed as a driver of economic growth and cultural exchange. Yet today it is also linked to climate change, biodiversity loss, cultural erosion, and social inequality. While the rise of sustainable tourism has been a step forward, sustainability alone is no longer enough. We need to move beyond doing less harm and start actively doing good.

As Hawken argues, "Sustainability is about not going backward; regeneration is about putting life at the center of every action."[14] Regeneration calls on us to rethink the very purpose of travel—not as a consumptive activity but as a means to restore ecosystems, revitalize communities, and strengthen cultural heritage.

But to achieve this, the industry must embrace five fundamental shifts that go far beyond surface-level change.

Five Systemic Shifts Toward a Regenerative Future

1 Regeneration must become the business model—not just a side project. Too often, sustainability is treated as an add-on: A certification plaque, a CSR program, or a seasonal marketing push. To drive meaningful transformation, regenerative principles need to be embedded at the heart of business operations. This means integrating regenerative goals into performance metrics, reinvesting profits into local communities, and measuring success not just in financial terms but in social, ecological, and cultural outcomes. Leading examples already exist: Fogo Island Inn in Canada reinvests all operating surpluses into the local community through the Shorefast Foundation, strengthening cultural and economic resilience,[15] while Intrepid Travel, one of the world's largest adventure companies, has been certified as a B Corp and explicitly links its regenerative efforts to business governance, environmental practices, and worker well-being.[16]

2 The industry must move from sustainability to what scholars call "post-green," regenerative models. While sustainability focuses on minimizing harm, regeneration aims to create a net positive impact—improving ecosystem health, supporting biodiversity, and enhancing community vitality. For example, the Berkeley Group in the UK commits to "net biodiversity gain" in its urban developments,[17] while Great Plains Conservation in Botswana and Kenya channels tourism revenue into wildlife conservation and ecosystem restoration.[18] In Costa Rica's Osa Peninsula, community-based tourism models have successfully balanced rainforest preservation with economic benefit for local residents.[19] Regeneration reframes tourism as stewardship, turning travelers into active participants in the restoration of place.

3 We must integrate Indigenous wisdom into governance and operations. Indigenous peoples protect more than 80 percent of global biodiversity despite representing just 5 percent of the population.[20] Yet their voices are often marginalized in tourism development. To build a regenerative future, Indigenous leaders must be included in governance roles, not just as advisors. Their knowledge systems must help shape business models, guest experiences, and conservation strategies. In Australia, Indigenous-owned businesses like Nitmiluk Tours and ranger programs not only preserve cultural heritage but also generate economic opportunities for Indigenous communities.[21]

4 Regeneration requires stronger public–private cooperation. No business, no matter how committed, can achieve systemic change alone. Governments, tourism boards, businesses, civil society, and local communities must work together to set shared goals, co-invest in regenerative infrastructure, and align their strategies. The European Capitals of Smart Tourism initiative, led by the European Commission, fosters partnerships between cities and businesses to enhance sustainability, accessibility, and cultural vibrancy.[22] Costa Rica's emergence as an ecotourism leader was made possible by decades of collaboration between government agencies, local entrepreneurs, and conservation groups.[23] Regeneration thrives when policy and business align.

5 Bold policy reform and financial incentives are needed to reshape the market. Governments and international bodies must rewrite the rules to favor regeneration over extraction. This could include visitor caps, as seen in Colombia's Tayrona National Park, where seasonal closures allow ecosystems to recover;[24] taxes on non-regenerative tourism models, such as mega-cruise ships or mass-market short-term rentals; and subsidies or low-interest loans for regenerative enterprises. The UNWTO Glasgow Declaration on Climate Action in Tourism, signed by hundreds of destinations and companies, commits the sector to cutting emissions in half by 2030 and embedding climate action into operations and value chains.[25] These kinds of frameworks offer blueprints for accelerating change. What's at stake is not only the future of travel but the future of the ecosystems, communities, and cultures that make travel meaningful.

> **GOVERNANCE CHECKLIST**
>
> ☑ Embed regenerative principles into the core business model, not as a side project.
> ☑ Involve Indigenous leaders and local communities in decision-making.
> ☑ Align with government, tourism boards, and local policies to prioritize regeneration.
> ☑ Establish clear, measurable regenerative goals across all departments.

Making Regeneration Work: Building Profitable, Scalable, and Impactful Tourism Models

The travel and hospitality industry is undergoing a profound transformation. No longer is it enough for businesses to merely minimize their environmental harm or offset their carbon footprints. Today's travelers, employees, and communities are increasingly demanding that tourism play an active role in regenerating ecosystems, cultures, and economies. This shift calls for companies not only to adopt regenerative practices but to demonstrate that such approaches are financially viable, scalable, and deeply embedded across business operations.

One of the most pressing imperatives is to build profitable, scalable regenerative models that prove regeneration can compete with, or even outperform, conventional business approaches. Research shows that consumer demand is moving rapidly in favor of businesses that embrace sustainability and social responsibility, with over 70 percent of global consumers indicating they would pay more for sustainable products and services.[26] Companies like Intrepid Travel, a certified B Corp, have successfully integrated regenerative principles into their business while maintaining robust profitability and international expansion, demonstrating that purpose and profit are not mutually exclusive.[27]

Alongside strong business models, regenerative companies must develop robust impact measurement tools to track, share, and improve outcomes. Too often, sustainability initiatives remain hidden from public view, or worse, devolve into greenwashing. Tools like EarthCheck and the B Impact Assessment platform enable companies to measure and communicate key indicators—such as carbon emissions, water use, biodiversity outcomes, and community investment—providing transparency and accountability. Importantly, these tools also engage guests, staff, and local stakeholders, allowing them to see and understand their role in driving positive change.

To make regeneration visible and credible, companies must reduce single-use plastics, waste, and emissions—actions that are both highly tangible and meaningful to travelers and staff. Recent data shows that travelers' interest in sustainable tourism has only intensified in recent years. According to Booking.com's 2024 Sustainable Travel Report, 75 percent of global travelers now express a desire to travel more sustainably over the next 12 months, reflecting a notable increase in consumer awareness and responsibility. Importantly, 45 percent of travelers report finding accommodations labeled as more sustainable more appealing, underscoring the growing importance of visible and credible sustainability practices in hospitality. Beyond preferences, these choices are tied to personal values: 43 percent of travelers acknowledge feeling guilty when they make less sustainable decisions, and many express concrete intentions to change their behaviors, such as reducing energy consumption (57 percent) and using more sustainable modes of transportation (54 percent) during their trips.[28]

This shift in consumer sentiment highlights a powerful opportunity—and challenge—for the travel and hospitality sectors. Businesses that prioritize and communicate authentic sustainability efforts, from eliminating single-use plastics to offering low-carbon transport options, are increasingly positioned to attract and retain conscious travelers. In short, sustainability has moved from a niche concern to a mainstream expectation, reshaping what success in travel looks like in the years ahead. Resorts like Six Senses Hotels have committed to eliminating all single-use plastics and sourcing energy from renewable sources, setting a gold standard in visible regenerative leadership.[29]

However, no regenerative strategy can succeed without the active participation of the workforce. Businesses must focus on employee engagement and empowerment, creating green teams, interdepartmental competitions, and targeted training to foster ownership and innovation among staff. Research shows that when employees perceive their organizations as environmentally responsible, they are more likely to engage in sustainable behaviors and feel greater job satisfaction.[30] Patagonia's environmental internship program offers a particularly effective model, encouraging employees to work with environmental organizations while building deep, values-based alignment within the company.[31]

Regeneration also requires a commitment to prioritize local supply chains and community benefit. Globalized supply chains often bypass local economies, weakening community resilience and increasing environmental costs. By contrast, local sourcing builds economic strength, protects cultural integrity, and reduces emissions from transportation. According to the United Nations World Tourism Organization, local procurement can amplify the positive economic effects of tourism by keeping income circulating within the destination.[32]

Finally, the guest experience itself must reflect regenerative values. Businesses should offer immersive, hands-on experiences that allow travelers to contribute meaningfully to local regeneration efforts, transforming passive consumers into active participants. Examples include coral restoration dives in the Maldives, regenerative farming workshops at resorts like Six Senses Douro Valley, or cultural preservation programs run by Indigenous communities. Not only do these experiences deepen guest satisfaction, but they also strengthen guests' connection to place, fostering a sense of shared responsibility that extends long after check-out.[33]

In conclusion, regenerating the travel and hospitality sector is both a moral imperative and an extraordinary business opportunity. By building profitable regenerative models, measuring impact, eliminating waste, engaging employees, strengthening local supply chains, and creating meaningful guest experiences, businesses can lead the way toward a travel industry that truly gives back to people and planet. Far from a niche trend, regeneration represents the next frontier of competitive advantage and industry leadership.

> **BUSINESS OPERATIONS CHECKLIST**
>
> ☑ Audit and reduce waste, emissions, and single-use plastics.
> ☑ Build local, ethical supply chains that benefit communities.
> ☑ Design employee engagement programs (green teams, competitions, trainings).
> ☑ Develop and use simple tools to measure and communicate impact to staff and guests.

How Tourism Can Inspire Change Through Communication

In the emerging landscape of regenerative tourism, operational change alone is not enough. How businesses communicate their efforts—through storytelling, messaging, and engagement—plays a critical role in shaping both guest behavior and industry transformation. While many sustainability campaigns have fallen into the traps of vague claims or virtue signaling, regenerative tourism demands a different approach: one rooted in authenticity, joy, community, and collaboration.

The first essential step is to use authentic, values-aligned messaging. Travelers today are not only skeptical of greenwashing—they are also increasingly sophisticated in detecting it. Research by the European Commission found that 42 percent of green claims made by companies across various sectors, including travel, were exaggerated, false, or deceptive, eroding public trust. [34] To regain credibility, tourism businesses must prioritize transparency and cultural respect in their communications. For example, the Indigenous Tourism Association of Canada has developed guidelines that help non-Indigenous operators communicate respectfully about Indigenous culture and avoid appropriation or distortion.[35] This type of authentic storytelling not only honors cultural heritage but also creates meaningful and trustworthy visitor experiences.

Equally important is the need to highlight joy and connection in regenerative narratives. Too often, sustainability messaging leans on guilt, sacrifice, or doom-laden warnings—messages that can alienate or overwhelm audiences. Behavioral science research shows that positive emotions like joy, hope, and connection are far more effective in driving long-term behavior change.[36] For example, the tourism project Rewilding Europe frames nature restoration not as an ecological obligation but as a joyful return to wild landscapes, inviting travelers to participate in the thrill of ecological recovery.[37] By positioning regeneration as something emotionally fulfilling, the industry can help travelers see sustainability not as a burden but as an opportunity to experience deeper meaning and purpose during their journeys.

Communication is not a secondary concern in regenerative tourism—it is a central tool for cultural transformation. By using authentic messaging, highlighting joy and connection, building long-term community engagement, and aligning language across the industry, tourism leaders can move beyond surface-level change toward deep, systemic impact. At its best, regenerative storytelling doesn't just market a destination or product; it invites travelers to join a movement that reshapes how we relate to the planet and to one another.

> **GUEST EXPERIENCE AND COMMUNICATION CHECKLIST**
>
> ☑ Offer immersive guest experiences that contribute to local regeneration (e.g., coral restoration, beach clean-ups).
> ☑ Share transparent, authentic stories—avoid greenwashing.
> ☑ Highlight joy, connection, and positive change in marketing messages.
> ☑ Create follow-up platforms for guests to stay engaged post-trip.

Education and Cultural Change in Travel

As the tourism industry moves toward a regenerative future, operational change and environmental standards are only part of the equation. Perhaps the most profound shift required is cultural: how we understand, communicate, and embody our relationship with the places we visit. Education and cultural change are at the heart of this transformation. By embedding regenerative thinking into education, equipping travelers to understand the difference between sustainability and regeneration, and inspiring a mindset of respect and reciprocity, the travel sector can help reshape not just how we travel—but why.

The first step is to start education early and across all generations. While much of the regenerative tourism conversation currently focuses on destinations and businesses, the deeper challenge is embedding regenerative thinking into schools, vocational programs, and public discourse. According to UNESCO's 2022 report on education for sustainable development, there is a global consensus that environmental literacy must start in childhood and continue throughout life if we are to meet climate and biodiversity goals.[38] Programs like the International Eco-Schools initiative, now active in over 70 countries, have shown success in instilling environmental values and stewardship among young people, creating a generation of travelers and citizens who carry those values into adulthood.[39] Integrating regeneration—

beyond recycling and conservation—into these curriculums can help shift the next generation's relationship to nature from one of use to one of care.

At the same time, it is critical to help travelers understand the difference between regeneration, sustainability, eco-tourism, and carbon offsetting. While sustainability aims to minimize harm, regeneration aims to actively restore and improve ecosystems and communities. Eco-tourism often focuses on nature-based travel with a conservation angle, while carbon offsetting tends to reduce the guilt of travel without changing the underlying systems. This confusion risks diluting the transformative potential of regeneration.

Perhaps most importantly, regeneration requires inspiring a mindset shift toward respect and reciprocity. Travelers need to move beyond a consumer mindset and begin to see themselves as guests, stewards, and partners in the well-being of the places they visit. Research in social psychology shows that feelings of gratitude and humility, when cultivated through experience and education, increase pro-environmental behavior.[40] In practice, this means designing travel experiences that invite guests to participate meaningfully—whether through volunteering, cultural exchange, or simply slowing down and listening to local voices. Initiatives like ReGeneration 2030, a youth-led Nordic-Baltic movement, actively work to foster intergenerational dialogue and civic engagement, encouraging travelers and residents alike to take responsibility for the places they love.[41]

Importantly, these educational and cultural efforts should not be limited to guests. Staff training within tourism businesses plays a vital role in ensuring that regenerative principles are lived, not just advertised. A 2023 report by the Global Sustainable Tourism Council emphasizes that workforce education is essential to embedding sustainability and regeneration into everyday operations and guest interactions.[42] This internal alignment can transform hotels, tour companies, and destinations into living classrooms of regenerative practice.

The journey toward regenerative tourism is not only a matter of policies and practices but of hearts and minds. By embedding regenerative thinking across generations, clarifying what regeneration truly means, and cultivating a sense of stewardship and reciprocity, the tourism industry can help shape a cultural transformation that extends far beyond the airport or hotel.

Regeneration, at its heart, is not just about restoring landscapes—it's about restoring relationships: with the earth, with each other, and with the generations to come.

> **EDUCATION AND CULTURE CHANGE CHECKLIST**
>
> ☑ Educate staff and travelers on what regeneration means (beyond sustainability).
> ☑ Provide opportunities for cross-cultural learning and Indigenous knowledge sharing.
> ☑ Design traveler materials that explain the "why" behind regenerative practices.
> ☑ Support community education initiatives, especially for young people.

The Future is Regenerative

As the global tourism industry faces mounting environmental and social challenges, it is increasingly clear that piecemeal solutions will not suffice. The shift toward regenerative tourism—where travel actively restores ecosystems, strengthens communities, and revives local cultures—requires more than operational tweaks. It demands a profound transformation in how travelers, businesses, governments, and communities think, behave, and invest. To realize this vision, the industry must advance two essential fronts: education and cultural change and infrastructure and innovation.

Cultural and behavioral shifts must be matched by investments in infrastructure and innovation. Without systemic support, even the most inspired travelers will face barriers to making regenerative choices. Our regenerative future must be shaped not solely by global companies or distant policymakers but by empowering local governance and control over tourism development. As a 2023 report from the World Bank emphasizes, decentralizing tourism governance enables communities to define what regeneration means in their own context, fostering more equitable and place-specific outcomes.[43] This includes giving local communities a decisive voice in setting tourism policies, managing visitor flows, and directing economic benefits toward community priorities.

The path to regenerative tourism runs through the intertwined domains of education, cultural transformation, infrastructure, and innovation. By embedding regenerative thinking into schools and society, equipping travelers with clear knowledge, designing awe-inspiring and reciprocal experiences, improving public transport, investing in sustainable energy, and empowering local governance, the industry can create a model of travel that truly gives back to people and planet. Regeneration, ultimately, is not just about restoring landscapes, it's about restoring relationships: between humans and nature, between visitors and hosts, and between current and future generations.

As we reach the end of this book, one truth stands above all others: Regeneration is not just a trend, a marketing strategy, or a niche movement within the travel industry, it is a profound shift in how we understand our relationship to the world.

Throughout these chapters, we have explored the many dimensions of regenerative tourism: From transforming business models and operations, to embedding Indigenous wisdom, to rethinking infrastructure, policy, and innovation. We have seen how regenerative principles challenge us to move beyond minimizing harm toward actively restoring ecosystems, revitalizing communities, and creating shared value that benefit both people and planet.

We have learned that education and cultural change are at the heart of this transformation. Without embedding regenerative thinking across generations, sectors, and societies, no amount of operational change will be enough. Regeneration calls on us to cultivate a mindset of reciprocity and respect, inviting travelers to see themselves not as consumers or spectators, but as guests, stewards, and partners in the healing of place.

We have explored how storytelling and communication play a critical role in this shift. Authentic, values-aligned narratives help avoid the trap of greenwashing, while positive, joyful messages inspire action. Community platforms and post-trip engagement tools deepen the traveler's connection to the places they visit, ensuring that the impact of regenerative travel extends long after the journey ends.

We have examined the importance of infrastructure and innovation, recognizing that the best intentions will falter without the systems to support them. Reducing reliance on long-haul aviation, investing in sustainable energy alternatives, and empowering local governance over tourism development are not optional—they are the foundations on which a regenerative future must be built.

Most importantly, we have seen that regeneration is as much about repairing relationships as it is about repairing landscapes. It invites us to reimagine the connections between visitors and hosts, between businesses and communities, between local wisdom and global systems, between the present and the generations yet to come.

For the travel industry, this is a moment of both reckoning and opportunity. Climate change, biodiversity loss, social inequity, and cultural erosion are no longer distant threats; they are realities that define our time. But within these crises lies the potential for extraordinary innovation, creativity, and leadership. By adopting regenerative practices, the industry has the chance to become not just a mirror of the world's challenges, but a laboratory for its solutions.

As we close, it is important to remember that regeneration is not a fixed destination—it is a journey, a practice, and a commitment. It is about learning, adapting, collaborating, and continually asking: How can we leave the places we touch healthier, stronger, and more resilient?

The work ahead belongs to all of us: Travelers, businesses, policymakers, Indigenous leaders, communities, scientists, storytellers, educators, and activists. Together, we can chart a new course for travel—one that honors the earth, uplifts human dignity, and regenerates the future we share.

The invitation is clear. The compass is set. The journey begins now.

Key Takeaways

Indigenous wisdom as the foundation:

- Indigenous peoples protect 80 percent of global biodiversity while being just 5 percent of population—their knowledge systems are essential for regenerative tourism.

- Indigenous worldviews treat humans as part of nature's web, governed by reciprocity and stewardship rather than extraction.
- Indigenous-led conservation consistently outperforms government or private management.

Five core principles for indigenous partnership:

- Power-sharing not tokenism—Indigenous communities lead governance and ownership decisions.
- Place-based design—Tourism reflects local ecology, history, and cultural meaning.
- Free, prior, informed consent with meaningful community benefits.
- Support living cultures through language and knowledge transfer.
- Respectful education guided by Indigenous hosts, not extractive storytelling.

Nature as stakeholder revolution:

- Grant legal rights to ecosystems—New Zealand's rivers and forests now have legal personhood.
- Companies like Faith in Nature appoint nature to their boards with formal voting rights.
- Indigenous co-management models prove conservation and tourism can thrive together.

Five systemic shifts required:

- Make regeneration the core business model, not a side project.
- Move beyond sustainability to net positive ecosystem and community impact.
- Embed Indigenous wisdom in governance, not just consultation.
- Strengthen public–private partnerships for systemic change.
- Implement bold policies: visitor caps, extraction taxes, regenerative subsidies.

Profitable regenerative business models:

- 70 percent of consumers pay more for sustainable services—regeneration drives profitability.

- Use transparent impact measurement tools to avoid greenwashing.
- Eliminate single-use plastics and engage employees through green teams.
- Prioritize local supply chains to strengthen communities and reduce emissions.
- Design immersive experiences that transform guests into active regeneration participants.

Communication that transforms:

- Use authentic messaging—42 percent of green claims are false or exaggerated.
- Focus on joy and connection, not guilt, for lasting behavior change.
- Create post-trip engagement platforms for ongoing relationships.

Education for cultural shift:

- Embed regenerative thinking across all generations and sectors.
- Teach the difference: sustainability minimizes harm, regeneration actively restores.
- Transform travelers from consumers to stewards through meaningful experiences.
- Train staff to live regenerative principles, not just market them.

Infrastructure and innovation imperatives:

- Invest in sustainable transport alternatives to reduce aviation dependence.
- Develop renewable energy infrastructure for regenerative operations.
- Empower local communities to control their tourism development.

Regeneration as relationship repair:

- Restore connections between humans and nature, visitors and hosts, present and future.
- Transform tourism from problem to solution for climate and biodiversity crises.

- View regeneration as ongoing practice requiring collaboration across all stakeholders.

Notes

1. United Nations. United Nations Declaration on the Rights of Indigenous Peoples, United Nations, 2007. raventrust.com/articles/a-necessary-resource-the-united-nations-declaration-on-the-rights-of-indigenous-peoples/ (archived at https://perma.cc/PUE9-MAWW)
2. K P Whyte. Indigenous science (fiction) for the Anthropocene: Ancestral dystopias and fantasies of climate change crises, *Environment and Planning E: Nature and Space*, 2018, 1 (1–2), 224–42.
3. F Berkes (2012) *Sacred Ecology*, Routledge, Abingdon.
4. S T Garnett, N D Burgess, J E Fa, Á Fernández-Llamazares, Z Molnár, C J Robinson and I Leiper. A spatial overview of the global importance of Indigenous lands for conservation, *Nature Sustainability*, 2018, 1 (7), 369–74.
5. P Hawken (2021) *Regeneration: Ending the climate crisis in one generation*, Penguin Random House, New York.
6. United Nations. United Nations Declaration on the Rights of Indigenous Peoples, United Nations, 2007. raventrust.com/articles/a-necessary-resource-the-united-nations-declaration-on-the-rights-of-indigenous-peoples/ (archived at https://perma.cc/PUE9-MAWW)
7. V Shiva (2020) *Reclaiming the Commons: Biodiversity, indigenous knowledge, and the rights of Mother Earth*, Synergetic Press, Santa Fe, NM.
8. Waitangi Tribunal. Whanganui River Settlement Summary, Waitangi Tribunal, 2017. www.waitangitribunal.govt.nz (archived at https://perma.cc/KGD6-ZQ3B)
9. Faith in Nature. We've made nature a board member, Faith in Nature, 2022. www.faithinnature.co.uk (archived at https://perma.cc/9865-REUZ)
10. Patagonia. Earth is now our only shareholder, Patagonia, 2022. www.patagonia.com (archived at https://perma.cc/J8VD-L7XU)
11. R Jones, C Rigg and L Lee. Haida marine planning: First Nations as a partner in marine conservation, *Ecology and Society*, 2010, 15 (1).
12. Tourism Australia. Indigenous tourism, Tourism Australia, 2024. www.tourism.australia.com (archived at https://perma.cc/9V4T-ZTL7)

13 P Hawken (2021) *Regeneration: Ending the climate crisis in one generation*, Penguin Random House, New York.

14 P Hawken (2021) *Regeneration: Ending the climate crisis in one generation*, Penguin Random House, New York.

15 Shorefast Foundation. About Fogo Island Inn, Shorefast Foundation, 2024. www.shorefast.org (archived at https://perma.cc/V8LF-S6ZX)

16 Intrepid Travel. Sustainability, Intrepid Travel, 2024. www.intrepidtravel.com (archived at https://perma.cc/JHU2-N9RA)

17 Berkeley Group. Sustainability report, Berkeley Group, 2023. www.berkeleygroup.co.uk (archived at https://perma.cc/87QU-7KCN)

18 Great Plains Conservation. Conservation tourism, Great Plains Conservation, 2024. greatplainsconservation.com (archived at https://perma.cc/VV98-J8FL)

19 M Honey (2008) *Ecotourism and Sustainable Development: Who owns paradise?* Island Press, Washington, DC.

20 United Nations. Indigenous peoples and climate action, United Nations, 2021. www.un.org (archived at https://perma.cc/5E9W-4GUQ)

21 Tourism Australia. Indigenous tourism, Tourism Australia, 2024. www.tourism.australia.com (archived at https://perma.cc/M8CV-U2GM)

22 European Commission. European capitals of smart tourism, European Commission, 2023. ec.europa.eu (archived at https://perma.cc/7YBA-FQUM)

23 M Honey (2008) *Ecotourism and Sustainable Development: Who owns paradise?* Island Press, Washington, DC.

24 WWF. Tourism in Tayrona National Park, WWF, 2023. www.worldwildlife.org (archived at https://perma.cc/SWU7-Y7NE)

25 UNWTO. Glasgow Declaration on Climate Action in Tourism, UNWTO, 2021. www.unwto.org (archived at https://perma.cc/HWX7-K6CK)

26 Nielsen. The sustainability imperative: New insights on consumer expectations, Nielsen, 2015. www.nielsen.com (archived at https://perma.cc/YHU9-QVV4)

27 Intrepid Travel. Sustainability, Intrepid Travel, 2024. www.intrepidtravel.com (archived at https://perma.cc/K87V-BNY8)

28 Booking.com. Booking.com Sustainable Travel Report 2024, Global Sustainable Tourism Council. www.gstcouncil.org/booking-sustainable-travel-report-2024 (archived at https://perma.cc/XK4U-KTQM)

29 Six Senses Hotels. Plastic-Free and Sustainability Goals, Six Senses Hotels, 2024. www.sixsenses.com (archived at https://perma.cc/YLT3-VE95)

30 T A Norton, H Zacher and N M Ashkanasy. Organizational sustainability policies and employee green behavior: The mediating role of work climate perceptions, *Journal of Environmental Psychology*, 2015, 43, 1–10.
31 Patagonia. Environmental internship program, Patagonia, 2024. www.patagonia.com (archived at https://perma.cc/4VVR-WNVM)
32 UNWTO. Tourism and local community development, UNWTO, 2021. www.unwto.org (archived at https://perma.cc/HWX7-K6CK)
33 H Goodwin (2016) *Responsible Tourism: Using tourism for sustainable development*, Goodfellow Publishers, Oxford.
34 European Commission. Screening of websites for 'greenwashing': Half of green claims lack evidence, European Commission, 2020. ec.europa.eu (archived at https://perma.cc/B3WJ-GK2U)
35 Indigenous Tourism Association of Canada. Guidelines for working with Indigenous tourism, Indigenous Tourism Association of Canada, 2021. indigenoustourism.ca (archived at https://perma.cc/6RYJ-E2TZ)
36 P E Stoknes (2015) *What We Think About When We Try Not To Think About Global Warming: Toward a new psychology of climate action*, Chelsea Green Publishing, London.
37 Rewilding Europe. Rewilding Europe: Making Europe a wilder place, Rewilding Europe, 2023. rewildingeurope.com (archived at https://perma.cc/G2Z2-ZKZS)
38 United Nations Educational, Scientific and Cultural Organization (UNESCO). Education for sustainable development: Roadmap for achieving the SDGs, UNESCO, 2022. www.unesco.org (archived at https://perma.cc/8T3M-DDX8)
39 Foundation for Environmental Education. Eco-Schools, Foundation for Environmental Education, 2023. www.ecoschools.global (archived at https://perma.cc/T4M8-BPHF)
40 M Rudd, J Aaker and M I Norton. Awe expands people's perception of time, alters decision making, and enhances well-being, *Psychological Science*, 2012, 23 (10), 1130–36.
41 ReGeneration 2030. Our mission, ReGeneration 2030, 2023. www.regeneration2030.org (archived at https://perma.cc/HYX7-KN9R)
42 Global Sustainable Tourism Council (GSTC). Destination criteria and guidelines, GSTC, 2023. www.gstcouncil.org (archived at https://perma.cc/2R3S-VHNE)
43 World Bank. Localizing tourism: Empowering communities for sustainable development, World Bank, 2023. www.worldbank.org (archived at https://perma.cc/L9TB-NV7K)

INDEX

'ABC Way' 133, 134
Aboriginal Cultural Tours 26
Accommodation Framework 233
advocacy 31, 42, 44, 75–77, 95–96
Africa 97, 214–15
   see also Botswana; Kenya; Rwanda; South Africa; Tanzania; Uganda
Africa Foundation 106
African Bush Camps 130, 131–34
African Bush Camps Foundation 131–32, 133
African Wildlife Foundation 31
agricultural regeneration 31, 88, 98, 107–08, 113
   see also farming; permaculture
agritourism 31, 168
Agriturismo 31
agroforestry 100–01, 107, 109–10, 255
air purification 106, 110
Airbnb 65
airline sector 38, 52, 53, 220, 233
Albergue, El 112–14
Alfama 65
Amaganyane team 90
Amboseli National Park 56
AndBeyond 6, 104–06
Angkor Wat 26
aquaculture 175–76, 177, 178, 180
Asociación Kuska 113
Association des Bassins d'Imlil 90
Australia 26, 27, 30, 76, 255, 257
authenticity 28, 42, 61, 165, 212–13, 224, 262

B Corp certification 223, 256, 259
B Impact Assessment 259
Bali 66, 71
Ban Magan 149
Barcelona 53, 65, 66, 67
Basata Eco-Lodge 203–07
Bastimentos National Marine Park 115–16
beaver reintroduction 103
Bedouin community 203–07
Belize 19, 139–43
benefits packages 134, 136
Berkeley Group 257
Bhagat, Maulik 144, 145, 146, 147
Bhutan 60–62, 75, 77, 156

biodiversity 103
   see also agricultural regeneration; aquaculture; blue carbon (coastal) ecosystems; ecological restoration; farming; fishing; forestation; grassland restoration; land degradation; pollination; rewilding; river restoration; soil fertility; watershed restoration; wetlands; wildlife
biodynamic farming 100
biophilia 146
biophilic design 144–46, 152, 153
   see also open-air architecture
birds 90, 106, 110, 114, 116, 117, 144, 147
Black Rhino Range Expansion project 105
blended finance 172–78
   see also investment; philanthropy
Blue Alliance 174–78
Blue Apple Beach 255
blue carbon (coastal) ecosystems 8, 54, 98, 177–78
   see also coral reefs
BNP Paribas 177
boma project (ABC Foundation) 133
Bonn Challenge 96
Botswana 257
Bowen, Alexis 217
Brack, Rebecca 219–24
Brathwaite, Angelique 175–78
Brundtland Commission 2
buddy systems 242
business operations 258–61
Bwindi Impenetrable National Park 57

Cambodia 26, 41, 185–88
Canada 27, 184, 185, 199, 255, 262
   see also Fogo Island Inn
Canggu 66
capacity building 13–14, 24–29, 46, 50–82, 186, 188–91
carbon credit programs 57, 98, 170, 177–78
carbon-negative status 61
carbon offsetting 31, 201, 218, 246
carbon sequestration 8, 31, 88, 96–99, 103–04, 108, 110, 169–70
   see also coastal (blue carbon) ecosystems
carbon sinks 8, 88, 92, 96–99, 103

Index

career development 136, 138, 150
Cayuga Collection, The 163–66
Celebrity Cruises 4
Certification for Sustainable Tourism 166
Charles III, King of the United Kingdom 148
cheetahs 105
Chile 33, 223
circular economy 94–95
climate change 1, 6, 7–8, 75
　see also environmental degradation
climate resilience 91–99, 103, 108
cluster calls 241–42
co-evolution (co-creation) 12, 13–14, 16, 17, 28, 69, 184, 252
coastal (blue carbon) ecosystems 8, 54, 98, 177–78
　see also aquaculture; coral reefs; marine ecosystems
Cobb, Zita 194–96, 201–02
cod fishing 201–02
collaboration see partnerships (collaboration)
Colombia 223, 255, 258
communication 261–63
　see also feedback mechanisms; reporting; storytelling
community-based tourism 36, 40, 55, 61–62, 156–57
　see also cooperative groups
Community Development Program (Woods at Sasan) 145
community empowerment 39–43, 46, 183–209, 219–21, 235–36, 252
　capacity building 63, 64, 67–69, 74
　ecological restoration 88, 94, 105–06
　see also capacity building; cooperative groups; cultural custodianship; economic viability; local sourcing
community engagement 185–88, 213, 224
　Blue Alliance 176–77
　capacity building 52, 58, 69–72, 79
　ecological restoration 91, 98, 101, 111–19
　and holistic wellbeing 126, 128, 129, 130–32, 137–43, 150–51
Community Forest User Group 150
community health initiatives 33, 72
community infrastructure 60, 90, 139, 164–65, 167, 168, 170, 186, 269
　see also healthcare; schools
Community Library (Woods at Sasan) 145
community power mapping 55–56
Community Support Partnership Programme 150
composting 110, 242
conscious consumerism 42, 43, 157–58, 165, 168, 180, 236, 259–60
consent 28, 253
Conway and Partners 4
cooperative groups 29, 36, 64, 74, 161, 164
　see also community-based tourism
COP26 244
COP27 203
COP28 244
COP29 245, 246
coral reefs 30, 54, 78, 79, 80, 103, 110, 175, 177, 206, 261
Costa Rica 13, 36, 158, 164–66, 180, 220, 223, 255, 257
Cotton, Marcus 149, 150
Covid-19 42, 57, 62, 138, 150, 167, 199, 215, 217, 227
cross-sector collaboration 73–74
culinary experiences 142, 146, 194–95
　see also plant-based meals
cultural change 263–65
cultural custodianship 28, 63, 67–69, 82
cultural empowerment 41–42
cultural exploitation 54–55
cultural heritage resilience 143–46, 219–24, 253
　capacity building 24–29, 46, 52, 61, 63, 64–69, 74, 75, 79
　and community empowerment 39, 41, 183, 190
　economic viability 165
　see also history of place
cultural sensitivity 28, 33–34, 61
Cultural Survival 29
cultural traditions 63

data 233–34
Datai Langkawi 77–81
Datai Pledge 78–81
Davey, Sally 230–34
Declaration for Enhanced Climate Action in Tourism 246
Destilería Andina 113
destination management companies (DMCs) 6, 211–28
destination management organizations (DMOs) 6
dialogic processes 25
diversification 57, 59, 62, 168
diversity 216
Dusek, Sarah 168–72

EarthCheck 80, 259
easyJet 52
EBITDA 169

Eco Tour (EMBOO) 95
ecological restoration 29–32, 46, 87–121
    see also natural capital
economic accountability 200
Economic Development Administration (US) 167
economic empowerment 40, 63, 186
economic integration 10, 31, 52–53, 191–202
Economic Nutrition labels 65, 193, 196–201
economic viability 27, 34–39, 40–41, 46, 59, 155–81
ecosystem services 106–11, 206
    see also water systems
ecotourism 31, 95, 107, 178, 206–07, 255, 257
Ecuador 220, 223
Eden Reforestation Projects 30
Edible Garden 146
education
    local community 43, 63, 65, 72, 78, 110, 137–39, 187–91, 204–05, 263–65
    traveler 43, 44, 63, 95, 184, 187, 189–90, 225, 253, 264
    see also schools
Education for All 188–91
efficiency 11, 34
El Albergue Ollantaytambo 112–14
El-Ghamrawy, Maria 206
El-Ghamrawy, Sherif 203, 204, 205, 206, 207
electric vehicles 94
elephants 90, 103, 105, 119, 132
Elsewhere 217–18
EMBOO 93–96
employees (staff) 36, 126, 128, 129, 130, 132–33, 134–38, 141, 150
    see also hiring practices
Endangered Language Fund 29
environmental degradation 1, 54, 235
    see also climate change
environmental stewardship 8–14, 26, 31–32, 38, 61, 143–47, 255
    community empowerment 183–84, 196, 204
    ecological restoration 88, 98
ESG 237
    see also environmental stewardship; governance; social empowerment
ethics 214–15
European bison 103
European Capitals of Smart Tourism 257
European Commission 231, 232, 257, 262
Ewaso Conservancy 57
Ezemvelo 105

fair trade 40–41
Fair Trade Tourism 41
Faith in Nature 254
farming 95, 100, 142–43, 201
    see also agricultural regeneration; permaculture
feedback mechanisms 187
female guide programs 132
Festival au Désert 26
Few and Far 169–70, 171
fishing 201–02, 204, 205
Flanders 9
Fogo Island Inn 19, 65, 74, 184, 193, 194–96, 197, 198–99, 201–02, 256
Fogo Island Workshops 196
Food and Agriculture Organization 106
forest bathing 33, 149
forestation 8, 92, 96, 103–04
    see also agroforestry; Kesambi tree; reforestation

G Adventures 4, 183
Galápagos' Islands 157, 179
'gardener' role 9–14
Gardiner family 89–90
gender equality 8, 132, 137, 141, 188–91
Geng Bersih Kampung (GBK) 78, 79
gentrification 64–67
Gir National Park 144
Glasgow Declaration on Climate Action in Tourism 244–45, 258
Gliricidia 109
Global Business Travel Association (GBTA) 231, 232
Global Fund for Coral Reefs 177
Global Impact Investing Network 173
Global Sustainable Tourism Council (GSTC) 2, 158, 184, 231, 232, 239–40, 241, 243, 264
Global Sustainable Tourism Partnership 35–36
global warming 7
Google 233
governance 41, 51, 55–57, 171, 173, 258, 265–66
grassland restoration 92, 97–99, 103, 170
Graves, Claude 70–72
Graves, Petra 70–71
Great Barrier Reef Restoration Program 30, 76
Great Plains Conservation 257
Green Climate Fund 174
Greenbuild Conference 5, 16
greenhouse gas emissions 1, 8
Greenland 68–69
greenwashing 262

Index

Growlers 196
growth 10, 12, 28, 36
GSTC 2, 158, 184, 231, 232, 239–40, 241, 243, 264
Guatemala 74, 164
guides 26, 61, 132, 144, 149, 158, 190
Gwaii Haanas National Park Reserve 255

Haida Nation 255
Hamanasi Adventure and Dive Resort 19, 139–43
Harry, Duke of Sussex (né Prince Henry 'Harry' of Wales) 230, 231
Hawken, Paul 7–8, 252, 255, 256
healthcare 33, 72
Hemaya Foundation 205–06
high-impact, low-volume tourism 60–62, 75, 77, 155–81, 168, 179
'High Value, Low Impact' policy (Bhutan) 60–62, 75, 77
Hillary, Sir Edmund 148–49
hiring practices 139, 141, 150, 164, 189, 191
history of place 15–19
Holdfast Collective 254
holiday rental properties 65–66
holistic well-being 31, 32–34, 46, 124–53
Hopkins 140
hotel chains 235–44
humility 11, 15–16, 44, 70, 264
Hwange National Park 130, 131
hydroponic farming 95

ikat weaving 67
Imlil Valley 190
immersive experiences 26, 33, 114–15, 117, 125, 127, 142, 148–49, 220–22, 260–61
impact investment 35–36, 176, 177, 178
impact reporting 241, 259
inclusion 39, 134, 137, 216
Indigenous Tourism Association of Canada 184, 185, 262
Indigenous wisdom 251–56, 257
Indonesia 66, 67, 70–72, 108–11, 175
Innovation Hub (EMBOO) 94, 95
InterContinental Hotels Group (IHG) 237, 241
Intergovernmental Panel on Climate Change 7
Intergovernmental Science-Policy Platform on Biodiversity and Ecosystem Services 87
International Eco-Schools 263
International Finance Corporation 174
International Union for Conservation of Nature 88

International Women's Day 141
Intrepid Travel 256, 259
Inuit drum dancing 68–69
investment 35–36, 37, 167, 169, 172–78, 245
Isla Palenque 164, 165
Italy 31
  see also Venice
Jamaica 137, 138–39
  see also Rockhouse Hotel
Japan 26, 28
Jawoyn stewardship 255
Juluchuca microwatershed 99, 101–02

Kadazandusun Penampang 68
Kahn, David 5, 16–17
Kahn, Sandra 5, 16–17
Kanshalife Project, The 78, 79, 80
Karaja Sumba 67
Kasbah du Toubkal 188–91
Kavango-Zambezi Transfrontier Conservation Area 90–91
kelp forests 103–04
Kenya 56, 57, 58–59, 74, 77, 93–96, 158, 174, 184, 257
Kesambi tree 110
khatta dhokla 146
Khwai 132
Khwai Community Concession 132
Khwai Leadwood 132
Khwai Lediba 132
Kimball, Jim 115–16, 117
Kimball, Renée 115
knowledge exchange 44, 241–42
Kodo Cultural Immersion programme 26, 28
Krauskopf, Dana 139–43
Krauskopf, David 139, 140–41, 143
Kunming-Montreal Global Biodiversity Framework 104
Kuska School 113–14
Kuta 71
Kwanini 159
Kwanini Foundation 160–63
KZN Wildlife 105

land agreement negotiations 71
land degradation 11, 30, 87, 107, 118
Langkawi 77–81
LEED 2, 10, 240
Leventhal, David 5, 15–19, 99–102
lime plastering 144, 145, 149
Lisbon 65–66
livestock enclosures 133
local power mapping 55–56
local sourcing 164, 166, 186, 191–93, 260
Local2030 Islands Network 167

Loïc 93, 94, 95
Lonely Planet 217
Lopesan Hotel Group 236
Luciernagas 166

Maasai Mara Conservancies 74, 184
Maasai Mara National Reserve 58–59, 93–96, 184
Machu Picchu 54
Mae Kampong Village 40
Makangale 161
Makhasa community 105
Malaysia 68, 77–81
Maldives 75, 237, 261
Mali 26
mangroves 91–92, 97, 98, 103, 108, 177
Manta Resort, The 158–63
Māori community 41, 74, 254
Marapu belief system 70
MareCet 79–80
marine ecosystems 8, 30, 79, 101, 110, 116, 161, 174–78, 187
  see also aquaculture; coastal (blue carbon) ecosystems; coral reefs
marine protected areas 174–78, 187
mass (traditional) tourism 12, 23, 25, 32, 34–35, 37–40, 52–54, 155, 215, 217
Matetsi Victoria Falls 89–91, 97
Maya Bay 54
McHugo, Mike 188–90
meal breaks 136–37
media, role of 53
Meishan Cultural Park 68
metrics (measurement frameworks) 20, 37, 173, 176, 241, 246, 256, 259
Millennial audiences 4
mindfulness 33, 148, 149
mindset 45
Ministry of Education (Jamaica) 138–39
Ministry of Environment (Egypt) 206
Ministry of Tourism and Ecotourism Kenya 95
Mnqobokazi community 105
Mohamed, Juma Bakar 159, 160
mohanthal 146
Monteverde Cloud Forest Reserve 36
Moremi National Park 132
Moroccan Tourism Board 4
Morocco 4, 188–91
Mountain Travel Nepal 148
Munywana Conservancy 105

Naboisho Conservancy 59
Namibia 56, 170
National Oceanic and Atmospheric Administration (US) 167

Nationally Determined Contributions (NDCs) 245, 246
natural capital 169–70, 181, 253–55
  see also ecological restoration
Nature Conservancy, The 142–43
nature immersion 33, 125
Ndlovu, Beks 130–34
Negril Community Library 138
Nepal 68, 148–51
New Zealand 41, 74, 254
Ngalung Kalla Retreat 108–11
NGOs 73, 79, 161, 241
  see also Blue Alliance
NIHI (Nihiwatu Resort) 70, 72
Nitmiluk Tours 255, 257
Norgay, Tenzing 149
Norway 75
Nurture Knots 80

Ocean Foundation, The 167
online travel agencies (OTAs) 232, 234
open-air architecture 109, 111
open skies agreements 53
Osa Peninsula 257
overtourism 53–54, 58–59, 66, 75

Pachamanca Farm Lunch 113
Pack for a Purpose 33
Pan Am 52
participatory tourism 43–44
  see also immersive experiences
partnerships (collaboration) 44, 52, 65, 73–81, 139, 163, 167, 184, 230–49
  see also community engagement; local sourcing
Pascal, Nicolas 177
Patagonia 254, 260
Patagonia National Park 33
peatlands 97
peer-to-peer learning 241–42
Pegasus Capital Advisors 237
Pemba Island 159–63
people, planet and profit 170–72, 176
permaculture 100, 109–10, 147
Pfister, Hans 163–66
philanthropy 72, 171, 172, 175
Phinda Private Game Reserve 104–06
photosynthesis 96
plant-based meals 8
Plastic Freedom Playbook (Six Senses) 242
Playa Viva 5, 15, 16–18, 19, 97, 99–102
policy advocacy 75–77
policy development 44, 56–57, 63, 65, 75–77, 104, 258
political empowerment 40
pollination 106, 107, 110
Pollock, Anna 9, 10–11, 11–12, 14–15

Index

Populus Hotel 235
'post-green' models 257
post-trip engagement 44
Prek Svay 185–86
private sector partnerships 36, 73, 171, 172–78, 207, 246, 257
Procolombia 6
profitability 171
Project Drawdown 7–8
public-private partnerships 36, 172–78, 207, 246, 257
public sector investment 36, 172–78, 207, 246, 257
purpose 45

qilaatersorneq 68–69
Quechua communities 114

rainwater harvesting 109
Randall, Ishmael 112
Randall, Joaquín 112, 113, 114
Rebecca Adventure Travel 220–24
reciprocity 76, 253, 264
Reed, Bill 5, 9, 10, 11, 12, 13–14, 16, 17
Reef Check Malaysia 79–80
reforestation 30, 96, 98, 99–102, 101, 107, 110, 112–14
ReGeneration 2030 264
regenerative tourism 3, 7–8, 10–15, 20–21, 23–24, 38, 39, 51–52, 179, 219
Regenerative Tourism Catalyst Grant Program 167
Regenerative Travel 5–7, 18–19, 21
Regenesis Group 16–17
regulatory standards 206
relationship building 26, 202–07
renewable energy 75, 174
reporting processes 37, 241, 259
resilience 55–56
    see also climate resilience; cultural heritage resilience
ReSiMar 101–02
restoration 13
'Return to the Neighborhood' program (Lisbon) 66
revenue-sharing models 58, 59, 193
rewilding 89–90, 91, 104–05, 164, 165, 262
Rewilding Europe 262
rhinos 105
ringan na oro 146
Ripple Score 183
river restoration 92
Roberts, Colonel Jimmy 148
Rockhouse Foundation 135, 138–39
Rockhouse Hotel 135–39
Rwanda 56, 57, 58, 59, 105

Ryanair 52

Sacred Valley 112–14
Sala Bai Hotel School 41
Salmon, Paul 135–39
Sami communities 75
Sattvic Meal Plan 146
Savanna La Mar Inclusive Academy 138–39
scalability 258–59
Schima-castanopsis woodlands 149
schools 113–14, 131–32, 138–39, 145, 150, 161–62, 188, 204–05, 263
SDF (Bhutan) 60, 61, 62
SDGs 88, 171, 173, 193
Sea, Christian 108, 109, 110, 111
sea otters 103–04
sea turtles 101
seagrass meadows 103
seaweed farming 142–43, 201
seed banks 242–43
Sele 161–62
Senda 165
sewage treatment 196
Seychelles 235
shinrin-yoku (forest bathing) 33, 149
Shiva, Vandana 253
Shorefast Foundation 74, 193, 194–201, 256
single-use plastics 259–60
Six Senses Hotels Resorts Spas 6, 35, 237–44, 260, 261
Skylark Negril Beach Resort 135
slow travel movement 33
Smith, Jeff 238, 240–41, 242, 243
social empowerment 27–28, 40, 41
social enterprises 41
social media 53
Social Progress Index 165
soil fertility 98, 106, 107, 108, 109–10
solar energy 56, 90, 94, 109, 196
Soneva Foundation 236
Soneva Fushi 237
Song Saa Private Island 185–88
South Africa 41, 56, 59, 104–05
South America 97
staff (employees) 36, 126, 128, 129, 130, 132–33, 134–38, 141, 150
    see also hiring practices
Starworks 4
stewardship 8–14, 26, 31–32, 38, 61, 143–47, 255
    community empowerment 183–84, 196, 204
    ecological 88, 98
    see also cultural custodianship
storytelling 4, 5–7, 195, 212–13, 224, 262

Sumba Foundation 72
Sumba Island 67, 70–72, 108–11
sustainability 2–3, 10, 75, 100, 109, 111, 142–47, 166, 222–24, 237–44
  see also composting
sustainability directors 242
sustainability revenue allocation 240–41
Sustainable Development Fee (SDF) (Bhutan) 60, 61, 62
Sustainable Development Goals (SDGs) 88, 171, 173, 193
Swadesh 146
Swiss Re Foundation 177
syntropic farming 100
systems thinking 3, 9, 14–15, 19, 32, 100, 125, 126

Tanzania 56, 57
Tarabine Bedouin tribe 205
Tayrona National Park 258
Te Urewera 254
technology 37, 52, 77, 232, 233
Thailand 40, 54, 236
Tiaki Promise 74
Tiger Mountain Pokhara Lodge 148–51
Tortuga Viva, La 101
tour operators 212, 214–16, 225
traditional (mass) tourism 12, 23, 25, 32, 34–35, 37–40, 52–54, 155, 215, 217
traditions 63
training 43, 74, 94, 110, 132, 134, 166, 189, 191, 241–42, 264
Tranquilo Bay 19, 97, 114–17
transformational relationships 26
transparency 186, 193, 234
  see also Economic Nutrition labels
transportation 43, 52
  see also airline sector
Travalyst 230–34
travel agencies 212, 214–16, 225, 232, 234
Travel Corporation, The 231, 232
Travel, Tourism and Outdoor Recreation program 167
Treaty of Waitangi 41
trust 71–72, 105–06, 141, 204–07
Tūhoe people 254

Ubud 66
Uganda 56–57, 58, 59
Uganda Wildlife Authority 56–57
Uma Mbatangu houses 70
Under Canvas 169
Underwater Room 158
Unguja 159
United Kingdom 254, 257

United Nations
  Sustainable Development Goals (SDGs) 88, 171, 173, 193
  UNESCO 25, 26, 27, 53, 68, 77
  United Nations Environment Programme 107, 126
  United Nations World Tourism Organization (UNWTO) 36, 183, 192, 193, 231, 232, 244–47, 258, 260
United States (US) 103, 167, 214, 235, 254
urban sustainability 242–44

Valery 93, 94, 95
Valle Sagrado Verde 96, 112–14
value supply chain 34, 37–39, 42–43
Venice 53, 75
Viola, Jay 115
Visit Flanders 9
Volcanoes National Park 57

Waitangi Treaty Grounds 41
waste management 61, 95, 186
water shortages 54, 66
water systems 72, 88, 93–94, 95, 106, 107, 109, 186
watershed restoration 88, 92, 99, 100, 101–02, 119
Weeks, Wendy 112
Weeva 234
well-being 31, 32–34, 46, 124–53
wellness retreats 32
wetlands 97, 103, 107
  see also mangroves
Whanganui River 254
Wild Impact 106
wildlife 30–31, 56–57, 73, 89–91, 101, 102–06, 110, 147, 158
  see also birds; elephants
Wilson, Edward O. 146
Woods at Sasan 144–47
World Animal Protection pledge 147
World Bank 54
World Resources Institute 107
World Sustainable Hospitality Alliance 232, 245, 246
Wright, Frank Lloyd 135
WWF 105

Yellowstone National Park 103

Zanzibar 159, 175
Zapatka, Craig 217–18
Zimbabwe 89–91, 97, 130, 131–34

Looking for another book?

Explore our award-winning books from global business experts in Marketing and Sales

Scan the code to browse

www.koganpage.com/marketing